Roads to Post-Fordism

Labour Markets and Social Structures in Europe

MAX KOCH
University of Ulster, Northern Ireland

ASHGATE

Published by
Ashgate Publishing Limited
Gower House
Croft Road
Aldershot
Hampshire GU11 3HR
England

Ashgate Publishing Company
Suite 420
101 Cherry Street
Burlington, VT 05401-4405
USA

Ashgate website: http://www.ashgate.com

British Library Cataloguing in Publication Data
Koch, Max
    Roads to post-Fordism : labour markets and social
    structures in Europe
    1.Labor economics 2.Social structure 3.Labor economics -
    Europe - Case studies 4.Social structure - Europe - Case
    studies
    I.Title
    331'.01

Library of Congress Cataloging-in-Publication Data
Koch, Max, 1966-
    [Arbeitsmärkte und Sozialstrukturen in Europa. English]
    Roads to post-Fordism : labour markets and social structures in Europe / by Max Koch.
        p. cm.
    Includes bibliographical references and index.
    A translation of: Arbeitsmärkte und Sozialstrukturen in Europa. Wiesbaden
: Westdeutscher Verlag, c2003.
    Originally presented as the author's Habilitationsschrift (Freie Universität Berlin, 2002) under the title: Wege zum Postfordismus.
    ISBN 0-7546-4308-5
    1. Labor market--Europe. 2. Industrial policy--Europe. 3. Europe--Economic conditions. 4. Europe--Social conditions. I. Title: Labour markets and social structures in Europe. II. Title: Labor markets and social structures in Europe. III. Title.

    HD5764.A6K64 2006
    331.101--dc22

                                                                    2006003908
ISBN-10: 0 7546 4308 5
ISBN-13: 978 0 7546 4308 1

Printed and bound in Great Britain by Antony Rowe Ltd, Chippenham, Wiltshire.

Contents

List of Figures

List of Tables

Preface

This book is based on my *Habilitation* (the 'second' doctoral thesis formally necessary for a professorship in the German-speaking world), which was accepted by the Faculty of Political and Social Science of the Freie Universität Berlin in October 2002. The original German version was published by *Westdeutscher Verlag* with the title *Arbeitsmärkte und Sozialstrukturen in Europa. Wege zum Postfordismus in den Niederlanden, Schweden, Spanien, Großbritannien und Deutschland* in 2003. After my move to the University of Ulster, and many discussions of this work – for example during the conferences of the *European Sociological Association* in Murcia and the *Industrial Relations In Europe Conference* in Utrecht – the idea took shape to write a theoretically and empirically updated version in English. Readers who also know the German version will realize that the theoretical body has been streamlined and that some elements – such as the section on closure theory – have been added. Empirically, the country studies now cover the years from the early 1970s up until 2003 (instead of 1997, in the original version). This has led to greater or lesser reinterpretations of the data material, especially in the cases of Sweden, Spain and Germany.

Acknowledgements

I would like to thank a number of people and institutions that have made this book possible. First the social sciences team of *Westdeutscher Verlag* (now *VS Verlag für Sozialwissenschaften*) for giving us permission to translate and adapt material from the original German publication. Second the German Research Council (*Deutsche Forschungsgemeinschaft*), who financed the original study (Project Code KO 1571/2-2). Third my colleagues at the *Freie Universität, Berlin* who critically supported me in conducting the study and during the *Habilitation* examination. Fourth my colleagues from the ERASMUS/SOCRATES network, coordinated by Erasmus University, Rotterdam, which organizes annual intensive courses with themes relevant to the EU, and which facilitated contacts enabling me to conduct interviews in Spain, Sweden, the UK and the Netherlands. Fifth my colleagues and students at the University of Ulster for encouraging me to see through the English version (living in Northern Ireland has also enhanced my 'European spirit' immensely). Special thanks go to the European Studies Research Unit of the Academy of Irish Heritage Culture who paid for the index. Sixth the Department of Social Policy at the University of Lund, where I – as a Visiting Scholar – finalized the manuscript. For ongoing support and partnership I am grateful to E.

Derry and Berlin, June 2006   Max Koch

List of Abbreviations

CC.OO.	Comisiones Obreras
CNV	Christian National Union
D-Mark	German mark
DIW	Deutsches Institut für Wirtschaftsforschung
EU	European Union
EUROSTAT	Statistical Office of the European Communities
FNV	Confederation of Dutch Trade Unions
FRG	Federal Republic of Germany
GATT	General Agreement on Tariffs and Trade
GDP	Gross Domestic Product
GDR	German Democratic Republic
ILO	International Labour Organization
IMF	International Monetary Funds
INEM	Instituto Nacional de Empleo
ISIC	International Standard Classification of all Economic Activities
LET	Ley del Estatuto de los Trabajadores
LO	Swedish Trade Union Confederation
LOLS	Ley Orgánica de Libertad Sindical
MAC	Unidades de Mediación Arbitraje y Conciliación
OECD	Organization for Economic Cooperation and Development
OPEC	Organization of Petroleum Exporting Countries
OSE	Organización Sindical Española
RCO	Council of Central Business Organizations
SAF	Confederation of Swedish Employers
SPD	Sozialdemokratische Partei Deutschlands
SER	Sociaal Economische Raad
STAR	Stichting van de Arbeid
UGT	Unión General de Trabajadores
UK	United Kingdom
US	United States
VHP	Union of White Collar and Senior Staff Associations
VNO	Federation of Dutch Industry

Introduction

After the 1970s, all Western European countries moved, at some point, from a period of prosperity and full employment to one shaped by stagnation and a crisis in employment. This is reflected in the academic debate insofar as the idea of a standard career with lower, middle, or higher educational qualifications, the corresponding professional career and pension dependent on the occupational position is now being treated as a thing of the past. It is more common that educational and professional careers are characterized by breaks and gaps; this means many more individuals experience social decline and *déclassement* today than a quarter of a century ago. In order to come to terms with these developments, since the 1990s, the term 'social exclusion' has come to be very widely used by politicians, policy makers, practitioners and academics. Although various conceptions of social exclusion were being developed as early as the 1960s and 1970s, recent years have witnessed an upsurge in the publication of a wide range of books and articles on the topic. Arguably, the growth in popularity of the term delineates attempts to understand and interpret new patterns of social division, particularly in relation to changing patterns in employment and unemployment, modifications in welfare provision, changing patterns in demographic mobility, both nationally and internationally, and changing definitions of eligibility for a variety of civil rights and duties.

If we take a wider temporal perspective by looking back to the changeable history of socio-economic development during the 20th century, it appears that 'good times' – with a great degree of social cohesion – and 'bad times' – with increasing social exclusion – alternate. Some great thinkers of the 20th century have therefore confronted the phenomenon of continuity and change in modern capitalism. Authors such as Luxemburg (2004), Kondratieff (1946), Polanyi (1944) and Boyer (1990) differ in many aspects of their analyses, but nevertheless agree on the fact that capitalist development is characterized by 'minor' and 'major' crises (Lutz, 1989). Although the basic structures of capitalist economy and society have remained remarkably unchanged, major changes have certainly taken place below this level. If we suppose that the development of capitalism is discontinuous rather that continuous, as the mentioned authors do, I would like to raise the issue once again of why, and under what conditions, relatively stable periods of development occurred in the past and if they could occur again.

In this book, I set out to do two things: first, I will develop a theoretical model for the understanding of the restructuring of labour markets and social structures of advanced capitalist countries on the basis of the 'regulation approach'; and second I will apply this approach to an analysis of the national trajectories of the Netherlands, the UK, Germany, Spain, and Sweden. In the initial stages of writing this book, I observed a dual gap in research: on the one hand, social structure played only a minor role in regulation theory and, in particular, in the debate on the transition from

Fordist to Post-Fordist growth strategies; on the other hand, regulation theoretical concepts have been hitherto rarely considered in the debate on social inequality and stratification. Grappling with the issue of how to contribute to close this dual gap in research, I found it necessary to focus on two things at the same time. First, empirically verifiable (and falsifiable!) hypotheses about long-term developments in labour markets and social structures were to be constructed from a regulation theoretical basis; and second, these hypotheses had to be applied to an analysis of the national trajectories of selected European countries, in the course of which the hypotheses could be empirically examined.

The structure of the book reflects this particular research interest. Chapter One is located on a rather high level of abstraction and contains a discussion of whether and to what extent the general features of the capitalist labour market correspond with particular tendencies in employment and, in particular, with the phenomena of labour market marginality and exclusion that make socio-economic regulation actually necessary. This discussion is founded on both the Marxian and the Weberian tradition as well as on contributions from state theory and the sociology of development. Chapter Two outlines the basic features and core concepts of the regulation approach, which are subsequently used to analyse employment and welfare regimes. The chapter further deals with rise and fall of Fordism as the predominant Western European growth strategy after World War II. Based on the debate on the crisis of Fordism, Chapter Three suggests hypotheses in relation to the long-term process of restructuring labour markets and social structures and delineates ideal-types of possible Post-Fordist growth strategies. It serves, at the same time, as the theoretical basis for the country studies in Chapter Four. These will be carried out against the background of the theoretical and practical issue of whether reforms in labour market and welfare regulation have sufficiently strengthened and increased in coherence in order to justify speaking of 'Post-Fordist' growth strategies. By reconstructing the five national trajectories consecutively, I will investigate how welfare capitalism developed after World War II, how it fell into crisis, and what solutions were sought to overcome this crisis. The analysis of concrete reforms in the labour market and welfare system will be based on the relevant scholarly literature and on interviews with experts in the fields of labour markets and social policy, which were carried out in the five countries. In order to portray the changes in the occupational and social structure, I will evaluate international labour statistics for the period 1970 to 2003.[1] Chapter Five interprets the country studies from a comparative perspective, and then the main theoretical and empirical results of this study are summarized with a view to further research in the concluding remarks.

---

1   The different stages of this enquiry are explained in detail in Section 3.3.

Chapter 1

Inclusion, Exclusion, and Capitalism

The issue in this chapter is the tensions or 'contradictions' inherent in capitalist development that, if not contained by institutional embedding or socio-economic 'regulation', may well lead to a decrease in social cohesion, to marginality and exclusion. This chapter discusses these issues at a relatively high level of abstraction in the sense that it refrains from analysing the particularities of national trajectories. The point of departure is the connection between the process of accumulation of capital and the development of employment based on Karl Marx's theorem of an 'industrial reserve army' (1.1). The picture of social inequality, inclusion and exclusion that emerges on that basis will subsequently be complemented by an analysis of social inequality and social struggles around the distribution of wealth in the Weberian tradition (1.2). Finally, we will consider the interaction between national economic locations and the international division of labour and discuss what new dimensions arise from this perspective for the concept of inclusion and exclusion in capitalism (1.3).

1.1   The Marxian tradition: The accumulation of capital and the development of employment

One does not need to be an old-fashioned materialist to consider the creation of profit on the basis of a rational organization of labour in private companies as the crucial orientation for economic action in a capitalist society.[1] In his analysis of the forms of value, Marx (1977, p. 150) shows that the characteristic form of the circulation of commodities c–m–c (commodity–money–commodity) produces an opposite cycle: m–c–m (money–commodity–money). The latter cycle has by definition 'no limits' as its extremes can only be distinguished according to their quantity. In fact it is the cycle m–c–m (money–commodity–more money) that expresses that value, in its manifestation as money, tends to increase its quantity, thereby approximating social wealth as such. Defined as value in motion, it is 'capital'. Max Weber (1986, p. 6) wrote that owners of capital are able to direct their economic practice towards the production of profit, because they have the power to determine the rational

---

1   Marx and Weber were united in this essential idea. The fact that Weber stressed different aspects in his analysis of the emergence and functioning of Western capitalism from Marx should not lead to the conclusion that these sociological classics are polar opposites. Interpretations of both theorists that stress their complementary mutuality are all too often neglected. See Ritsert (1988) and Koch (2000) for alternative views.

organization of the work process that is required in this instance – if necessary, against the wishes of the wage-earners. Marx added that, since employees normally work and produce value for their employers for a longer period than corresponds to the amount of time necessary to earn their living, the employees' working day is divided into a paid and an unpaid part. It is during the latter that the wage-earners produce a surplus for the employer.

Marx (1977, p. 225) further explains the distinction between the time necessary for a worker to earn his or her living and surplus for the employer when dealing with the conflict that arises when working hours are determined. At this point he suggests an 'antinomy' between 'collective capital', which claims its right as a purchaser of labour power by fixing working hours as long and – one would add today – as 'flexible' as possible, and 'collective labour'. The objective interest of the latter is to keep working hours within certain limits and to organize labour flexibility in ways that allow for professional and private life to be successfully planned on a regular basis. As the interests of these poles, collective labour and capital, appear to be equally deducible and legitimized in the principles of exchange relations (1.3) – in Marx's words, they both bear 'the seal of the law of exchanges' – employers and employees continue 'working out' this conflict by representing their respective interests in, at times, tense struggles.

These struggles are not limited to the quantitative regulation of working hours but also include qualitative dimensions of the organization of the work process. The profitability of a company can not only be improved by increasing the working hours of the wage-earners (Marx referred to this as the production of 'absolute surplus value') but also by shortening that part of their working day that is necessary for the workers' physical and social reproduction ('relative surplus'). Marx explains a reduction in the price of labour power (and, all other things being equal, the magnification of the employers' profit) through increases in productivity in those branches of production that are part of the consumption patterns of the wage-earners. However, he also stresses, following his assumption that labour is the only source of value, that the realization of such a relative surplus value is linked to an immanent contradiction: individual owners of capital are permanently motivated to optimize the technological and organizational basis of the work process in order to be one step ahead of their competitors. This is normally carried out by a substitution of workers by machinery or by an improved organization of the internal division of labour. The employers whose productivity level is above average can thus make extra profit since they are able to sell their commodities at prices below the normal level.[2] But such an improvement of production methods tends towards generalization, and the extra profit moves towards zero, since competing companies have no choice but to copy the new methods or even to optimize them. Since this improved level of productivity

---

2   It is controversial whether or not the average time necessary to produce a given commodity constitutes an empirically identifiable 'value' of a commodity that can be defined independently from its price. See Heinrich (1999) for an detailed overview on the transformation problem of labour values into prices.

gradually becomes the new social standard, a given quantity of commodities is now produced with less labour effort than previously. The price of a single commodity decreases as a result. Marx concludes that the methods of production of relative surplus result in workers being driven out of the production process. On the one hand, the rate of surplus of the employed workers increases; however, on the other hand, the absolute volume or mass of surplus value (and, other conditions being equal, the mass of profit) decreases since fewer workers are needed to produce a given amount of commodities than previously. In order to keep the volume of profit stable, despite this dilemma, there is no alternative but to expand the overall scale of production; in other words, accumulation.

'Accumulation' means that employers do not consume all the profit they produced during the preceding cycle of production, but instead that they reinvest at least some of it into the elements of the production process (labour power, which Marx defines as 'variable capital' as it adds value to the original capital value in the production process; and raw materials, machines, etc., understood as 'constant' capital because these capital constituents merely pass their value onto the new product) so that it functions as additional capital alongside the original capital. For systematic reasons, Marx first analyses the demand for labour power under the conditions of constant labour productivity. In these circumstances, in which the 'organic composition' of capital (the proportion of constant and variable components) remains the same, companies employ more people in direct proportion to the expansion of the scale of production. A national economy is then soon characterized by full employment and, in turn, wage rises; but also by a lack of technological and organizational innovation. In practice, however, this case is the exception; the rule is the tendency, mentioned above, towards an increase of relative surplus value, which is normally achieved through an increase in the organic composition of the capital used in the production process: the constant constituent of capital increases relatively at the expense of the relative constituent. In this case, the absolute number of employees can only increase, if the entire scale of production (constant *plus* variable capital) is advanced in greater proportion than the rise of the constant capital components against the variable element. However, this arrangement is also only found during particularly prosperous periods of capitalist development. In general, Marx is able to demonstrate that there is a permanent danger that the accumulation of capital results in a 'relatively redundant population of labourers' (Marx, 1977, p. 590).[3]

Marx distinguishes between three types of relative surplus population: the 'floating', the 'latent', and the 'stagnant'. The floating type is typical for industrial centres where 'the labourers are sometimes repelled, sometimes attracted again'. He understood the agricultural population ('latent' surplus population) as a reserve of

---

3 Marx was not the first political economist to raise the issue of unemployment and exclusion in the context of the accumulation of capital. John Barton, Richard Jones, George Ramsay, and David Ricardo should also be mentioned. It was Ricardo who coined the term 'redundant population', a kind of superfluous stratum at the margins of economy and society.

labour that was required during the Industrial Revolution in the quickly expanding cities (Marx, 1977, p. 601). Finally, wage-earners in irregular and precarious conditions of employment are referred to as 'stagnant' surplus population. Probably Marx had qualified craftsmen and women in mind whose skills were devalued in the course of the restructuring of the economy and who had no alternative but to compensate this inferior rate of productivity through increasing self-exploitation. This precarious employment often took the form of self-employment at home. However, it would be inappropriate to dismiss such individualized ways of production as mere historical phenomena. More recently, under the auspices of globalized production, the outsourcing of particular tasks within the work process to small businesses has become especially lucrative. It is well known, for example, that in the textile industry most of the fabrics supplied by western companies are produced in South East Asia. Less well known however is the fact that these companies make the most of the advantages of these locations in a strict economic sense. The often highly capable craftsmen and women, low wage levels, and the lack of prohibition or, at least, the tolerance of child labour, all belong to the 'locational factors' that enjoy especial popularity among multi-national corporate groups.

Finally, Marx mentions the 'lowest sediment' of the relative surplus population; the social groups that most approximate what was later labelled the 'underclass' (Herkommer and Koch, 1999). The *Lumpenproletariat*[4] consists of three categories. First, there are those who are still able to work whose number increases and decreases in accordance with the stages of the business cycle. The second category is the group of 'orphans and pauper children', who are likewise, 'speedily and in large numbers', enrolled in the active army of labourers during economic growth periods. One might add that the precise circumstances of this enrolment depend on the particular integration of a national location into the international division of labour at a particular stage of capitalist development. The third category encompasses those unfit for work, 'chiefly people who succumb to their incapacity for adaptation, due to the division of labour; people who have passed the normal age of the labourer ...' (Marx, 1977, p. 602–3). Given that the welfare state limits the risks of wage-earning the individual consequences of being unfit for work become less dramatic. But the reverse is also true, when such arrangements are removed. Individuals must then increasingly rely on themselves and their capacity to make private provisions to cover for these risks. Since from the standpoint of capital valorization, the costs of inability to work, for example, belong to the *faux frais* of production, it is a matter of socio-economic regulation, whether capital succeeds in moving these costs, 'from its own shoulders on to those of the working-class and the lower middle-class' (Marx, 1977, p. 603) or whether these classes are able to establish a modus vivendi of cost sharing, in which the employers take part.

---

4   I leave it open at this point whether or not Marx's expressions: Lumpenproletariat, 'lowest sediment', or 'dangerous classes' have contributed to the establishment of a jargon that stigmatized these strata into the undeserving poor.

To sum up the results so far, the logic of the capitalist production and accumulation process presents itself as 'exclusive' in the sense that a section of the wage-earners must permanently take the risk of being removed form the active production process and moved into the reserve. The same reasons that improve the productivity of labour, and, at the same time, the rate of accumulation, lead, other circumstances being equal, to a progressively decreasing input of human labour. The distinction between full-time membership in the production process, merely sporadic participation, and complete exclusion, is not just of academic interest, but has significance for the identification of the employee with his or her job, and, more generally, with his or her sense of self-esteem. Elaborating on Marx, Herkommer (1985) argues that the degree of an employee's autonomy and identification results from his or her particular position in the production process in its dimension as work process. In this determination, this process is shaped and codetermined by workers according to their skills and preferences.[5] Just as important it is for the individual to prove his or her worth as part of a larger organism through employment, this individual will experience devaluation and self-destruction if it is no longer possible to bring his or her specific interests and skills into the work process. Like a businessperson, who owns only outmoded machines, a person's labouring capacity has then ceased to have economic value. Since it cannot be deployed productively, there is no alternative but to enhance the 'investment' in a person's own skills in order to achieve re-entry into the labour market. If it is a 'misfortune' (Marx) to be a productive worker, since in capitalist circumstances this is associated with exploitation, then it is a personal disaster to be excluded from this process altogether.

The American sociologist Erik Olin Wright (1997) emphasizes that the unemployed are not involved in an exploitative relationship with the owners of capital. Nonetheless, he understands unemployment, labour market marginality, and poverty as being inherent in a socio-economic structure shaped by the capitalist mode of production in Marx's sense. Localizing the unemployed and economically marginalized in this structure, Wright distinguishes between exclusion, which he refers to in terms of 'economic oppression', and 'exploitation'. Exclusion denotes a situation in which the material benefits of one group are acquired at the expense of another group, coercive practices being an essential part of the process. Exploitation is then a specific form of exclusion: 'In exploitation, the material well-being of exploiters is causally dependent on their ability to appropriate the fruits of labor of the exploited' (Wright, 1994, p. 40). Therefore, the welfare of the exploiter depends on the effort of the exploited, whereas in non-exploitative exclusion there is no labour transfer from the excluded to the excluding group. The welfare of the latter is due to a denial of access to certain societal resources for certain social groups, but not to their efforts. Thus, the crucial difference between exploitative and non-

---

5 Things look different if we analyse the production process in its second determination as the valorization of capital. As such, the production process is indifferent to the concrete use of specifically skilled labour power, and self-fulfilment through the self-confident use of physical and intellectual capabilities is demoted to subordinate significance.

exploitative exclusion is that the exploiter needs the exploited, whereas in the case of non-exploitative exclusion, the excluding group might sometimes be happier if the excluded group simply disappeared.

The distinction between exploitation and exclusion is significant not only within the terms of reference of a theory of stratification but also for an understanding of the different conditions for the representation of interest. The basis for the wage-earners' influence and their degree of autonomy in the work process is the fact that employers are just as dependent on employees as employees are on employers (Ganßmann, 1999, p. 100). Due to this interdependence,[6] the largely repressive control of employees often proves cost- and labour-intensive and does not lead to optimal results in relation to productivity and efficiency. Often these determinants of profitability are best achieved where wage-earners have a relatively large level of autonomy and identification with their own work. Repressive forms of surveillance of workers are typical for the peripheral regions of the world market, while the locational advantages of Western European nation-states are due to the advanced development of the division of labour in combination with investments in skills and the corresponding active integration of wage-earners in the work process. The representation of the interests of the unemployed is more difficult since the capital-owning classes are not in any way dependent on their cooperation. As the existence of the unemployed is, so to speak, not economically founded, special efforts must be made to further their interests in the political arena, and here, especially though the mediation of the state (1.3). These interests refer to simple biological and cultural reproduction, on the one hand, and to the access to those resources that could make the labour power 'marketable' again (above all, training and further education), on the other.

1.2   The Weberian tradition: Exclusion, usurpation, and citizenship

The Marxian tradition views exploitation and exclusion as inherent features of capitalist societies. While it pays special attention to exclusion as a result of the

---

6   To state interdependence between employers and employees does not assume a symmetrical balance of power. Ganßmann (1999, p. 100) mentions several social facts that point to the structural advantage of the employer side: a) employers have money and therefore – through investments – are capable of determining the level of activity of the economy; b) employers can 'rent' employees, but, due to their limited access to loans, it is a rare event that employees rent capital; c) wage reductions lead to deflation if the development of prices is primarily determined by real wages. Once there is an oversupply of labour power, this is likely to remain as there are physical and social limits on the unemployed to reduce the price of their commodity, labour power. Even if they are prepared to do so, unemployed persons then face a closure of the labour market that further advantages the employer side; d) employees find themselves under pressure if full employment can only be achieved at wage levels that are below the level of subsistence; e) the periods of time in which the labour market parties can hold out in a conflict are different. Employers normally have more resources and are therefore in an advantaged position.

particular capitalist organization of the division of labour, the Weberian tradition has been especially, but not exclusively, interested in the different forms that exclusion takes at the level of the distribution of social wealth and in non-economic social fields. Max Weber's differentiation between open and closed relationships is generally seen as the starting point of such a theory of exclusion. An open relationship 'does not deny participation to anyone who wishes to join', whereas a relationship is defined as closed against outsiders 'so far as, according to its subjective meaning and its binding rules, participation of certain persons is excluded, limited, or subjected to conditions.' (Weber, 1978, p. 43) Exclusion (or 'social closure') is hence a process through which social groups maximize advantages by limiting access to privileges and life chances – 'rights' in Weber's terminology – to an inner circle of selected persons. To achieve this aim, that is, the monopolization of life chances and the definition of outsiders, practically any feature – language, race, class, gender, religion – can be singled out. Although this definition appears to point to a general concept of exclusion, in his practical work, Weber discusses the issue mainly with reference to economic relationships. Here, 'usually one group of competitors takes some externally identifiable characteristic of another group of (actual or potential) competitors ... as a pretext for attempting their exclusion.' And – rather casually – he goes on to say that 'such group action' of exclusion 'may provoke a corresponding reaction on the part of those against whom it is directed' (Weber, 1978, p. 342). However, Weber did not develop the concept of 'corresponding reactions' as systematically and as generally as his notion of exclusion. The idea therefore remained unexplored in Weber's writings and it was some time before it was revisited by scholars.

Frank Parkin (1972; 1979) and Raymond Murphy (1988) were foremost in developing Weber's original ideas and this led to a general analysis of all kinds of relations of dominance in which 'corresponding reactions' on the part of excluded groups play a significant role. Inclusion and exclusion are thought of as a socio-political process in which two reciprocal collective strategies are involved: exclusion and usurpation, 'both being means for mobilizing power in order to enhance or defend a group's share of rewards or resources' (Murphy, 1988, p. 10). Exclusion refers to all social action that serves the monopolization of societal chances, privileges and resources, while usurpation strategies are directed at the reduction of the share of resources claimed by dominant groups, and the questioning of their privileges. Excluded groups normally have to rely on forms of 'solidaristic' amalgamations, which can take different forms. According to Murphy (1988, p. 77), there is first 'inclusionary' usurpation, which can be described as a 'reformist' strategy orientated at the inclusion of an excluded group within the present social order, while 'revolutionary' usurpation 'makes a direct attempt to change the structure of positions in society and in some cases to change the structure of nation states'.

From this theoretical standpoint, the idea of the simple and trouble-free accomplishment of the interests of dominant groups must be rejected as long as the counterstrategies of excluded groups are not systematically considered. Exclusion and usurpation are seen as reciprocal strategies, which, in combination, constitute a conflict, the outcomes of which is open in principle. Possible conflict outcomes, in which the dialectics of exclusion and usurpation are temporarily balanced, seem to include the three following forms: first, an excluding group can push through its interests without concessions to the excluded, sometimes in a repressive way, for example, by making use of the state monopoly of physical violence. Here, the relations of dominance remain unchanged (as in China during the student movement of 1989); secondly, the usurping group succeeds in carrying out a revolution and abolishing the *ancien régime*. Examples include the storming of the Bastille of 1789 and of the Winter Palace in 1917 in Russia, and, as history shows, following the revolutionary strategy, the previous usurpers run the risk of becoming an excluding group themselves in the 'new society'; and finally, the area of conflict between excluding and usurping groups can be expressed in a third type of outcome, which was, in my view, not adequately considered by Parkin and Murphy. Social resources and benefits, which were appropriated through the furthering of a collective strategy, do not always, and not under all circumstances, coincide with corresponding losses of the counterpart, but can also turn into win–win situations that benefit both sides. In these cases, the conflict settlements that are typically negotiated often take the form of an institutionalized compromise, expressing the interests of both groups in some way. Such kinds of agreements often emerge through the mediation of third actors or parties and/or the shift onto another level of action, so that the interests of the actors of the old conflict change while new actors and interest groups emerge. Conversely, existing agreements between interest groups can become unbalanced and might well be cancelled by one group. An example for this is the post-war class compromise of setting up a universal welfare state in Western Europe and North America, which was later partly cancelled by governments and employers' organizations (Chapter 3).

A good example for social exclusion processes is the disputed access to citizenship (Mackert, 1998). Thomas H. Marshall (1977) argues in his classic essay on 'Citizenship and Social Class' that for an adequate notion of citizenship it is necessary to subdivide it into civil, political and social elements. The *civil element* considers basic individual freedoms, such as personal liberty and freedom of speech. The *political element* includes the right to participate in the political process. The practice of this right normally requires corresponding institutions, such as parliament and local administration. Marshall thought that civil and political citizenship remained incomplete without a *social element* by which he mainly referred to socio-economic welfare. The extension of citizenship in general is tied to the commitment of the capitalist economy to bringing about social justice, and, according to Marshall, this was to be ensured through a corresponding set of institutions such as the welfare state.

Marshall was perfectly aware of the fact that social achievements such as an encompassing welfare state did not just appear out of the blue, but were hard-won in sometimes difficult social struggles. As the post-war period was above all shaped by the building of the welfare state, which Marshall saw as capable of regulating capitalism and avoiding its worst anomalies, it is understandable that he saw the working class as the crucial collective agent in establishing elements of social citizenship. The conflict between the imperatives of a formally rational capitalist economy and the value of universal citizenship was acknowledged by Marshall (1981), but he was probably too influenced by the *zeitgeist* of the post-war class compromise in order to systematically consider the possibility of a one-sided cancellation of this particular regulation of capitalism. But, as Ruth Lister (1997, p. 35) rightly objects, citizenship standards that have once been achieved are 'not static but always open to reinterpretation and renegotiation'. This was precisely the case towards the end of the 1970s, when governments started to take back some of the welfare state elements from 'above' at a time when the working class movement was not strong enough to defend them.

Against this background, it would appear that Marshall's concept of the extension of citizenship is too static. Furthermore, the close link he suggests between this development and the practice of the working class seems questionable. Pointing out the relatively late introduction of female suffrage, feminists have argued that the extension of political rights proceeds in anything but an automatic and linear manner. In addition, women, in practice, are prevented from exercising their social rights, because, in the first instance, they are responsible for looking after children and caring for elderly and ill people (Jones and Wallace, 1992). Drawing on his experiences in Australia and the US, Bryan S. Turner (1993) drew the attention of sociologists towards ethnic conflicts. He shows that such conflicts can be as important, and sometimes crucial, for the debate on civil, political, and social standards of citizenship as class and gender. It follows from these criticisms that the extension of citizenship rights does not proceed in linear and simultaneous ways and that social theory should seek a way of incorporating this fact.

I would argue that the non-linear and non-simultaneous ways of accomplishing citizenship rights and social resources in general can be addressed adequately in a theory of stratification that combines arguments from both the Marxian and the Weberian tradition. From a Weberian perspective, a historical standard of citizenship rights and distribution of social resources appears as both a result and a requirement of strategies of closure and usurpation in different societal fields. The corresponding social struggles are not simply reduced to the conflict of capital and labour, but also include other relationships of dominance such as those built on gender and ethnic affiliation. A too static picture of the social structure is avoided through the emphasis of the dynamic character of the relations between excluding and usurping groups. As it is in the interest of both parties to maximize their respective share of resources, if necessary, against the resistance of the opposite group, we should rather start from the hypothesis of a delicate and fragile balance of their mutual relations, whereby the withdrawal of resources and rights that have been achieved can always occur.

In the Marxian tradition, the class conflict in capitalist society and the antagonism of nobility versus commoners are not just exclusionary but also exploitative relationships since they are located in the process of production of wealth. As shown in the previous section, the welfare of the capitalists/nobles depends directly on the effort of the working class/commoners in the *work process*, while in the cases of patriarchy and ethnic conflicts, located at the level of *distribution* of wealth, the

Table 1.1   Social resources and citizenship rights as areas of conflict of exclusion/exploitation and usurpation

Citizenship rights	Disputed resources	Social relationships of exclusion/exploitation
Civil rights	Personal freedom; Freedom of speech; Freedom of property	*Feudal system*: nobility vs. 'commoners', freemen vs. serfs;
Political rights	Equal participation in political system	*Patriarchy*: men vs. women; *System of rule based on ethnic affiliation*: Whites vs. Blacks, Christians vs. Jews vs. Muslims; colonial powers vs. colonized peoples;
Social rights	Access to labour market; Codetermination in work process; Distribution of societal wealth; Welfare state entitlements	*Class conflict*: surplus-producing vs. surplus-appropriating classes

welfare of men/ruling ethnic groups is due to the exclusion of women/ruled ethnic groups from access to certain societal positions and resources, but not to their efforts in the work process. With regard to the extension of social rights, it follows from these examples that it would be advisable to conceptualize each exclusionary relationship as a separate case. This is because the parties, resources and stakes vary from field to field and according to different principles. For example, the intellectual capital necessary to progress in academia is of a different kind from the requirements needed to make it to the top of a private company (Bourdieu, 1977; 1986). Taken from this angle, the usefulness of Parkin's concept of 'dual closure' (1979, p. 89) becomes obvious: to talk of 'dual' or 'multiple' exclusion means to consider the possibility that social groups, who are dominant in one field, are excluded in others.

The perspective suggested considers the fact that the extension of social rights proceeds in fits and starts rather than in a smooth linear way. The social structure is characterized by the simultaneous existence of disputed terrains and conflicts of excluding/exploiting and excluded/exploited groups who attempt to usurp the established order in different societal fields. This does not exclude, in certain historical circumstances, the possibility of a temporal dominance of one relationship of exclusion/exploitation over others. At the level of empirical analyses of concrete societies, this will frequently be the case. By and large, Marshall's division of periods is correct in dating the extension of civil rights to the eighteenth century, political rights to the nineteenth, and social rights to the twentieth century. However, in the twentieth century, the accomplishment of both civil and political rights was still an issue. The working class's usurpational gains against the bourgeois class did not automatically lead to an improvement of the situation of women and of the dominated ethnic groups of the time, even though it no doubt contributed to the development of a civil society, which itself facilitated corresponding social struggles. Instead, political and social citizenship rights for women and non-mainstream ethnic groups had to be achieved by independent civil movements. This organizational autonomy was necessary, not least, because trade unions and socialist parties, for example, were in many countries dominated by males and whites.

1.3   The state and the international dimension

Both the Weberian and Marxian tradition regard the state as crucial in shaping economy and society, for the maintenance of social cohesion, and, at the same time, for the reproduction of social inequality. Parkin (1979), representing the Weberian tradition, stresses that strategies of exclusion and usurpation are not chosen arbitrarily. Rather, they are normally preceded by legal definitions of subordination by the state: 'In all known instances where racial, religious, linguistic, or sex characteristics have been seized upon for closure purposes the group in question has already at some time been defined as legally inferior by the state. Ethnic subordination, to take the commonest case, has normally occurred as a result of territorial conquest or the forced migration of populations creating a subcategory of second-class citizens within the nation-state' (Parkin, 1979, p. 96). Parkin shows that the main example of exclusion within the working class occurs when groups singled out for exclusion by the labour movement of the culturally dominant group are typically those 'that already suffer the disabilities of marginal political status, and whose own organizing and defensive capacities are seriously diminished' (Parkin, 1979, p. 96).

For the Marxian tradition, the point of departure for the notion of the state was always the question of why it does not take the form of a 'private apparatus' but of an unpersonal one removed from society (Paschukanis, 1929). The answer for this question was sought in an analysis of the structural prerequisites for the exchange of labour equivalents. In order to establish a circulation of commodities based on the principle of equivalence, individuals must 'recognize one another reciprocally as proprietors' (Marx, 1973, p. 243). This includes a 'juridicial moment' since exchange relations are only possible if the acting individuals are not prevented from entering them, for example, by feudal rule. Neither is it a legal or legitimate way of appropriating commodities through the use of violent means. On the contrary the motto is 'voluntary transaction; no force on either side' (Marx, 1973, p. 244). The state enters the equation as a formally independent institution that guarantees the legal and economic independence of the owners of commodities: their equality, legal security and protection. In an advanced division of labour, this guarantee cannot be ensured in accordance with common law but must be personified in a third party. The state does this, *inter alia*, through the monopolization of the legitimate use of physical force (see also, Weber, 1991, p. 78). The modern state, under the *rule of law*, guarantees private property, the principle of equivalence, and the legal security of the economic subjects.

Marx and Weber were in agreement that, in capitalism, the social cohesion of individuals is initially produced in the market, where they offer their commodities for sale. It was Marx, who stressed that this circulation of commodities is an 'abstract sphere' insofar as, if we analyse it in its simple form, we do not know how the owners of commodities originally came to possess these commodities. The only assumption possible on this basis is that, at some previous stage, the owners of commodities must have carried out work themselves so that, subsequent to this original work, their commodities now embody value. At a more concrete level of abstraction, however, Marx clarifies that exchange relations are not reduced to the exchange of use values, which are differentiated by their material features only, but that they also include the particular exchange between owners of capital and wage-earners in the production and accumulation process of capital. This exchange formally respects the rules of appropriation that correspond to the simple circulation of commodities – the principle of equivalence and the assumption of property being the result of a person's previous work – as far as the price of the labour power is concerned, but, more importantly, it initiates the real exchange between labour and capital in a production process that is based upon its exact opposite: the appropriation of surplus labour without equivalent. The second dimension of our understanding of the state in a capitalist society is therefore its role of ensuring and legitimizing *social inequality*. As state under the rule of law, it ensures the violence-free interaction of individuals on the market, the respect of private property, and the principle of equivalence. It thereby contributes enormously to the socio-economic inclusion of the economically active population. But as it not only guarantees private property in general but especially the private property of the means of production, it guarantees the private appropriation of the labour of others and the exclusion of particular social groups from privately monopolized resources (Bader *et al.*, 1983, p. 373). Exploitation and exclusion, on the one hand, personal freedom, independence, legal equality, and the idea of private property resulting from own achievements, on the other hand, are the two sides of a social structure that, in good times, are held together by the intermediation of the state.

Finally, the state can be defined as an autonomous political sphere, in which not economic characters but citizens interact. Whether in the form of political parties or communities of interest, members of all social classes and groups attempt to represent their interests in the political arena. The extent to which society is shaped by social policies that constitute an alternative to mere market regulation is largely dependent on the ability of organized labour and its political allies of influencing this process; our understanding of the state is then completed by its welfare dimension. The expansion of that dimension is most likely in cases where different social forces und interests are united in common projects of prosperity and growth, and where, in particular, the employers' interest in profits is not divorced from the welfare interests of the wage-earning classes. However, it is important to reiterate that the state is not only the location for the political regulation of class conflicts but also of those following the lines, for example, of gender and ethnic affiliation. Political parties do not normally represent such interests directly but tend to combine the interests of different social groups so that race, gender, and class and also religion, age, and the environment are sometimes in the focus of the political struggle, only to be superseded by other issues at a later point in time. State policies can therefore not be reduced to the strategic action of single actors, rather they develop as a result of the dynamics of different interests, social relations, and struggles (Hirsch, 1995). In its disparate forms, for example, economic policy, social policy, minority and asylum policy, these policies are of major significance for the cohesion or disintegration of society. The concrete forms of these policies vary and can only be understood in the context of empirical research.

The world market is constituted within the competition of economic spaces that are largely organized along the borders of nation-states. If the state harmonizes different interests of social classes and groups at the national level, at the international level, it then ties them in opposition to similar coalitions of interests of other countries. The relative strength or weakness of national locations in global competition depends greatly on whether or not governments succeed in allocating to particular group interests a subordinate status in comparison to goals of general national interest such as a common foreign-trade strategy. Governments can put pressure on organized labour, for example, by arguing for wage restraint in order to ensure the competitiveness of a national location. Outwardly, the state ties and represents national interests, and inwardly, it focuses the international balance of power back into the processes of internal policy-making (Hirsch, 1995).

While the existence of a multitude of heterogeneous national economic spaces is the result of internal and external political struggles, it is also a prerequisite for global accumulation of capital. The juxtaposition of these spaces, to which different forms of production and exploitation correspond, allows for the emergence of different markets for commodities, capital, and labour power. At one end of the spectrum, there are countries that attempt to improve their position in global competition by keeping wages low, working conditions bad, and political participation limited; at the other end, priority is placed on technological progress, education, and political and socio-economic inclusion. Indeed, the accumulation of capital at the global level appears to be largely founded on the possibility of combining different forms of the division of labour; and this systematically includes the (over)exploitation of cheap labour power in the peripheries.[7] When dealing with the accumulation of capital and the different dimensions of the state in socio-economic regulation, we stated that

---

7   I use the terms centre and periphery in a social rather than in a topographic sense. I understand the world market not as a geographically fixed structure but as a variable one in which both the 'promotion' of previously peripheral regions to the centre and the 'demotion' of ex-central regions to the periphery are, in principle, possible. In reality, however, for structural reasons that are described by Scholz (2000), such a promotion will only be an option for some regions or nation-states.

under capitalist circumstances social inclusion and the development of citizenship is produced in particular, contradictory forms. Now when considering the international level, is seems as if the expansion of inclusion and citizenship is largely limited to the central regions of the world market. The accumulation of poverty in the periphery corresponds to the concentration of welfare and democracy in the centre, a structural duality with a long history that does not appear to be dwindling.

Finally, the relationship between the national and the international level has a symbolic component. With his distinction of 'mechanical' and 'organic' solidarity, Emile Durkheim (1964) pointed to the fact that, under conditions of an advanced division of labour, social cohesion can no longer be based on regional rites, local societalization or courtly rules. Weber and Marx elaborate on this by arguing that modern capitalist society tends to dissolve previously isolated communities and to regroup its inhabitants according to new spatio-temporal structures that largely follow the borders of the developing nation-states. The idea of the 'nation' plays an important role in providing a new form of identity based on language, descent, morals and norms (Poulantzas, 1978). Feelings of belonging and cohesion, which have been lost in the process of economic uprooting and spatial restructuring, are symbolically reconstructed and recomposed in accordance with the new socio-economic territory. At times, however, this includes the dissociation from everything that is perceived – often on the grounds of ascriptive features such as colour of skin or accent – as foreign, external, and ex-territorial (Balibar and Wallerstein, 1998). What was symbolically won in the ideal of the nation – a new sense of belonging after the dissolution of local identities following the uprooting of pre-capitalist communities – is then felt as coming under a new sort of threat from the foreign and unknown. Faced with this threat, the integration of non-mainstream ethnic groups is justifiable only under extraordinary economic circumstances: 'The more there is a demand for its [the foreigner's labour force] service by the host society, the more flexible the host society will be in accepting it. ... But when the demand for its services [declines] during the recession, these foreigners [start] to be the target of all kinds of rejection, discrimination and exclusion' (Sabour, 1999, p. 224).

1.4   Looking back, looking forward

Our notion of socio-economic inclusion and exclusion has developed and taken on new forms that correspond to the various core structures of capitalist economy and society that we have considered. The analysis of the accumulation process of capital, based on Marx's critique of political economy, showed that the possibility for the emergence of labour market marginality, unemployment, and exclusion is a constant feature of the capitalist mode of production. We discussed the theorem of the 'industrial reserve army' at a very high level of abstraction and this appears to be in need of elaboration when applied to concrete societies, but the principle remains correct in that those causes that result in an increase in the productivity of work – the substitution of workers by machinery, for example – normally do not lead to a decrease of the workload of individuals, but – other factors being equal – lead to the production of a 'superfluous population'. The latter takes on different forms such as underemployment, precarious employment and (temporal or permanent) unemployment. Different forms of labour market marginality correspond to different interests on the part of those exposed to it and to different conditions for their representation. In relation to the current debate on inclusion and exclusion, it appears to follow from this perspective that the social sciences would be well advised to start from the hypothesis of a systematic link between the conditions and changes within the sphere of production and the emergence of unemployment, poverty, and exclusion beyond this sphere.

While the strengths of the Marxian tradition lie in its explanation of social practices of exploitation and exclusion in the context of a particular mode of *production*, the Weberian tradition has its merits in addressing inequality at the level of the *distribution* of wealth and in non-economic fields. In particular, it provides us with a non-linear and multi-dimensional notion of the process of the extension of citizenship rights and of social inequality in general. The analysis of very different aspects of inequality such as gender, class, and ethnic groups can be carried out in using the same theoretical terms of reference. Furthermore, the dynamic character of the collision between excluding and usurping groups is highlighted: the balance of a relationship of exclusion in a particular social field, as it appears in a historical moment, is always unstable, insofar as both parties struggle to assert their interests, against the resistance of the counterpart, if required. In contrast to Marshall's linear concept of the extension of civil, political and social rights, it is difficult to predict whether these rights will be maintained, since it is entirely possible that they either increase or decrease.

Again, our understanding of inclusion and exclusion was increased through the brief consideration of the state and the world market. The state plays the dual role of representing the hegemonial interests of a national economic space in the international arena, and of refocusing the international balance of power into internal debates. At the same time, nation-states, or federations of states, mediate the international and sometimes global process of the accumulation of capital by representing different types of labour organization and different types of socio-economic regulation. Against this background it must be suggested that the extension of economic prosperity, social welfare and inclusion in the centres is linked to the reproduction of economic stagnation, social antagonisms, and disintegration in the peripheries. Finally, the symbolic dimension should not be underestimated when developing a sociological model of inclusion and exclusion that is in keeping with the times. The notion of a 'nation' remains an empty phrase without the consideration of the standardization of time and space as part of the emergence and development of the capitalist mode of production. The social construction of the national, however, implies the dissociation from everything that is perceived as 'foreign', 'other' and 'alien'. The form and extent of dissociation and exclusion appear to vary with the economic cycle: in times of high unemployment, the probability increases that human beings, who due to ascriptive features are not regarded as part of the native 'race', are exposed to sometimes violent practices of exclusion, while they are relatively welcome in times of economic prosperity in combination with great demand for labour power.

In short, our general and abstract analysis of inclusion, exclusion and capitalism suggests that there are ongoing contradictions and tensions inherent to this kind of society. Alongside exploitation, exclusion and inequality, however, we have also found elements of equality, inclusion, and citizenship. Why one of the two aspects predominates at a certain point in time and in a particular region of the world over the other cannot be defined in general theoretical terms. For an adequate understanding of the restructuring of labour markets, welfare regimes and social structures in countries of the European Union, further dimensions must be considered. The 'regulation approach' is an attempt to bridge general theories of capitalist development with empirical research on employment systems and socio-economic regulation.

Chapter 2

The Regulation Approach

The analysis of economic categories such as commodities, money, capital, accumulation, the state, and the world market and their corresponding social relationships suggests that societal coherence in capitalism cannot be taken for granted. On the contrary, major and minor crises and, in their wake, social disintegration are always a possibility. When approaching the dialectics of continuity, crisis, and change, the abstract features of what Marx called the capitalist mode of production appear to have remained remarkably constant, while significant changes seem to have taken place beneath this level. Despite considerable differences in their particular theoretical lines of argument, authors such as Polanyi, Schumpeter, Wallerstein or Kondratieff are united in the hypothesis of a non-continuous development of capitalism, one that proceeds in a series of qualitative breaks. This is also the starting point of the 'regulation approach'. This chapter deals with the general features of this theoretical movement (2.1), before introducing the concept of Fordism as the predominant growth model of the post-war era (2.2). Using the regulation theoretical literature, we raise the issue of how both regime of accumulation and the mode of regulation were intertwined to enable such a long-lasting period of growth and prosperity. Thereafter, we consider the debate on the crisis of Fordism with special emphasis on the changing conditions for policy making and the articulation of growth strategies at the national level (2.3).

2.1 Socio-economic development and inclusion from a regulation theoretical perspective

The regulation approach is not a unified and generally accepted body of theory; rather it encompasses a set of different ideas that have been interpreted as a research programme in the social sciences; Bob Jessop (1990) discusses seven different regulation approaches within this research programme. In the following section, I will concentrate on what he calls the Parisian school, associated with writers such as Michel Aglietta (1987), Alain Lipietz (1987, 1998), and Robert Boyer (1995). The origins lie in the late 1970s and 1980s, when Michel Aglietta (1987) published his groundbreaking analysis of long-term political and economic trends in the US. The debate on his work was, at the same time, the point of departure for a re-interpretation of the crisis cycle of capitalist development. The researchers from the Parisian CEPREMAP Institute, around which the discussion was concentrated, stated that the Marxist discourse of the 1960s and 1970s allowed only for very abstract, general and partly inconsistent insights into the understanding of capitalism after World War II. In France especially, structuralism was influential at the time. Although Althusser and Balibar (1998) insisted that it was necessary to resist the temptations of determinism and reductionism, their theory remained largely concerned with epistemological problems within Marxism, without actually addressing concrete processes of crises and development, let alone subjecting their theories to empirical verification.

As his 'rebellious sons' (Lipietz) and daughters, regulationists went critically beyond Althusser. On the one hand, they held onto the most important insights of Marx's *Critique of Political Economy* such as the differentiation between a 'mode of production' and 'social formations'. As with Althusser and Poulantzas, it was argued that empirically 'concrete' social formations cannot be derived from concepts that correspond to the analytical level of the mode of production. But, on the other hand, regulationists went beyond structuralism by stressing the fact that continued capital accumulation depends on a range of social, cultural and political factors. Economy and society in the US or France of the 1970s, for example, were seen as an *objet trouvé*, the understanding of which required theoretically guided historical and empirical inquiry. Aglietta's original work can be read as a double critique of textbook economics and of a Marxism that does not go beyond the limits of the 'mode of production'.

On the one hand, neo-classical economists are criticized for their notion of a delimited economic space, which is to be found in a stable equilibrium and, if disturbed by external shocks, returns to this equilibrium spontaneously. In addition, rather than accepting the assumption of the trans-historical *homo economicus*, regulation theory conceptualizes economic incentives as dependent on changing economic structures and norms. On the other hand, the regulation approach breaks with the conventional Marxist view that capitalism will ultimately collapse in a series of crises due to its internal contradictions. On the contrary: regulationists assume that capitalism 'develops through a series of ruptures in the continuous reproduction of social relations. Crises are resolved through an irreversible transformation which allows the fundamental or "determinate structure" of capitalism to continue' (Friedman 2000, p. 61). In short, while regulationists regard the abstract features of capitalism as largely trans-historical, both crises in the accumulation process and phases of expanded production must be addressed in the context of their institutional, social and political embedding. The institutional settings necessary for continued and expanded capital accumulation are socially, culturally and politically constructed and contested in a myriad of societal struggles, in which the relations both within and between social classes, play a prominent role (Koch, 2001).

As this historical, empirical and comparative research project unfolded, regulationists felt the need to employ intermediary concepts, which were located at a level of abstraction between the mode of production and concrete analyses of economic conjunctures and social issues. These concepts were designed to express, on the one hand, the largely invariant social conditions of the agents involved in the relations of production and exchange, and, on the other hand, the historical changes these relations undergo during different phases of capitalist development

(Aglietta, 1987). Furthermore the new concepts emphasized that the articulation of a social formation in time and space corresponds with particular structural features and institutional forms (Hurtienne, 1988, p. 187). It was assumed that the latter are valid over a long period of time and make a crucial contribution to the stabilization of the underlying structures of the mode of production in particular ways. *Regimes of accumulation* are associated with certain historical phases and development paths, which are characterized by economic growth, 'under which (immanent) crisis tendencies are contained, mediated or at least postponed' (Tickel and Peck, 1995, p. 359). Such growth takes the form of compatible commodity streams of production and consumption, which are reproduced over a long period of time. It is also normally associated with a particular industrial paradigm, a dominant principle of the division of labour. A *mode of regulation* comprises an ensemble of social networks as well as rules, norms, and conventions, which facilitates the trouble-free reproduction of an accumulation regime.

A mode of regulation itself comprises five subdimensions or *institutional forms*: the wage relation or 'wage–labour nexus' (Bertrand, 2002); the enterprise form; the nature of money (Guttmann, 2002); the state; and international regimes (Aglietta, 2002)[1]. It also includes a geographical and temporal dimension, which Jessop (2002, p. 21) calls *spatio-temporal fixes*. These determine the main spatial and temporal boundaries within which structural coherence is ensured. Within a given spatio-temporal fix, different regulatory institutions deal with different issues on different scales and over different time periods. Regulationists refer to a historical situation, in which a regime of accumulation and a mode of regulation complement each other sufficiently to secure a long era of economic expansion and social cohesion, as a *growth model* or a *model of development*. The stability of such a growth model is further enhanced when shared values and norms help to bring about a common sense value system that is subscribed to by members of all social classes. Regulationists such as Lipietz (1998) and Becker (2002) use Antonio Gramsci's notion of a *hegemonic block* with respect to those social classes and groups, which adhere to these values and are the carriers of them. Other authors have begun to link the regulation approach with the sociology of Pierre Bourdieu, and, in particular, with the concept of *habitus* (Dangschat, 1998; Koch, 2003, pp. 38–43, Herkommer, 2004). This concept is particularly helpful as it considers the perspective of the actors. Bourdieu goes beyond Marxist approaches to the issue of ideology by enlarging the focus of research to the preconscious and 'natural' dimensions of the reproduction of the social order. In doing so he takes very seriously the fact that social structures are inscribed not only in the minds but also in the bodies of the dominated.

For the present analysis, the wage relation, and the state (both in its role in socio-economic regulation at the national level and in its relationship to the international

---

1   The distinction of several (five) institutional forms and the corresponding openness in relation to the number of national capitalist configurations marks the major difference between regulation theory and the 'Varieties of Capitalism' approach (Hall and Soskice, 2001), which attempts to 'dichotomize the distribution of the various forms of capital' (Boyer, 2005: 529).

division of labour) are the most relevant institutional forms. Robert Boyer defines the wage relation as a 'set of legal and institutional conditions that govern the use of wage-earning labour as the workers' mode of existence' (Boyer, 2002a, p. 74). It refers 'to the type of means of production; the social and technical division of labour; the ways in which workers are attracted and retained by the firm; the direct and indirect determinants of wage income; and lastly, the workers' way of life' (Boyer, 1990, p. 38). While the wage relation is a more general concept, which has complementary relations with other institutional forms – the monetary regime, forms of competition, and the international division – in this book, we deal especially with the procedures and contents of wage determination. The latter can be understood as the process by which wage norms are generalized within an economic space. In advanced capitalist societies, wage determination processes, as with socio-economic regulation in general, is normally mediated through bipartite or tripartite bargaining at company, sector or national levels.

The debate on the role of the state in socio-economic regulation in the 1970s resulted in the thesis that the emergence of a state apparatus formally separated from all economic agents 'and the resulting institutionalized division between "politics" and "economics" is a structural requirement for the stable reproduction of capitalist societies' (Hirsch, 2000, p. 110). Market forces alone cannot reproduce the basic categories of the capitalist mode of production – private labour, the securing of private property, and the respect of the principle of equivalence in exchange relations – but depend on a formally independent institution that, above all, monopolizes the legitimacy of physical force and is therefore capable of enforcing the validity of these categories if necessary. Regulationists elaborated on this notion and analysed the state as an institutional form. As such it was seen as both 'an active party in the economy (via public finances and money) and as constitutive of the environment of the commodity economy (through the interaction of public policies)' (Théret, 2002, p. 123). The nation-state is especially well suited for the formation of a long-lasting combination of a regime of accumulation and a mode of regulation. Its relatively clear spatial structure provides a sounder basis for the emergence of common values, agency orientations, and, hence, class and/or group alliances than, for example, confederations of states. In addition, such a consensus is more likely to be reached within the boundaries of a nation-state as it tends to define its institutional structure while dissociating itself from 'external' factors. Lipietz (1985) therefore uses the nation-state as a starting point and interprets the changes in the international division of labour from the perspective of the developments and crises of single countries. This approach, however, does not prevent him from considering the particular features of international exchange relations, institutions and dependencies with regard to their repercussion on national growth strategies.

More generally, the regulation approach addresses the relationship between the international regime and national economies as 'a doubled set of connections' (Hirsch, 2000, p. 105). On the one hand, the growth and development potential of national locations depend on the ways in which they are embedded in the international division of labour, and, on the other hand, the latter is itself determined by the structures and development of national formations which are themselves results of negotiations and struggles between different classes and social groups. The position of a country in the world market is essentially influenced by its internal social structure, and above all by the composition of its elites and the particular forms of institutionalization of conflicts. The issues of whether an agricultural reform results in the abolition of extensive landed property or not, or whether industrial or financial capital factions actually dominate, for example, is of great significance for the structure of internal power relations and, in turn, for the growth strategy of the country in the world market. Equally relevant for such a strategy is the composition of the wage-earning class and the particular nature of industrial relations, within which workers are tied to the employers of a national location. Industrial relations can be gradually differentiated in a continuum from uncoordinated and conflict-oriented to coordinated and consensus-oriented models.

Thus, the room to manoeuvre of national growth strategies corresponds with different combinations of two parameters (the particular way a country is integrated into the international division of labour and the country's internal socio-economic structure), while the structure of the world market is seen as a 'field of possible positions' that allows for the simultaneous existence of a 'range of mutually compatible national regimes' (Lipietz, 1987). In contrast to prior *dependencia* theories (Cardoso and Faletto, 1978) and the World System approach (Wallerstein, 1979), regulationists do not interpret the international division of labour as a socially and spatially invariable and homogeneous block – a fixed 'core–periphery' relationship – but rather as a ' ... variable network. The global movements of capital are constantly modified via national formations' (Hirsch, 2000, p. 106), and the socio-economic struggles that underlie them. If the world market were constructed as a fixed set of relations of dominance with consistent poles and not, as in regulation theory, as an unstable balance of dominant and peripheral regions, then neither the 'catching-up' nor the relative decline of locations could be explained. On the one hand, the process of globalization remains determined by competitive, largely national economic spaces, on the other hand, once a hierarchy in the international division of labour has been established, the room to manoeuvre of national growth strategies is significantly reduced: nation-states can be 'successful' only to the extent to which they are integrated within the global context and the extent to which they respect the imperatives of the world market.

The issue of social cohesion can be approached against the background of those contradictions and dilemmas inherent to capitalism that necessitate regulation (1.1). Jessop (2001; 2002) summarizes Marx's theory in that there are basically three forms of these contradictions, which have to be dealt with in any kind of capitalist society. Firstly, there is the inability of capitalism to reproduce itself wholly through its inherent logic of commodification. Reproduction, by contrast, depends on a range of non-commodity forms of social relations as well as on 'fictitious' commodities such as land, money, knowledge, and, above all, labour power.[2] An eventual commodification of everything – a pure capitalist economy – is impossible. Uneven waves of commodification, decommodification and recommodification result and normally coincide with processes of territorialization, deterriorialization and reterritorialization. Secondly, many of the contradictions of capitalism can be traced to the basic contradiction between exchange and use value in the commodity form: productive capital is both an abstract value in motion and a concrete stock of time- and place-specific assets that have already been invested; the worker is both an abstract unit of labour power substitutable by others and a concrete individual with specific skills, knowledge and creativity; the wage is both a cost of production and a source of demand; money functions both as an international currency exchangeable against other currencies and as national currency; land functions both as a form of property and as a natural resource that is more or less renewable; knowledge is both the basis for intellectual property rights and a collective resource; state economic and social policy is not only responsible for securing certain key conditions for the valorization of capital and the reproduction of labour power but is also responsible for the maintenance of social cohesion in a socially divided, pluralistic social formation. Taxation is hence both an unproductive deduction from private revenues and a means to finance collective investment and consumption to compensate for 'market failures'. Thirdly, despite being inherent in the capitalist mode of production, these structural contradictions nonetheless assume different forms and different weightings in different countries. They are also, more or less, manageable depending on the particular institutional regulation, the specific spatio-temporal fixes and the hegemonic blocks with which they are associated.

In the face of these tensions, it cannot be taken for granted that a relatively stable regime of accumulation that is able to provide a correspondence between both the norms of production and of consumption and a successful mode of regulation will emerge. Such a productive combination, itself a product of the rather fortuitous and fortunate convergence of relatively independent parameters and developments in different societal fields, may or may not emerge. However, the extent to which such coherence is established is not only crucial for the success of the economy but also in order to avoid far-reaching socio-political crises. It is an absolute necessity for the maintenance of social cohesion. Conversely, socio-political disasters such as the emergence of fascist regimes in Germany and southern Europe were facilitated by crisis situations, where an accumulation regime did not harmonize with an outdated regulatory network, and where, for example, a deficit in effective demand led to major under-utilization of productive capacity. The results of such an imbalance include over-accumulation of capital, mass unemployment and social exclusion.

---

2   'Fictitious' in the sense that labour power, for example, is bought and sold on the labour market but is not itself created in a profit-oriented labour process (Jessop, 2002, p. 13).

2.2 Fordism as the predominant model of the post-war era

The regulation approach suggests that growth models achieve the greatest extent of sustainability if their regimes of accumulation are characterized by an optimal coherence of both the norms of production and consumption. Historically, the accumulation of capital took various forms: intensive forms alternated with extensive ones; export-oriented with import-oriented forms; and the main focus of accumulation was either on the production of the means of production or on the production of consumption goods. Equally, the institutional forms through which the accumulation of capital was regulated – the wage relation, monetary policies, and state intervention, especially – changed over time. The division into periods of capitalist development in regulation theory largely corresponds to Kondratieff's approach of *longues durées* (Kondratieff, 1946). According to Alain Lipietz (1998), a largely extensive accumulation regime dominated in the second half of the nineteenth century. This was based on the merely formal subsumption of wage labourers and therefore remained dependent on the subjective knowledge and skills of these workers. The regulation system embodied the liberal 'night-watchman' form of state that guaranteed the free movement of prices, wages and scale of production. This growth model was followed by a period of monopolist and imperialist economic and political relations. Taylorism began to be generalized as an industrial paradigm as early as World War I. However, this was not accompanied by a simultaneous increase in consumption by wage-earners. The Great Depression of the late 1920s can therefore be understood as the result of a lack of compatibility between the new production methods and an unchanged mode of regulation, which did not enable wage-earners to increase their consumption. It was only after the end of World War II that mass production was combined with mass consumption.

The great economic slump of the early 1930s, the seizure of power by fascist regimes in a range of European countries, the war, and – last but not least – the new challenge following the emergence of a competing non-capitalist social system in Eastern Europe moved the restructuring of capital–labour relations in Western Europe to top of the post-war agenda. In spite of different interests, which from time to time led to serious conflicts, most political parties and actors in industrial relations contributed substantially to the rebuilding of national economies. While trade unions began to accept new management methods, in return they established that wage-earners would benefit from productivity gains through direct wage increases. On the one hand, managers were recognized as having the leading role in the organization of the production process and in making strategic choices about markets and investments, while, on the other hand, the unions struggled to achieve a fair share of the profits arising from productivity increases for their members. The emerging new growth model soon came to be labelled 'Fordism'[3] after the production model developed and applied by Henry Ford in his automobile factories.

---

3   The first author to use this label was the Italian communist and Marxist philosopher Antonio Gramsci (1971), who, in the 1930s and 1940s, analysed the American New Deal in

Fordism did not exist in pure form anywhere. In what follows I outline the main features of Fordism as an 'ideal-type'. This theoretical construction will be subsequently used as a kind of analytical yardstick in the analysis of the 'real types' of national trajectories.[4] As a regime of accumulation, Fordism was characterized by a parallel restructuring of both the technological and organizational basis of the production process and the lifestyles and consumption patterns of the wage-earners. The economy was dominated by large, vertically integrated companies, which applied mass-production technologies, while the work organization in the factories largely followed the principles outlined in F.W. Taylor's 'Scientific Management' (1947). The latter involved a clear distinction between conception and execution, production and sales, marketing and finance, etc. Unlike the previous industrial paradigms, which had continued to depend on the wage-earners' subjective abilities and skills, the entire work process was now designed to be emancipated from the specific qualifications of individual workers and so ensured that one worker could be substituted by another. The function of workers was largely reduced to carrying out simple and repetitive functions within the work process, while skills, control assets and qualifications were increasingly concentrated within the planning department. Productivity continued to rise through economies of scale together with strict control over the majority of employees who mainly worked on the assembly line.[5] Furthermore, assembly line workers required a minimum of training which lead to large savings in costs. Fixed capital quickly was written off and amortization costs were incorporated into prices (Friedman, 2000, p. 59).

One of the favourable conditions for the success of this new regime of accumulation was the fact that pioneers such as Henry Ford could count on an 'infinite' demand for mass-produced goods such as automobiles, televisions, and washing machines. Unlike the 1930s, when solvent consumers were scarce, during the era of the post-war reconstruction, there was stable and expanding demand for both consumer goods and the means of production to build them. Since most households did not yet own these durable commodities, mass production could become the technological basis for their fast generalization. The turnover of fixed capital was accelerated by the continuing increase in the number of products, which reduced the costs of a single product. Corporate philosophy suggested a neutralization of costs through the expansion of the volume of production (Revelli, 1997, p. 3). Profits were supported by consumer demand that, in turn, was based on high and increasing wages, which were usually determined by collective agreements at the sector or central level and tied to an expected growth in productivity. Centralized collective bargaining, the increased mobility of workers seeking the best-paid jobs, and the creation of minimum-wage schemes, created not only increasing real wages but also, compared

---

his prison notebooks.

4   It should go without saying that it is above all the discrepancies between ideal-types and real-types (in Max Weber's classical sense) that is important in social research.

5   It was not by accident that Robert Reich (1997), Secretary of Labour in the first Clinton Presidency, compared the Taylorist division of labour with military command structures.

to pre-Fordist periods, stabilized wage differentials. Whereas in the nineteenth century and the inter-war period, labour struggles created wage differentials across skill levels, sectors and regions, within the Fordist system of wage determination, wage rises in one sector often led to wage increases at the national level (Reynauld, 2002; Koch, 2005).

As a mode of regulation, the Fordist type of enterprise involved a significant amount of separation between ownership and control in large corporations, in which mass production provided the spur to economic growth (Jessop, 2001). This does not exclude the fact that companies applying mass-production methods also employed other labour processes as well, or were tied to these labour processes in production networks within a given economic sector. The wage relation rested on the recognition of trade unionism and centralized collective bargaining in which the state played an active role (Boyer, 2002a). The trade unions, for their part, respected the management's power to control the labour process. Wages were indexed to productivity growth, while monetary emissions and credit policies were oriented towards the creation of effective aggregate demand in national economies. The state helped to secure this by means of policies designed to integrate the circuits of the capital and consumer goods industries, and by mediating the conflicts between capital and labour over the individual and social wages (Hirsch and Roth, 1986). Further, it helped to achieve growth and productivity agreements between employers' organizations and trade unions by promoting capital accumulation through public infrastructure spending and permissive credit and monetary policies. The state also carried out substantial income redistribution through Keynesian countercyclical economic policies. These developments were to culminate in the creation and expansion of the welfare system. In most advanced capitalist countries, both political parties and corporate actors agreed on the establishment of social funds and/or insurance systems to cover risks such as old age, sickness, and unemployment. Usually both employers and employees contributed to the financial maintenance of these funds.

Fordism would have been unsustainable without international regulation. Towards the end of World War II, the International Monetary Fund (IMF) and the World Bank were created by the agreements reached at Bretton Woods in 1944. The breakdown of the system of coupling national currencies to a national economy's available gold reserves was seen as an important contributory factor to the crisis in the 1930s. Following these agreements, the international financial and loan system was liberated from the gold standard; subsequently, national central banks had a much greater degree of autonomy in their monetary policies. Crucial economic decisions on parameters such as the convertibility of national currencies or the determination of whether, and to what extent, a trade partner was creditworthy were not taken more or less automatically on the basis of the gold standard but increasingly through central banks and national governments. The prime important role of the World Bank and the IMF was to determine a system of fixed rates of exchange, within which both institutions could give loans to nation-states in order, for example, to compensate for deficits in the balance of payments. In this way, differences in economic development between different states could be accommodated and sometimes reduced (Hall and

Midgley, 2004). The introduction of the General Agreement of Tariffs and Trade (GATT) in 1947 led to a gradual reduction of national tariff and trade barriers. By continuing to tie its own currency to the gold standard, the US supported this international regulation of money and loan transfers. The dollar functioned as 'world money' and thus it was possible to compensate for deficits in the balance of payments, which accompanied the foreign trade surplus of the US after World War II. However, the international regulation of Fordism was far from being altruistic. Non-capitalist countries, including former World War II allies, were, from the beginning, excluded from this support toward the reconstruction of devastated economies.[6]

As a mode of societalization, Fordism led to a historically unprecedented and encompassing level of social cohesion. However, this also took on a contradictory form. On the one hand, the productivity growth associated with the general achievement of economies of scale was a prerequisite for the simultaneous and proportionate development of the two departments of social production (production goods and consumption goods). The percentage of wages within total employers' costs decreased (or in Marx' terms, the 'organic composition' of capital grew), but the real wages of workers also increased. Employment could grow because the total volume of capital rose by a greater proportion than the increase in the number of workers made redundant due to productivity gains in the work process; hence, Fordism constituted one of the historically rare conjunctures in which the inherent tendency of capital to produce a 'redundant' population (Chapter One) was temporarily overcompensated by the fast growth of the total volume of capital. The cheapening of industrial products raised the purchasing power of wage labourers, so that both the employers' profits and the employees' real wages increased. The state benefited from this favourable situation and used its growing income from taxation for the expansion of a welfare state system, which, in turn, provided a guaranteed minimum standard of living for those who did not participate in the labour market. Not only was the working class actively integrated in the growth project of Fordism, but, for the first time, the unemployed and recipients of welfare entitlements, pensioners, and students (in some countries) received independent incomes, which the state raised via taxation and subsequently redistributed to these groups (Koch, 2001). The Fordist mode of societalization can be summarized in the simple formula:

> Fast growth rates of GDP and productivity
> + increase in real wages
> + <u>high levels of state income and welfare expenditure</u>
> = high degree of system and social integration[7]

---

6   Generally, anti-communism should not be underestimated as an ideological tool that helped to establish consensus in the western capitalist world and to create a 'hegemonic project' (Gramsci, 1971) to which large parts of the population – including huge sections of the working class – subscribed.

7   In the sense of the still valuable and useful notion of integration at system and social levels by David Lockwood (1992).

On the other hand, social inclusion remained somewhat incomplete since women were partially or completely excluded from economic activity. Until the 1970s, most European countries were characterized by almost full capacity utilization of the male workforce; for most women, however, gainful employment was only acceptable until the onset of marriage and motherhood. With the exception of the Scandinavian countries, this was ideologically enforced in the stylization of the nuclear family as the exemplary lifestyle of the time.[8] As women's income remained largely dependant on the outcomes of the informal exchange relations with the 'male breadwinner', Fordism confirmed and reinforced the basic structures of patriarchal division of labour.

Finally, comparative regulationist research demonstrated how the Fordist wage relation was applied in different nation-states, and it referred to the roles that the collective actors as well as particular institutions played in these processes (Boyer, 1995; Tickel and Peck, 1995; *Initiativgruppe Regulationstheorie*, 1997; Koch, 2004b). While most capitalist countries were shaped by the main features of Fordism as ideal-typically described above (above all by the parallel development of profits and wages, and the synchronous expansion of the welfare state), there was always a great deal of heterogeneity at the level of 'real-types'. In the 'periphery', a range of countries attempted to achieve a delayed Fordist development through policies of industrial import substitution, in which the state played the key role. It supported the industrialization processes through a range of measures, ranging from high tariffs to protect the domestic market and cheap loans and tax advantages for local investors to direct state investments in employment and infrastructure. In the case of larger countries such as Brazil, Mexico or South Africa, authors such as Feldbauer *et al.* (1995) talk of a 'peripheral Fordism'. In relation to the countries of the 'centre', there were also significant differences. The welfare state, for example, was much more advanced in Western Europe than in the US. Also, within Western Europe, growth strategies were heterogenous from the beginning. On the one hand, Torfing (1997) reports from Denmark that Taylorist mass production remained a marginal phenomenon there, while Fordist norms of consumption nevertheless became dominant. On the other hand, *Initiativgruppe Regulationstheorie* (1997, p. 15) reminds us that in many countries the export sector became the motor for the development of mass production, while the advancement of Fordist norms of consumption lagged behind. Chapter Four will elaborate on these contributions by reconstructing the national trajectories of the Netherlands, Sweden, the UK, Germany, and Spain.

In summary, Fordism, as an ideal-typical concept, was based on the parallel change of the production and accumulation processes of capital on the one hand, and the change in lifestyle of the middle and working classes on the other. This led

---

8   Leading sociologists tended to amplify this view. Talcott Parsons, like many others, described the nuclear family as best suited for the functioning of the social system. In doing so, the functionalist tradition failed to grasp the internal power relations of the nuclear family. Non-mainstream forms of family life were usually not even mentioned.

to historically unprecedented and comprehensive social cohesion. In Marxist terms, the relative surplus of the labour power increased due to the reduction of the time necessary to learn the skills necessary for the labour process and, at the same time, real wages increased due to the reduction of the prices of commodities available for mass consumption. In combination with the introduction of Keynesian economic and social policies and the creation of the welfare state, a 'class compromise' (Peter von Oertzen) between capital and workers was attained. Not only was the working class actively integrated in the growth project of Fordism, but non-economically active persons also benefited to a certain extent. As long as the Fordist growth strategy could ensure the participation of these heterogeneous groups in social wealth, it enjoyed extraordinary broad support and legitimacy. As both subjective aspirations and the actors' objective positions in the occupational system and in social space normally remained intact, the development strategy was welcomed by a great majority of a population whose composition cut across social classes.

2.3   The crisis of Fordism as challenge for national growth strategies[9]

The rise of Fordism advanced under circumstances of virtually unlimited markets. The only barrier to accumulation appeared to be the existing scale of production. By contrast, the awareness of the limited nature of the world is a hallmark of Post-Fordist times. Geographically, the Fordist market was largely limited to the nation-state but appeared to be economically inexhaustible. In time, however, firms began to encounter markets, which were geographically boundless but – in the medium-term – economically saturated; markets that did not 'grow' sufficiently fast to accommodate the rising amount of commodities that were produced due to the increased productivity of work, but remained at best stable (Revelli, 1997). Once the demand for mass-produced goods could no longer be taken for granted, sales and the market in general ceased to be secondary and dependent variables and became primary and independent. Management strategies were to change accordingly.

In addition to the crisis caused by deficits in the demand for mass-produced goods, there were also limits to the expansion of Fordism to every branch of production, including services. The 'growing capital intensity of production and dependence of economies of scale on full capacity utilization increased the strike power of organized labour; and the continuing search for productivity increases through work intensification led to growing alienation on the shop floor' (Jessop 2002, p. 81–82). The potential for accumulation and expansion under Fordist conditions was further hampered by the fact that it depended greatly on the availability of oil at decreasing costs in real terms. The two major increases in the price of oil following the formation of the Organization of Petroleum Exporting Countries (OPEC) in 1960 heightened the crisis. The capacity to integrate different social strata into the post-war class

---

9   I do not intend here to deliver an exhausting treatise on the different dimension of that crisis; these are touched merely in so far as they are relevant for the understanding of adjustments of national growth strategies.

compromise was further undermined by the political emergence of new social movements (Hirsch and Roth, 1986). Alongside ecological movements, whose goals and orientations often went beyond and, at the same time, below national borders by addressing issues at the global and regional level, it was above all the women's movement that questioned the patriarchal division of labour and thereby weakened one of the cornerstones of the Fordist mode of regulation and societalization: the nuclear family. This, in turn, led to changes in demand for state support, particularly for single parent families and elderly people. Finally, these changes were accompanied by a re-adjustment of the spatial dimension of capitalist regulation: social problems of housing, health, single households tended to be concentrated in urban areas, which had been in many cases abandoned by the middle classes.

In an attempt to achieve further economies of scale and to compensate for the relative market saturation of their home markets, companies began to expand into foreign markets. They also began to utilize foreign credit and tax havens to reduce the costs of both borrowing and transfer payments; this contributed to the undermining of the nation-state as the main unit of economic management. As the internationalization of the economy proceeded, national governments could no longer act as if their economic space were hermetically enclosed. This, in turn, had major implications for the financial base underpinning Keynesian economic and social policy. The tax revenues available to finance social security payments were reduced – particularly in welfare regimes where these payments were tied to wage labour – at a time when unemployment was increasing. At the same time, the contributions of employers to state revenues fell because of diminishing gross profits. Ironically, the declines in profit levels were often compensated for through the introduction of tax reductions and/or tax exemptions by national governments, which, in turn, aggravated the fiscal crisis of the state. The emergence and expansion of new information and communication technologies enabled capital to become increasingly mobile and to circumvent and even avoid the tax regime of the nation-state.

In the post-war decades, the international division of labour was comprised predominantly of advanced industrial countries producing both capital and consumption goods, and of poorly developed countries, which mainly exported raw materials. From the late 1970s, corporations found it increasingly lucrative to transfer the production of commodities to the developing world. The work process became fragmented and this was accompanied by the increasing heterogeneity of the entire economic space. Special tasks could be carried out in virtually any place in the world as long as this outsourcing ensured the most efficient combination of capital and labour. Fröbel *et al.* (1981, p. 15) were among the first to identify this tendency as a 'trans-national reorganization of production'. In this new spatio-temporal fix, the location of production is determined not simply by the supply of natural resources but also by factors that can be supplied 'artificially' such as infrastructure, skills, labour costs, and taxes. The existence of local networks based on mutual trust is likewise an important determinant of international competitiveness. According to Altvater and Mahnkopf (1996), global competition and local competitiveness can be understood as two simultaneous dynamics of modern (market) societalization. The term 'glocalization' expresses the two intertwined tendencies that transform the Fordist spatio-temporal fix, that is, the disembedding of economic processes from traditional social and political ties, and the emergence of new group ties and networks at a given location.

Important changes also occurred within the international regulation of economic relations. In the post-war decades, the dollar was the only currency tied to the gold standard; it was generally used as 'world currency'. According to the agreements reached at Bretton Woods, dollar reserves from other countries remained exchangeable against gold in the US. European and Japanese exports began to increase at a faster rate than those of the US, whose productivity advantage began to erode. At the same time, there was an expansion of US direct investments overseas and this resulted in a further outflow of the dollar from the US, mainly towards Europe. In the US, a rapidly growing deficit in the balance of payments emerged and started to undermine the commitment to exchange foreign-held dollars for gold. The gold cover of the dollar turned out to be fictitious to the extent that the deficit in the balance of payments increased (*Initiativgruppe Regulationstheorie*, 1997, p. 15). By the early 1970s, a devaluation of the US dollar seemed to be inevitable. The US government withdrew its commitment to convert foreign dollars into gold and this signalled the beginning of the end of the international currency system negotiated at Bretton Woods. The system of exchange rates was now to become more flexible. The use and the exchange rate of the US dollar in the currency markets declined. The dollar did not lose its function as a world currency but was supplemented by the D-mark and yen, and, more recently, the euro, which have increasingly taken on the role of reserve currencies. With regard to international trade, the transition to flexible exchange rates resulted in greater market uncertainty due to the fact that currencies were now free-floating. At the same time, the potential for currency speculation grew enormously and new investment possibilities emerged for financial capital that became increasingly available as the crisis of Fordism unfolded.

Further opportunities for capital valorization opened up as the new information and communication technologies facilitated the ready availability of necessary information on markets and permitted the purchase of blocks of shares anywhere in the world. This meant it was now possible, and increasingly expected, to be active in financial transactions twenty-four hours a day in different time zones. The enormous growth of financial capital, which could no longer be profitably invested in industry to a satisfactory extent; the deregulation of financial markets; and technological innovation fuelled an enormous expansion in financial operations, which grew faster than the volume of world trade and gross national products. For example, the total value exchanged in stock markets increased by a massive 1500 per cent between 1980 and 1999. During the same period, however, the GDP within the OECD countries merely doubled (Koch, 2003, p. 57); a phenomenon that is often referred to as decoupling of 'real' and 'monetary' accumulation (Novy *et al.*, 1999).

The immediate response to these structural changes at the first G7 summit at Ramboillet (France) in 1975 was 'Keynesian' in the sense that the maintenance of global demand was given priority (Lipietz, 1998). The World Bank and the IMF were given the task of coordinating this policy. However, these priorities were subsequently reversed. The demand side was no longer seen as the cause of the crisis. Instead, the supply side was increasingly identified as the main obstacle to profitability. The main pieces of evidence used to justify this about-turn included the slowdown in the growth of productivity; the rise in labour costs; and the alleged burden of welfare state transfer payments. The core principle of 'Reaganomics' in the 1980s was the creation of favourable conditions for the investment of financial capital in the US. The exchange rate of the dollar recovered following the rise of interest rates in the US. The impact of this development on other countries was, however, disastrous, particularly for the planned economies in Eastern Europe and the peripheral countries in Latin America and Asia.[10] Many of these countries had obtained loans at favourable interest rates in the early 1970s and were now confronted with ballooning interest repayments. Despite making enormous repayments, the debts of developing countries increased from 616 billion US dollars in 1981 to 2177 billion in 1996 (*The Economist*, 26.04.97). After the 'lost decade' of the 1980s, a range of developing countries agreed restructuring and adjustment plans with the IMF and the World Bank. These contained, among other things, freezes on wages and prizes as well as cutback policies, especially in the area of social services, in order to ensure the debtor nations were creditworthy (Hall and Midgley, 2004).

There is general consensus among authors in the fields of industrial relations, political economy and social policy that the dimensions of the crisis of Fordism, in particular those at the international level, have a huge impact on the options of decision-makers at the national level. However, *how* precisely these options are affected remains controversial. A majority of authors seem to assume a close connection between external constraints such as 'globalization' and internal policy choices: deregulation of the institutional settings (which typified the Fordist era of capitalism) and the reduction of state expenditure, especially for social affairs, are seen as the only options open to decision-makers in the areas of labour market and social policy. This idea is taken for granted to such an extent that empirical studies on reforms of labour markets and social structures are often not even initiated. Empirically, however, the hypothesis that nation-states have no option but to compete against each other in order to undercut social and ecological standards cannot be validated until its defenders provide proof that real labour market and welfare reforms, carried out since the late 1970s, indeed led to mere deregulation, and that they one-sidedly served the interests of employers. Conversely, the possibility that deregulation could turn into re-regulation, and into some form of Post-Fordist growth pact in which trade unions play a meaningful role should not be excluded by definition. Theoretically, too, the overly hasty reduction of locational factors to merely those of low tax and cheap labour remains unconvincing (Hirst and Thompson, 1996; Garrett, 1998). While it is true that large corporations invest in those countries and regions that promise the biggest net profit, profit margins depend

---

10 For the Chilean case, see Koch, 1998a: 44-46.

not only on the costs of the factors of production, but also on their comparative productivity. A country with relatively high taxes can therefore remain attractive to international capital as long as it offers a highly qualified labour force able to produce high quality commodities.

In the debate on the changing role of nation-states following the crisis of Fordism, regulationists work from the 'hypothesis that the nation-state is still a relevant unit of analysis, even when a high level of internationalisation is de-establishing many of the institutional compromises of each country' (Boyer, 2002b, p. 231). Following the conceptualization of the relationship between world market and national economies as 'doubled set of connections' (2.1), national trajectories are assumed to be shaped by two factors: the particular integration of a country in the international division of labour and the country's internal power relations and socio-economic composition. The world market is not seen as a homogenous structure with stable core–periphery relations. By contrast, the very process of 'globalization' itself is understood as codetermined by state growth strategies. From this perspective, economic and political internationalization does indeed threaten the functioning of national economic spaces, but it does *not* follow that the role of national governments and collective actors in areas such as labour market and social policy is reduced to one of transmission of global 'constraints'. While there is a consensus among regulationist researchers that there is a general shift towards a relative opening of national economies that triggers a piecemeal transition in regulation from demand management towards supply management in order to guarantee and/or improve the competitiveness of a national location – Bob Jessop (1999, p. 355) talks of a 'Schumpeterian state' in so far as it 'tries to promote permanent innovation and flexibility in relatively open economies' – in the following chapter, I would like to argue that this transition can be carried out in different ways.

Chapter 3

New Directions in Comparative Research into Labour Markets and Social Structures

The first section of this chapter suggests two ideal-types of possible Post-Fordist growth strategies that Western European nation-states can follow (3.1). The likely effects these new growth strategies have on the social structure will be discussed in the next section (3.2). These theoretical reflections will at the same time serve as point of departure for the empirical analysis of labour markets and social structures in five Western European countries. The design of this inquiry will be introduced in the last section (3.3).

3.1   Capital-oriented and negotiated growth strategies

The Fordist growth model became crisis-prone in the late 1970s (2.3). The economic dimensions of this crisis were multi-layered and extended from the exhaustion of the productivity potential of economies of scale, through the changing demand structures for industrially manufactured goods and the spatial reorganization of the work process, to the new role of financial capital and investment practices. All these separate factors combined to undermine the crucial structural basis for the ascendancy of the Fordist mode of societalization: the parallel enhancement of profits and wages and the accompanying redistribution of income by the state. For national decision-makers the pressure increased to either change established forms of regulation – the levels and the content of collective bargaining, in particular – or to optimize the leeway of a given model by changing the content and orientation of collective bargaining (Koch, 2004a).

In relation to the changing relationship between world market and national economies, regulationists work from the hypothesis of a 'doubled set of connections' (Hirsch) between the nation-state and the world market, whereby the latter is not viewed as a fixed structure external to nation-states. National governments, especially, are seen as relevant actors that decisively contribute to the shape of the features of the world market. The possibilities and limits of the growth strategies of particular states are hence defined at the intersection of two factors: the particular nature of a country's integration into the international division of labour and the country's internal socio-economic structure. The fact that this dual relationship shapes national locations in different ways is the structural background for the simultaneous existence of different national formations and their greater or lesser 'success'. Hence, while there is as yet no agreement between regulationist researchers on the precise features of Post-Fordist accumulation regimes with corresponding alternative modes of regulation, it is nevertheless possible to theoretically construct two opposing 'Roads to Post-Fordism' that Western European nation-states can follow. Both roads stress the increasing importance of more flexibility, of enabling organizations to adapt quickly to rapid development in technology, of greater diversity in labour markets, and of growing international competition.

The first ideal-type of a Post-Fordist growth strategy could be called the capital-oriented road. It features a lack of wage coordination (typically achieved by bargaining at company or individual level) and a general orientation towards (short-term) capital interests (for example, through reforms that improve the conditions for capital valorization without much consideration of other parameters such as the development of real wages or economic participation). Collective bargaining is decentralized and flexibility manifests itself in negotiations between employer and the individual employee, or at company level. Wages are no longer index-linked and this is accompanied by structural weakening of the unions. Work organization and working hours will, for the most part, be arranged to achieve short-term gains in competitiveness, and new technologies will be introduced largely to decrease labour costs and to reinforce controls without actually transcending Taylorism. At the same time, contributions made by employers to pension schemes, holiday pay, health insurance, etc. are reduced, while public services are increasingly privatized. Legislation is introduced to facilitate hiring and firing, and dismissals lead less often to legal penalties for the employer. During individual or company level bargaining, employees rarely experience work situations that allow them to coordinate and manage their professional and private life. Part-time work is organized in a way that maximizes the insecurity of workers: it is involuntary and flexible according to the changeable, competitive needs of the employer. The role of the state is weak as it carries out reforms that are exclusively in the short-term interest of capital-owners (for example, the attraction of international capital through low labour costs and reduced taxes and contributions, while demoting previous goals of state regulation such as full employment and the avoidance of greater income inequalities). Once these reforms are achieved, the state withdraws from any active role in regulation and leaves it to 'market forces'.

At the opposite end of the spectrum is what could be called the negotiated road. Here, wage coordination continues to take place either at the national or sector level and is oriented towards achieving a balance between capital valorization, productivity growth, wage developments, and labour market participation. The company's internal distribution of work will not only consider competitive interest in the short-term but also the workers' interest in long-term employment contracts and the enhancement of his or her commitment to the job. The flexibility of working hours and overtime will be organized within defined limits and related to the length of the working week. Part-time work also increases in this system, but since it is

Table 3.1   Two Post-Fordist growth strategies

Features of growth strategy	Capital-oriented	Negotiated
General orientation	Extensive: capital valorization through decrease of costs; orientation at (short-term) capital interests	Intensive: capital valorization through optimization of technological basis of working process; combination of capital interests and employment rights
Wage determination	At individual or company level	At sector or central level
Level of employers' contribution to public funds	Low	High
Role of trade unions	Weakened	Important
Labour market and welfare system	Deregulated to accommodate capital interests; welfare level quantitatively reduced	Re-regulated: qualitatively restructured but maintained at quantitatively high level
Working hours	Changeable according to needs of employing company: 'generous' margins for overtime and short-time work	Flexibility of working time within defined limits; part-time workers are entitled to additional public transfer income
Role of the state	Initially strong achieving capital-oriented reforms; makes itself redundant and becomes 'weak' thereafter	Strong and engaged: continues with its active role in managing the economy and to invest, for example, in key technologies and infrastructure

subject to central bargaining, combining professional and private life is easier here than in the capital-oriented road. Information technologies will be used in order to modernize industries and to find an alternative to Taylorism. The role of the state remains strong or is strengthened as supply-oriented policies are combined with the maintenance of employment rights. Such an 'engaged state' is generally oriented towards rationalization, rather than the downsizing of the labour market and the welfare state, and continues to invest in key technologies, infrastructure and/or in active labour market policy.

3.2   Decomposition and recomposition of the social structure

The regulation theoretical perspective suggests that major changes in labour market and social structure are dependent on the 'grand' conjunctures in the historical development of capitalism. Having said this, two things seem to be all the more surprising: first, that the social structure has hitherto played an, at best, subordinate role in the debate on the transition from Fordist to Post-Fordist growth strategies; and second, that regulation theoretical approaches and problems have so far hardly found any echo in the international discussion on social stratification and inequality.[1] With the aim of contributing to the closure of this double gap in research, this section presents four hypotheses in relation to the changes in labour markets and social structures in the transition towards Post-Fordist growth strategies in Europe, which will, at the same time, serve as the point of departure for the empirical analysis in the following chapter. According to the first hypothesis, there is or has been a social structure that corresponds or has corresponded to the Fordist stage in the development of capitalism. This 'Fordist social structure' itself is subdivided into growth and decline phases. The second hypothesis relates to the growth period of Fordism. This phase was shaped by fast productivity growth achieved through mass production and the 'scientific' organization of the division of labour. With the enormous reduction of prices in essential consumer goods, the conditions for what Burghart Lutz (1989) called 'internal takeover' (*innere Landnahme*) were established: the participation of the 'masses' in commodified forms of consumption that had hitherto been monopolized by the dominant classes. Among the structural features of the growth period of Fordism are a rising percentage of industrial employment, full employment and full-time jobs, but also – due to the predominant male breadwinner model – a low percentage of female economic activity. With the continuing standardization of the work process and its spatial concentration, a relatively homogeneous working class emerges that learns to defend and represent its interests self-confidently. At the same time, this standardization leads to an expansion in the size of the units of production, and this coincides with a concentration of capital in fewer and fewer companies. The quantitative expansion of the working class is accompanied by the decrease in the number of economic units, which is statistically expressed by the increase of dependent labour at the expense of self-employment. In a nutshell, Fordism was based on a previously unknown coherence in the movements of both production and consumption: the synchronous expansion of the scale of production and of mass consumption was the economic foundation for a relatively high level of inclusion of the population in labour market and society.

The advancement of Fordism and the corresponding social structure reached its climax in the early 1970s and, with the crisis in the mid-1970s, turned into decline thereafter. The third hypothesis claims that those labour markets and social structures that had emerged in the course of the growth of Fordism, began to be decomposed during the crisis of Fordism. Features of this process (of structural decomposition) are: diminishing growth rates in both GDP and productivity, the decentralization of locations and units of production, decreasing employment and increasing unemployment rates, especially in the industrial sector, the stagnation of real incomes and a heterogenization of class positions. These developments are accompanied by a general disorganization of the labour market, which takes the

---

1   See Dangschat (1998) for an exception to this rule.

form of an increase in segmentation, precarization, and de-regulation. Marginal and informal work, fixed-term and non-standard employment expand, while inequalities in real incomes rise so that wages no longer secure sufficient domestic demand for mass-produced commodities. By and large, Fordist prosperity comes under pressure from both the supply and the demand side: On the one hand, due to the exhaustion of the potential for productivity growth of mass production, fast growth rates in GDP and productivity can no longer be achieved; on the other hand, wages stagnate and neither allow for sufficient demand nor for state policies towards a redistribution of profits as in the heyday of Fordism. A general disintegration of economy and society, including increasing wage inequality and relative poverty, is the result.

The fourth hypothesis is the least well grounded and so is in special need of empirical scrutiny. It claims that after the Fordist crisis and the corresponding decomposition of the social structure, a process of recomposition of labour markets and social structures starts, whereby the concrete features of this process are dependent on the kind of road to Post-Fordism followed by a country. In countries where a capital-oriented and labour extensive growth strategy predominates, the return to fast growth rates in GDP and to full employment is carried out at the expense of slow productivity growth. The social structure is characterized by relatively long working hours, due to the labour-extensive orientation of the growth strategy, and huge wage inequalities due to the low level of wages at the lower end of the occupational system and to the decreased level of state transfer payments. Relative poverty is therefore advanced, often taking the form of *working poor*. Part-time workers are especially likely to be affected by poverty. Self-employment will rise, often motivated by despair caused by the lack of satisfactory alternatives in the formal occupational system.

In negotiated growth strategies, new technologies will be used to modernize industries and to find an alternative to Taylorism. The use of labour is intensive, enabling productivity to recover much faster from the Fordist crisis. Real wages can therefore remain at a relatively high level, thereby minimizing the percentage of the working poor. The welfare state supports this through the continuing provision of benefits, especially for part-time workers. As in capital-oriented growth strategies, self-employment will increase, but in this model, it will be supported by national and regional planning as well as by intensive training programmes. In a nutshell, the high productivity orientation allows the return to full employment combined with rising real wages, relatively short working hours, stable wage inequalities and, consequently, a low level of poverty. This growth strategy is therefore a genuine class compromise, clearly going beyond short-term interests in competitiveness and actively embracing the participation of employees.

In the following chapters, I assume that labour markets and social structures of advanced capitalist countries go through the three phases of economic and political development outlined above: the growth of the social structures that correspond with Fordism, followed by their de- and recomposition depending on the type of Post-Fordist growth strategy followed by a country. Differences in national trajectories are to be expected even if we only consider the possibility that one country might

Table 3.2   Labour markets and social structures in capital-oriented and negotiated growth strategies

Labour market and social structure indicators	Capital-oriented	Negotiated
Use of work force	Extensive	Intensive
Working hours	Many	Few
Productivity	Low	High
Wage inequalities	High	Low
Level of state expenditure for labour market and welfare purposes	Low	High
Level of state transfer income	Low	High
Relative poverty	High (often working poor)	Low
Unemployment	Low	Low
Part-time work	Rising (insecure, unregulated)	Rising (negotiated in tripartite bargaining; part-time workers are entitled to additional welfare payments)
Self-employment	Rising (often due to lack of alternatives in dependent work)	Rising (supported by state programmes)

maintain its Fordist forms of socio-economic regulation, while another might already have proceeded to the stage of deregulation and/or re-regulation. The concrete forms of recomposition of labour market and social structure in a particular country are mediated through the practice of a multitude of social and political struggles. The social sciences, in so far as they operate at the level of 'pure' theory, have to content themselves with outlining the limits within which these struggles take place. The two scenarios outlined above – capital-oriented and negotiated growth strategies – are an attempt to theoretically construct these limits. Issues of concrete national trajectories, however, can only be treated in the context of an historical and empirical analysis. This will be the next step: five Western European countries will be analysed in relation to their political and economic development, their reforms in labour market and welfare regulation, and the changes in their social structure. It is only in this context that the suitability of the suggested scenarios for the comparative understanding of labour markets and social structures in the transition from Fordism to Post-Fordism can be assessed.

3.3 Labour markets and social structures in five European countries: Design of a comparative empirical investigation

After focussing on theoretical issues in the context of the crisis of Fordism and possible Post-Fordist growth strategies, we shall now consider the historical and empirical process of deregulation and re-regulation of labour market and welfare systems in the Netherlands, Sweden, Spain, the United Kingdom, and Germany. First, I comment on the selection of countries (3.3.1), and then, I introduce both the different steps of the empirical enquiry and the databases used (3.3.2).

3.3.1 Selection of countries

The Western European countries selected for the purpose of comparative investigation represent the theoretically constructed Post-Fordist strategies (3.1) in the broadest possible way. The UK (4.4) was assumed to be closest to the capital-oriented road to Post-Fordism due to its tradition of company-level bargaining and the fact that its Conservative governments began 'liberating market forces' earlier than other governments. The corresponding measures of privatization and deregulation were also presumed to be most far-reaching. As a consequence, features of a Post-Fordist social structure with capital-oriented hallmarks were expected in the UK rather than in other countries. Sweden (4.2), on the other hand, was presumed to be close to a negotiated growth strategy, since it has a tradition of tripartite bargaining at central level and a strong active state, which created employment, and, via taxation and intervention, has contributed to limiting socio-economic inequalities and to safeguarding a maximum of social inclusion. Germany (4.1), due to its tradition of bargaining at the sector level, was viewed as taking a path between capital-oriented and negotiated growth strategies. Two further countries were chosen to be investigated as they have been in the focus of international debate on labour market and welfare regulation for a considerable period of time: Spain and the Netherlands. In the case of Spain (4.3), it was hypothesized that there would be a high level of economic and social disintegration, since the country was shaped by high unemployment rates for much of the 1990s. The González and Aznar governments reacted to this with a range of reforms with the main aim of making the industrial relations system more flexible. The investigation of the impacts of these reforms on employment appeared to be a promising endeavour. And finally, as a 'counterpart' to the Spanish situation, the Netherlands were considered (4.5); many experts in labour market regulation and industrial relations have recommended the emulation of the country's labour market reforms. The Netherlands came to be known as the 'European champion' in terms of employment growth, and this is normally seen as being related to an offensive strategy of redistribution of work and income.

3.3.2   Deregulation and re-regulation of labour markets and welfare systems and the occupational and social structure

The economic and social system of each country is first analysed separately; particular emphasis is placed on the procedures and contents of wage determination, the political and social processes that generalize wage norms in a national economy. The second focus is on the changing role of the state as an institutional form in these regulatory processes. Thereafter, again with a special emphasis on wage determination procedures and the role of the state, the issue of reforms in labour market and welfare systems in the last two decades is raised. These first two steps are based on a detailed study of relevant literature and on interviews with experts in the field of labour market and welfare carried out in Madrid, Glasgow, Rotterdam, Lund, and Berlin.

The next step is the analysis of the transformation of the occupational and social structure in the five countries. This uses datasets provided by the International Labour Organization (ILO), the Organization for Economic Cooperation and Development (OECD), and the Statistical Office of the European Communities (EUROSTAT). Together, these institutions provide a wealth of information on the occupational and social structure that previous comparative investigations have not yet utilized exhaustively. The crucial advantage of these datasets is that internationally comparable statistical series, beginning with the 1960s, can be compiled. This is necessary for the understanding of long-term tendencies in the restructuring of the occupational and social structure. More recent databases provide more detailed information on individual countries, but not normally in comparable form, and not over a long period of time. Where opportune, however, some of the more recent and national databases are considered as additional sources of information. A further advantage of official international statistics is the fact that nearly all of the relevant tables can be compiled for women and men separately.

The point of departure of the data analysis is the investigation of growth of GDP, 'productivity, wages, and unemployment since 1961'. On the basis of EUROSTAT data (European Commission, 2004), the core thesis of regulation theory of a dramatic crisis in economic growth and employment in the 1970s and 1980s, but also potential tendencies of economic recovery and a recomposition of the social structure since the 1990s are considered. In the second step, demographic development with long-term tendencies in labour market participation and unemployment is contrasted using ILO data.

The third step is a class-specific analysis of the economically active population. The class structure is of relevance in this research in so far as it builds primarily on the qualitative difference between owners of capital and dependent employees. In particular, we focus on the dialectic of increasing and decreasing self-employment within total economic activity. The theoretical discussion suggests that self-employment decreases as a result of the concentration and centralization of capital during the growth period of Fordism. While economies of scale were characterized by large companies that tended to concentrate on the purchase, fabrication, and sales of goods under one roof, and while this led to a decrease in the total number of companies, a trend in the opposite direction can be hypothesized when Fordism becomes less important. During the transition towards Post-Fordist growth strategies, a re-articulation of the accumulation regime takes place. On the basis of the literature on the crisis of Fordism, we can assume a tendency towards the outsourcing of some of the production chain and some increased use of external services. In addition, where capital-oriented growth strategies are followed, the increasingly exclusive nature of the labour market will force a growing number of participants in the market to become self-employed. Therefore, typical features of a Post-Fordist labour market are that the number and the percentage of self-employed persons increase, while the percentage of dependently employed persons decreases. To validate this hypothesis, ILO data are evaluated with respect to the changes in the percentage of self-employment in the total economically active population over time.

Fourth, we look at wage-earners by economic sector and examine the movement of the formerly agricultural population, either to the industrial sector or directly to the tertiary sector. A second focus will be on regroupings within the industrial sector and whether patterns of change followed the classical model: an initial expansion of the industrial sector was followed by its contraction during the transition towards a post-industrial society. Our comparative perspective will particularly focus on the temporal dimension: in one case, a relatively early de-industrialization could have emerged, while in a second case, the process of decline in industrial employment could have started later and to a lesser extent. Of special relevance is the development of the service sector; the regrouping of traditional lower-middle class jobs in the retail trade, food and hospitality sectors, for example, in relation to modern highly-skilled services in the financial and high-tech sector, and the social services (health and education sector, in particular). Issues to be raised include: what sort of service economy was created in the Netherlands, the alleged employment miracle? What kind of impact did the UK's market-oriented growth strategy have on the service sector in comparison with the Swedish state-centred strategy? Is Spain, traditionally known as economically underdeveloped, characterized by a predominance of traditional services (personal services, hotels and restaurants, etc.)?

In order to understand the changes in different employment sectors over time, I use the third revised categorization of the *International Standard Classification of all Economic Activities* (ISIC) (ILO, 1999, p. 1307). 'Agriculture' includes tabulation categories A and B of the ISIC: *Agriculture, Hunting and Forestry* as well as *Fishing*. 'Industry' includes tabulation categories C to F: *Mining and Quarrying, Manufacturing, Electricity, Gas and Water Supply* as well as *Construction*. In order to further differentiate between diverse service sector jobs, I follow Max Haller's (1997) suggestion and subdivide them into three groups: 'Services I' consists of tabulation categories G to I: *Wholesale and Retail Trade; Repair of Vehicles, Motorcycles and Personal and Household Goods* as well as *Hotels and Restaurant*; 'Services II' includes financial services (tabulation categories J and K, *Financial Intermediation* and *Real Estate, Renting and Business Activities*); and 'Services III' includes the social and personal services (tabulation categories L to Q, *Public Administration and Defence, Compulsory Social Security, Education, Health and Social Work, Other Community, Social and Personal Service Activities, Private Households with Employed Persons* and *Extra-territorial Organizations and Bodies*).

The fifth step is an overview of annual hours worked, part-time employment, long-term unemployment, and labour market policy using statistical data provided by the OECD.[2] The information on the volume of work and the relative weight of part-time work within total employment, viewed both comparatively and over time, allows an approximation of whether a country followed a labour-intensive or labour-extensive growth strategy. Long-term unemployment is a crucial indicator of the temporal aspect of socio-economic exclusion. It makes a great deal of difference whether unemployment is short- or long-term. In the latter case, complete exclusion from all labour market activity is a real possibility, which can trigger strategies of self-exclusion and/or resignation on the part of those exposed to it. The criteria of the OECD define long-term unemployment as that which lasts more than one year. Labour market policy is considered in terms of a country's expenditure on passive and active labour market policy as a percentage of the gross domestic product (GDP). From this information, we conclude whether a national government is actively involved in socio-economic affairs or does so to a lesser degree.

The empirical investigation is concluded by the consideration of income inequality and relative poverty since the late 1960s in order to test our hypothesis, put in Section 3.2, that different Post-Fordist growth strategies correspond with different degrees of income inequality and relative poverty. For this purpose, I use data from the *Luxembourg Income Study*,[3] which counts households and their members as 'poor', if they earn up to 50 per cent and 60 per cent, respectively, of average disposable income. Relative poverty is further analysed in terms of different age groups. The dataset also allows the investigation of the question of whether, and to what extent, the elderly and children are disproportionately exposed to poverty. Finally, the *Luxemburg Income Study* provides the *Gini coefficient* over time and across countries. The *Gini coefficient* is a popular measurement of income inequality that condenses all income distribution into a single number between zero and one: the higher the number, the greater the degree of income inequality. A value of zero corresponds to the absence of inequality, so that, having adjusted for household size and composition, all individuals have the same household income. In contrast, a value of one corresponds to inequality in its most extreme form, with a single individual having command over the entire income of the economy.

---

2   The OECD counts all work as part-time work that takes less than 30 hours a week.
3   See, for further details, <www.lisproject.org>.

Chapter 4

The Country Studies

4.1 Germany

4.1.1 Economic and social system

West Germany's post-war growth strategy was based on a specific Fordist wage determination process. This was done by separating the sector level, where wages and the length of collective agreements were discussed (*Tarifvertragssystem*) from the company level, where daily work relations were addressed (*Betriebliche Mitbestimmung*). Even though there was no wage bargaining at the social level, wages were normally negotiated for one sector in one federal state (*Bundesland*) – often in the metal industry in Baden-Württemberg – and the result served as a model for further bargaining rounds in other federal states and in other industries. Since these bargaining rounds did not result in great differences from the original wage level, a general distribution of wage norms was ensured. Collective agreements (*Flächentarifverträge*) were negotiated between the trade union and employer's organization representing the relevant sector. While these agreements defined minimum standards in relation to wages, working hours, holidays, dismissal protection, and so on, arrangements within individual companies were made at the level of work councils (*Betriebsräte*). General agreements were therefore interpreted and implemented extremely heterogeneously at company level, an issue that is often underestimated (Ganßmann and Haas, 1999, p. 151). This is also stressed by the Sachverständigenrat (a think-tank of economists that advises the government): the lack of flexibility at company level is often caused not by restrictions resulting from agreements at sector level but rather from the utilization of flexibility within these agreements by the companies themselves (*Sachverständigenrat*, cited in Ganßmann and Haas, 1999, p. 151). Furthermore, it was possible to include particular cases where a company could legally deviate from the collective agreement, known as 'opening clauses' (*Öffnungsklauseln*).

In companies with at least five employees, employees were given the right to be represented in works councils. As mentioned above, their main function was to ensure the application of collective agreements according to the particular needs of the company. The works councils codetermined, for example, payment methods and systems, bonuses and performance-related pay, holiday scheduling, recruitment, and dismissal. In companies with over 500 employees, more extensive codetermination rules were agreed (*Unternehmensmitbestimmung*). Federal governments guaranteed the autonomy of the labour market parties (*Tarifautonomie*) and restricted themselves to setting basic parameters for bipartite bargaining (for example, maximum number of working hours, legislation for fixed-term contracts, and the legal regulation of industrial conflicts). The state's capacity for direct intervention was limited both vertically and horizontally (Streeck, 1997). Vertical limitation refers to the federal structure of the political system and to the fact that the federal government and the governments of the *Länder* often consist of different coalitions of political parties, making political change rather slow. Horizontally, much of the power of socio-economic regulation was given to independent authorities such as the Bundesbank or the Federal Cartel Office. Governments, therefore, could normally not initiate Swedish-style industrial policies. The state was more 'enabling' and moderating than étatiste (Streeck, 1997, p. 38).

This institutional setting had a positive impact on the international competitiveness of (West) Germany for quite a long period of time. Germany's foreign trade relations are extensive and amount to a percentage of more than 10 per cent of global exports, sharing the position of leader with the US and Japan. In contrast to these latter countries, where foreign trade relations are distributed more widely, 70 per cent of Germany's exports remain within Western Europe. Therefore, in relation to Germany, it is more apt to speak of enduring Europeanization than globalization. The competitiveness of traditional industrial areas (mechanical engineering, the chemical sector, vehicle production) has always been especially strong. This is supported by the dual education system, which, particularly with regard to highly skilled vocational training, is extremely wide-ranging and produces a diversified and skilled labour force. The social democratic Friedrich Ebert Foundation summarizes the main features of the German economic and social model as based on a functioning infrastructure, economic growth, exports, and full employment alongside job safety and a stable currency (Zukunftskommission der Friedrich Ebert Stiftung, 1998, p. 47).

The pillars of the German welfare state are insurance schemes to provide cover for risks such as old age, disability, sickness, the need for nursing or care, and unemployment. The means-tested social assistance benefit (*Sozialhilfe*) functions as 'last resort' in cases of individual need. The model is not geared towards equality and redistribution but towards the conservation of the status quo. Given that benefits (and the duration of these payments) depend directly on the contributions paid into the insurance fund, then a person's occupational status is largely transferred to unemployment benefits and pensions. Social citizenship rights depend greatly on a person's (previous or current) occupational position; this is why Esping-Andersen (1990) labelled the German welfare state conservative. The fact that the functioning of the economic and social system is linked to a traditional gender-based division of labour also contributes to the conservation of a social position. The husband functions as the 'breadwinner', whereby it is assumed that his salary is sufficient to provide for his wife and children. The continuation of marriage as the predominant type of household in the Fordist era was further 'supported' by the fact that women as 'housewives' were normally only entitled to very low payments from the social insurance system. Women remained dependent on their husbands as it was only their status as 'wives' that guaranteed the receipt of pensions comparable to those of their husbands. Relatively generous pensions for widows ensured that women who had not been economically active maintained their socio-economic status.

The conservative German welfare state has been hit especially hard by economic crises because revenues from social insurance increase and fall in direct proportion to the number of people in employment. The system is pro-cyclical: if the number of employed people decreases, the revenue of the social insurances is also reduced, and, due to increasing unemployment, expenditure rises. Financial limitations of social insurances are the inevitable result. However it is not only the level but also the type of employment that has a crucial effect on the financial situation of the insurance system since not all economically active groups contribute to it. Civil servants, above all, do not contribute to their own pension schemes and so this burden must be met by scarce public funds. German governments can react in three ways to reduced social insurance revenues: by increasing contributions, cutting benefits, increasing the Federal Subsidy for Social Insurance (*Bundeszuschüsse*), or a combination of all three. However, this usually has negative side effects. Cuts in benefit, on the one hand, lead to decreasing transfer incomes, which, in turn, limit domestic demand and aggravate the crisis of economic growth and employment; all in all, a vicious circle. Increased contributions, on the other hand, raise labour costs to which employers generally respond with rationalization strategies and increased redundancies. The consequence for the social insurance schemes is again decreased revenues. If the 'old' Federal Republic of Germany (FRG) had to cope with considerable problems in relation to economic growth and employment – full employment ended in 1975 and the country has been characterized by structural unemployment since this time – the decision of the citizens of the former German Democratic Republic (GDR) to join the FRG led to additional financial strains. The extraordinary event of German reunification triggered a routine response from the political system that boosted the vicious welfare without work cycle (Hinrichs, 2002). Enormous public transfers followed from West to East Germany that increased public debt to such a level that it was difficult to meet the criteria of the Maastricht treaty.

4.1.2   Deregulation and re-regulation in Germany

Despite the advanced employment crisis and the adjustment problems caused by unification, only gradual reforms were carried out in the German labour market and welfare system in the 1980s and 1990s. The following reforms sought to improve the competitiveness of national companies:

- Increased opportunities for fixed-term contracts
  (*Beschäftigungsförderungsgesetz*);
- Adjustment of the *Arbeitsförderungsgesetz*: employees, who are indirectly affected by a strike in the same economic sector but in a different region

(*Tarifbezirk*) lose their entitlements to wage substitution payments;
- Adaptation of working hours legislation to suit employers' competitive interests (*Arbeitszeitrechtgesetz*);
- Relaxation of the law governing the hours of trading (*Ladenschlussgesetz*).

The impact of these reforms, however, was limited. Recent studies (Keller and Seifert, 1998) indicate that the increased opportunity for fixed-term contracts did not create many new jobs, and that, despite the reforms of the working and trading hours, work on Sundays and public holidays has hardly increased. Additionally, the formal procedures of wage determination and codetermination were left untouched. Thus, it was argued that the German model has remained 'firmly intact' (Klickauer, 2002). While this is formally correct, 'opening clauses' have been used more often in the last decade than ever before. This led some authors to propose that the *Flächentarifvertrag* was being slowly undermined (Hinrichs, 2002) or that the entire system of industrial relations was being eroded (Hassel, 1999). Despite the formal continuity of the wage determination system, a more or less disguised trend towards company-level bargaining at the expense of the sector level can be observed.

The Christian Democratic governments (1982–1998) retained the tradition of the 'moderating' state without carrying out far-reaching reforms in labour market and welfare regulation. Paradoxically, it was the SPD/Green coalition (in power from 1998 to 2005) that, after a very slow first term brought about fare-reaching changes. Under the umbrella of the Agenda 2010 (a term coined in 2003) an entire catalogue of reforms in taxation, health, pensions, and, above all, the labour market and welfare system have been implemented or are being implemented. With regard to taxation, tax levels of both citizens and businesses have been reduced. Between 2000 and 2005, the basic income tax rate was reduced from 26 to 15 per cent, and the top rate from 53 to 42 per cent. According to the SPD/Green government, the main beneficiaries were employees, families on low and average incomes, and small and medium-sized businesses. The government also claimed that the tax reform was balanced in social terms (see evaluation in Table 4.1.18). In the health sector, increased competition and personal responsibility of individuals was agreed between government and opposition parties in order to ease the burden on statutory health insurers by 23 billion euro by 2006. The aim for average rate contributions to fall below 13 per cent from 2005 onwards has mainly been realized through the elimination of 'non-insurance' benefits such as maternity benefits, funeral payment allowances, and one-off child-related benefits. Since 2005, a separate premium is payable to cover dental treatment, and since 2006 the same applies to sick pay. The statutory pension insurance was supplemented by private pension schemes. In 2002, the Federal Government introduced a capital-funded state supplement, the Riester pension (after the then secretary of labour, Walter Riester). Any contributions to this pension are non-taxable. Additionally, some measures had immediate effect and were designed to keep the rate of pension contributions at 19.5 per cent of gross income. These included freezing pensions in 2003 and 2004. From 2005, the annual pension increase will be calculated on the basis of a new formula that takes the changing ratios between persons paying into the pension scheme and those receiving pensions into account.

At the heart of Gerhard Schröder's Agenda, however, were the reforms in the labour market and welfare system. Similar to the UK, these follow the guiding principle of 'incentives and demands' and aim to give the largest possible number of unemployed people the chance to re-enter the labour market. Pushed through in a 'Great Coalition' with the Christian Democrats in both chambers of parliament, which thus accelerated the normally slow process of political change in Germany, employers now pay fewer taxes and lower social security contributions. The 'Hartz laws' (after the then senior manager at Volkswagen, Peter Hartz), introduced against trade union resistance, limited entitlement to unemployment benefits (*Arbeitslosengeld*), which is salary-related, to one year (Unemployment Benefit I, *Arbeitslosengeld I*). *Arbeitslosenhilfe*, previously paid indefinitely and likewise salary-related, has become part of welfare benefits (*Sozialhilfe*) through the creation of Unemployment Benefit II (*Arbeitslosengeld II*). This new benefit is dependent on means-testing and fixed at the level of the former welfare benefit entitlements. Finally, the pressure on unemployed persons to accept employment in other parts of the country and below their level of skills has been increased.

4.1.3 The transformation of the occupational and social structure

4.1.3.1 Growth of GDP, productivity, wages, and unemployment

All indicators selected to measure the degree of the population's inclusion in economy and labour market peak in the 1960s and early 1970s (years we came to know as the prime of Fordist accumulation and regulation) show that considerable growth in GDP was achieved on the basis of labour productivity growth of 4 per cent. This went hand in hand with an almost full capacity utilization of the available workforce. Full employment, in turn, facilitated the bargaining position of trade unions. In the 1960s, real wages rose steeply by 5.5 per cent. Then, after a period when GDP, productivity, employment and wages rose in a parallel manner, growth in GDP, productivity and wages slowed down, while, from the mid-1970s, unemployment continued to increase.

The increase in growth in GDP from 1.7 per cent in the period from 1974 to 1985 to 2.7 per cent in the period of 1986 to 1995 is mainly due to the short-lived post-unification boom. In 1990 and 1991 GDP growth rates were 5.7 and 5.0 per cent respectively, falling back to below 2 per cent after this period (Koch, 2003, p. 86). Overall, the data do not provide any indications of a return to high economic growth rates generally seen as the precondition for a reduction in unemployment. The fact that growth in labour productivity has been decreasing for three decades – in a country with a traditional high productivity/high-wage growth strategy – is especially worrying.

In public discourse, not least in Germany, it is often held that two things are paramount for the creation of employment and a decrease in unemployment. First, it is often argued that real labour costs are too high making it unattractive for

Table 4.1.1 **GDP growth, labour productivity growth, real unit labour costs, real wages per head, unemployment rate: 1961–2005***

Year	GDP growth**	Labour productivity growth***	Real unit labour costs****	Real wages per head*****	Unemployment rate******
1961–1973	4.3	4.0	0.5	5.5	0.7
1974–1985	1.7	1.9	-0.3	1.4	4.2
1986–1995	2.7	1.8	- 0.4	1.9	6.5
1996–2005	1.3	1.0	- 0.5	0.2	8.7

* *1961–1990: West Germany.*
** *Gross domestic product at 1995 market prices; annual percentage change.*
*** *Gross domestic product at 1995 market prices per person employed, annual percentage change.*
**** *EUROSTAT definition; annual percentage change.*
***** *Real compensation per employee, deflator private consumption; national income; annual percentage change.*
****** *EUROSTAT definition.*

Source: European Economy, No. 73 and No. 4 (2004).

employers to employ new staff. Secondly, it is hypothesized that wage restraints reduce unemployment (see, for example, Lapp and Lehment, 1997; for a critical view, see von der Vring, 1999, p. 121). However, Table 4.1.1 does not validate these assumptions in relation to Germany. Instead, we observe that real labour costs have been decreasing for more than 30 years, that real wages per head have hardly increased at all in the last 10 years, and that, in the same period, unemployment has risen to 8.7 per cent.

4.1.3.2 Population, economic activity, employment and unemployment
Table 4.1.2 gives information about the development of both Germany's total and economically active population between 1970 and 2003. In absolute terms, population (II) increased slightly, whereby opposing trends can be observed in East and West Germany.[1] While the number of inhabitants of former East Germany fell by 362,000 between 1991 and 1994, in West Germany, population increased by 1,901,000. Overall, the population grew by 2.625 million between 1991 and 2002; in 2002, the absolute population reached 82.455 million; this equals an annual growth rate of 0.3 per cent.

---

1 The ILO provides data for East and West Germany separately for the years 1991 to 1994. Before and after this period, data only exist for West Germany or unified Germany respectively.

The number of persons capable of gainful employment (III) rose from 54,743 million in 1991 to 55,643 million in 1997; then it fell to 55,228 by 2002. Here again, East and West Germany show opposing trends: while the number of those capable of gainful employment decreased by 45,000 in East Germany, it increased by 642,000 in West Germany. However, for this group, the overall growth rate between 1991 and 2002 was 0.08 per cent annually, a considerably slower rate than that of the total population. While the percentage of those aged between 16 and 64 was 68.5 per cent in 1991, it fell to 67.0 per cent in 2002. Reduced pressure on the labour market appear, therefore, to result not from economic conjuncture but from demographic trends.

Due to the increase in the population's average age, increasingly more people are becoming economically inactive and hence do not appear in (un)employment statistics. The downside is the additional burden on those who actually pay into social insurance schemes. The dilemma becomes obvious when we take the example of old age pension schemes. In order for pensions to remain constant, contributions would have to rise. But since this is precisely the result recent social policy aimed to avoid, the level of statutory pensions will decrease. As private pensions are only a realistic alternative for a section of the population, it must be assumed that more pensioners will be exposed to age-related poverty in the future.[2]

In West Germany, the number of the economically active (IV) increased until 1993. The proportion to the overall population (V) and to the population capable of gainful employment (VI) grew from 42.5 per cent in 1976 to 49.2 per cent in 1993 and, respectively, from 65.8 per cent to 71.8 per cent. Likewise, the effects of the economic cycle are observable; between 1970 and 1982 and between 1976 and 1982 both percentages declined.

In Germany as a whole, the 1990s were characterized by a falling activity rate (VI), and this trend was not reversed until 2000. In East Germany, shortly after the fall of the Berlin Wall, the activity rate had been much higher than in West Germany (81.8 per cent versus 71.0 per cent). However, the proportion of the economically active (IV) in the East German population capable of gainful employment (III) dropped by more than 5 per cent in only three years (between 1991 and 1994). As this percentage rose by 0.8 per cent in West Germany, the overall activity rate fell from 73.1 per cent in 1991 to 71.6 per cent in 1997. In absolute terms, the number of the economically active declined from 40,022 million (1991) to 39,823 million (1997). By 2002, the 1991 level had again been reached.

In West Germany, the number of employed people (VII) fell by more than a million between 1970 and 1982. In the subsequent period, 1982 to 1993, occupation grew to peak at 29,873 million, followed by a decline of roughly half a million. The employment rate (VIII) moved in the same direction and fell throughout the 1970s and early 1980s. Afterwards it recovered to reach 66.7 per cent in 1993. In East

---

2 The imbalance between the contributors and recipients to statutory pension schemes could be eased through continuing immigration. However, apart from a few thousand green cards for IT experts, this approach has not been followed by German policy to date.

Table 4.1.2   Population, economic activity, occupational system and unemployment

	I Year	II Population (1000)	III Population 16–64 (1000)	IV Economically active population (1000)	V IV in II (%)	VI Activity rate (IV in III) (%)	VII Employed (1000)	VIII Employment rate (VII in III) (%)	IX Unemployed (1000)	X Unemployment rate (IX in IV) (%)
West	1970	60650	–	26493	42.5	–	26344	–	149	0.6
West	1976	61886	39422	25957	41.9	65.8	25059	63.6	898	3.5
West	1979	61516	40529	26253	42.7	64.8	25516	63.0	737	2.8
West	1982	61660	41809	26996	43.8	64.6	25177	60.2	1819	6.7
West	1985	61196	42837	28779	47.0	67.2	26627	62.2	2152	7.5
West	1988	61077	42826	29466	48.2	68.8	27366	63.9	2100	7.1
West	1991	63889	44069	31295	49.0	71.0	29684	67.4	1611	5.1
East	1991	15941	10674	8727	54.7	81.8	7761	72.7	966	11.1
Total	1991	79830	54743	40022	50.1	73.1	37445	68.4	2577	6.4
West	1993	65433	44794	32162	49.2	71.8	29873	66.7	2289	7.1
East	1993	15667	9718	8076	51.5	83.1	6599	67.9	1477	18.3
Total	1993	81100	54512	40238	49.6	73.8	36472	66.9	3766	9.4
West	1994	65790	44711	32090	48.8	71.8	29397	65.7	2693	8.4
East	1994	15579	10629	8147	52.3	76.6	6678	62.8	1469	18.0
Total	1994	81369	55340	40237	49.5	72.7	36075	65.2	4162	10.3
Total	1997	82029	55643	39823	48.4	71.6	35805	64.3	4018	10.1
Total	2000	82160*	55433*	39731 *	48.4	71.7	36046	65.0	3685	9.3
Total	2003	82455	55228	40022	48.5	72.5	35815	64.8	4207	10.5

* This data is from 2002.

Germany, the employment rate was much higher (72.6 per cent in 1991) and fell by 10 per cent within three years. In absolute terms, employment decreased considerably from 7,761 million in 1991 to 6,678 million in 1994. Overall, the employment rate stood at 64.8 per cent in 2003 – well below the 1991 level in West Germany.

In West Germany, the unemployment rate (IX) climbed continually until 1985 and became a structural feature. We can talk of structural unemployment in cases where the unemployment stock, which is to be observed when comparing the lower turning points of different economic cycles, constantly increases. In East Germany, the labour market partially collapsed after 1990. The unification with West Germany and therefore the transformation of East German society led either directly to unemployment or often resulted in occupational downward mobility. Educational capital acquired in the GDR could not be adequately transferred to the new labour market (Koch, 1998b, p. 181).

Overall, two development trends appear to have caused the very high rates of unemployment in Germany (the absolute number was more than four million in 2003). On the one hand, growing unemployment rates since 1976 indicate that the West German labour market had not recovered from the Fordist employment crisis that began in the mid-1970s. On the other hand, this situation was aggravated when, in the course of the collapse of the East German labour market, additional millions of employees were made redundant. The 'luckier' ones then entered a tense labour market at best; many simply dropped out of the economically active population altogether.

Tables 4.1.3 and 4.1.4 provide insights into gender-related access to the labour market. In West Germany, the female activity rate stood at 49.4 per cent in 1976. By 1991 it had increased to 58.7 per cent. Despite this increase, the difference between this and the male activity rate, which stood at 83 per cent in 1991, remained considerable. It follows that if we have referred to the Fordist mode of societalization as one of a high degree of system and social integration, this is, strictly speaking, only true for the male population. The positive labour market performance of the 1960s (Table 4.4.1) is not least due to the fact that women were normally economically active only until marriage and motherhood. Fordism in West Germany was, among other things, a period of far-reaching male dominance in economic life. Its crisis coincided with the questioning and politization of this gender dominance.

In East Germany, the proportion of economically active males stood at 86.3 per cent in 1991 and was therefore higher than in the West. The rapid decline in the absolute number of the economically active from 4,555 million in 1991 to 4,200 million in 1994 is remarkable. Since then, the activity rate of East German men has been below that of West German men. The crucial difference between East and West, however, was the much higher economic activity of East German women, which stood at 77.4 per cent in 1991; a level close to that of West German men. While employment rates of East German women (VIII) fell quickly to the level of West German women, unemployment rates of East German women (X) were twice or even three times as high. In the mid-1990s, almost every fourth economically active East German woman was unemployed, and so they should be identified as

Table 4.1.3 Population, economic activity, occupational system and unemployment: men

	I Year	II Population (1000)	III Population 16–64 (1000)	IV Economically active population (1000)	V IV in II (%)	VI Activity rate (IV in III) (%)	VII Employed (1000)	VIII Employment rate (VII in III) (%)	IX Unemployed (1000)	X Unemployment rate (IX in IV) (%)
West	1976	29538	19182	15967	54.1	83.2	15531	81.0	436	2.7
West	1979	29383	20018	16172	55.0	80.8	15855	79.2	317	2.0
West	1982	29495	20724	16437	55.7	79.3	15454	74.6	983	6.0
West	1985	29252	21328	17535	59.9	82.2	16402	76.9	1133	6.5
West	1988	29323	21553	17833	60.8	82.7	16759	77.8	1074	6.0
West	1991	30947	22382	18558	60.0	82.9	17719	79.2	839	4.5
East	1991	7601	5281	4555	59.9	86.3	4156	78.7	399	8.8
Total	1991	38548	27663	23113	60.0	83.6	21875	79.1	1238	5.4
West	1993	31843	22837	18983	59.6	83.1	17712	77.6	1271	6.7
East	1993	7539	5333	4200	55.7	78.8	3675	69.0	525	12.5
Total	1993	39382	28170	23183	58.9	82.3	21387	75.9	1796	7.7
West	1994	32008	22742	18758	58.6	82.5	17270	75.9	1488	8.9
East	1994	7525	5366	4257	56.6	79.3	3717	69.3	540	12.7
Total	1994	39533	28108	23015	58.2	81.9	20987	74.7	2028	8.8
Total	1997	39971	28257	22631	56.6	80.1	20549	72.7	2082	9.2
Total	2000	40080	28066	22371	55.8	79.7	20472	72.9	1899	8.5
Total	2003	40282*	27925*	22318*	55.4	79.9	20022	71.7	2296	10.3

* This data is from 2002.

Source: ILO, Yearbooks of Labour Statistics; various volumes.

Table 4.1.4   Population, economic activity, occupational system and unemployment: women

	I Year	II Population (1000)	III Population 16–64 (1000)	IV Economically active population (1000)	V IV in II (%)	VI Activity rate (IV in III) (%)	VII Employed (1000)	VIII Employment rate (VII in III) (%)	IX Unemployed (1000)	X Unemployment rate (IX in IV) (%)
West	1976	32348	20240	9990	30.9	49.4	9528	47.1	462	4.6
West	1979	32133	20511	10081	31.4	49.1	9661	47.1	420	4.2
West	1982	32166	21085	10559	32.8	50.1	9723	46.1	836	7.9
West	1985	31944	21510	11244	35.2	52.3	10225	47.5	1019	9.1
West	1988	31754	21273	11633	36.6	54.7	10607	49.9	1026	8.8
West	1991	32942	21689	12737	38.7	58.7	11965	55.2	772	6.1
East	1991	8340	5390	4173	50.0	77.4	3605	66.9	568	13.6
Total	1991	41282	27079	16910	41.0	62.4	15570	57.5	1340	7.9
West	1993	33590	21958	13179	39.2	60.0	12161	55.4	1018	7.7
East	1993	8127	5283	3829	47.1	72.5	2924	55.4	905	23.6
Total	1993	41717	27241	17008	40.8	62.4	15085	55.4	1923	11.3
West	1994	33782	21971	13332	39.5	60.7	12127	55.2	1205	9.0
East	1994	8054	5262	3890	48.3	73.9	2961	56.2	929	23.9
Total	1994	41836	27233	17222	41.2	63.2	15088	55.4	2134	12.4
Total	1997	42058	27386	17192	40.9	62.8	15256	55.7	1936	11.3
Total	2000	42080	27367	17360	41.3	63.4	15574	56.9	1786	10.3
Total	2003	42173*	27303*	17704*	42.0	64.8	15793	57.8	1911	10.8

* This data is from 2002.

Source: ILO, Yearbooks of Labour Statistics; various volumes.

the main losers of reunification. Considering the fact that East German women were as well qualified as men (Geißler, 1992, p. 239), the indications are that gender domination played a more important role in the processes of marginalization and exclusion of the East German labour force from the work process than, for example, educational capital or 'economic factors' in a more narrow sense. Overall, the female employment rate stagnated at 55 per cent in the 1990s before it rose to 57.8 per cent in 2003. Unemployment peaked at 12.4 per cent in 1994 and stood at 10.8 per cent in 2003.

With regards to the unemployment rate, the gap between that of East German and West German men is not as great as that between East and West German women. Here, employment trends appear to follow economic cycles more directly: the crisis-prone phase towards the end of the 1970s/early 1980s is mirrored in an increase of the unemployment rate as are the adjustment problems after reunification in the 1990s. Overall, the male employment rate has declined throughout the whole period of observation. In 2003, it stood at 71.7 per cent – almost 10 per cent below 1970, while the unemployment rate surpassed the 10 per cent mark.

4.1.3.3   Class-specific analysis of the economically active population
In 1970, the absolute number of economically active West Germans stood at 26,493 million (Table 4.1.2) of which 22,350 or 84.1 per cent were wage earners and 4,227 million or 15.9 per cent were self-employed (Table 4.1.5). The latter class was subdivided in 2,571 million capital owners (9.7 per cent in all economically active) and 1,656 million (6.3 per cent) contributing family members. By 1993, the percentage of wage earners increased to 90.1 per cent, and the proportions of capital owners and contributing family members decreased to 8.4 per cent and 1.5 per cent, respectively.[3] In East Germany, a class of capital owners had yet to re-emerge, and so its percentage within all economic activity was relatively small (5.3 per cent). Overall, until 1993, data confirm the long-term tendency of an increase in wage earners within the class structure – a trend, to which Thomas Hagelstange (1988), among others, referred to as 'proletarianization'.

In line with our theoretical expectations (Section 3.2), this trend has not continued in recent times (1993–2003). During this period, the proportion of total self-employment within all economic activity rose to 11.4 per cent. The fact that the great majority of this class are own account workers appears to validate our additional assumption that, after a Fordist period dominated by huge companies with an increasing concentration of the economically active population, there is a transition towards a new era characterized by the decentralization and outsourcing of companies, including one-person service-providers.

---

3   The decline of the proportion of contributing family members is mainly due to the shrinking relative weight of the agricultural sector, where the bulk of family members are occupied, within self-employed employment. For a sectoral analysis of self-employment over time, see Koch, 2003, p. 94.

Table 4.1.5   **Self-employment as percentage of total employment**

	Year	Employers (%)	Contributing family members (%)	Own account workers (%)	All self-employed (%)	Total employment (1000)
West	1970	9.7	6.2	–	15.9	26577
West	1993	8.4	1.5	–	9.9	30935
East	1993	5.3	–	–	5.3	8065
Total	1993	7.8	1.2	–	9.0	39000
Total	1997	4.9	1.0	5.0	10.9	35805
Total	2000	4.9	0.9	5.0	10.8	36604
Total	2003	4.9	1.1	5.4	11.4	36172

Source: ILO, Yearbooks of Labour Statistics; various volumes.

Table 4.1.6   **Self-employment as percentage of total employment: men**

	Year	Employers (%)	Contributing family members (%)	Own account workers (%)	All self-employed (%)	Total employment (1000)
West	1970	12.0	1.8	–	13.8	17043
West	1993	10.7	0.4	–	11.1	17793
East	1993	7.1	–	–	7.1	4196
Total	1993	10.0	0.3	–	10.3	22160
Total	1997	5.7	0.4	6.8	12.9	20549
Total	2000	6.7	0.4	6.0	13.1	20680
Total	2003	6.9	0.5	6.5	13.9	19996

Source: ILO, Yearbooks of Labour Statistics; various volumes.

In 1970, the self-employed class was made up of 4.240 million people of which 2.352 million or 55.6 per cent were male and 1.888 million or 44.4 per cent were female (Tables 4.1.5–4.1.7). However, while the vast majority of self-employed men were employers (12.0 per cent in total male employment, and 87.0 per cent in male self-employment), most women were contributing family members (14.2 per cent in total female employment, and 71.7 per cent in female self-employment). Among the capital owning class (employers plus own account workers without contributing family members), 2.045 million or 79.3 per cent were men but only 534.000 million or 20.7 per cent were women. By 1993, in West Germany, the percentage of women in that class had increased to 26.3 per cent, while in East Germany it was higher and stood at 30.4 per cent. Overall in Germany, the female proportion of the capital owning class was 26.9 per cent. Finally, in 2003, this class consisted of 2.679 million

Table 4.1.7   Self-employment as percentage of total employment: women

	Year	Employers (%)	Contributing family members (%)	Own account workers (%)	All self-employed (%)	Total employment (1000)
West	1970	5.6	14.2	–	19.8	9534
West	1993	5.3	3.0	–	8.3	12971
East	1993	3.4	–	–	3.4	3869
Total	1993	4.8	2.3	–	7.1	16840
Total	1997	3.8	1.8	2.5	8.1	15256
Total	2000	2.6	1.5	3.8	7.9	15924
Total	2003	2.5	1.8	4.1	8.4	16176

Source: ILO, Yearbooks of Labour Statistics; various volumes.

men and 1.068 million women. With a composition of 71.5 per cent men versus 28.5 per cent women, it was still largely a male domain. The alleged 'feminization' of the workplace seems to take place, above all, among the wage-earning class.

The fact that women face huge obstacles when they attempt to reach higher class positions becomes even more obvious if we focus on the most privileged positions: employers. While the proportion of male employers in total employment rose from 5.7 to 6.9 per cent between 1997 and 2003, the percentage of female employers shrank from 3.8 per cent to 2.5 per cent. In absolute terms, the number of female employers decreased from 580,000 in 1997 to 404,000 in 2003, while the number of male employers increased from 1.171 million to 1.38 million. Despite the growing economic activity of women, their representation among employers decreased from 33.1 per cent to 22.6 per cent during the same period. The economic downturn in Germany goes hand in hand with a process of exclusion of women from privileged class positions.

4.1.3.4   Wage-earners by economic sectors

In 1970, paid employment was characterized by Fordist features in so far as almost one half of all wage-earners worked in the industrial sector; the agricultural sector still amounted to 8.6 per cent. By 1988, the percentage of industrial workers had decreased to 40.4 per cent, which corresponds to an absolute job loss of just over two million. In the same period, agricultural employment decreased by 1.1 million and stood at just 4.2 per cent. These trends continued after reunification.[4] In 2003, the industrial sector's percentage amounted to about a third of all dependent employment while the percentage of the agricultural sector went back to 1.4 per cent. These percentages and numbers confirm the hypothesis that the Fordist period of capitalist

---

4   In relation to their level of industrialization, there was no great difference between East and West Germany. In 1991, in both parts of the country, it was just above 40 per cent (Koch, 2003, p. 99).

development led to a decrease in agricultural employment and to a historical peak in industrial employment. Since the beginning of the crisis of Fordism (1979 in Table 4.1.8), the employment system has been characterized by the continuing reduction of the industrial sector – both in absolute and relative terms.[5]

The tertiarization of the distribution of work began in the 1970s. In 1970, the percentage of all service jobs was 43.9 per cent. Towards the end of the 1970s, the service sector began to be the only dynamic employment sector in the sense that employment was actually created. Between 1970 and 1988, the number of West German employees in the service sector increased from 11.6 million to 15.2 million. In Germany in total, this number grew from 19.5 million (60.6 per cent) in 1995 to 21.2 million (66.1 per cent) in 2003. Employment was created, especially in the social services, the percentage of which grew from 16.7 per cent to 32.1 per cent, and in financial operations. Nearly four million people worked in insurance, consulting and other financial services.

Table 4.1.8   **Wage-earners by economic sector (%)**

	Year	*Agriculture*	*Industry:* manufacturing, mining, electricity and water, construction	*Services I :* wholesale and retail trade, transport, hotels and restaurants	*Services II :* financial operations	*Services III :* social services	**N** **(1000)**
West	1970	8.6	49.3	20.3	4.2	17.5	26493
West	1979	5.8	44.2	21.2	6.3	23.0	25516
West	1988	4.2	40.4	20.4	7.5	27.5	27366
Total	1995	1.7	37.7	21.9	8.9	29.8	32230
Total	2003	1.4	32.6	22.3	11.7	32.1	32043

* *1970–88: total employment by economic sector.*

Source: ILO, Yearbooks of International Labour Statistics; various volumes.

Again, we see a different picture if we look at the transformation of the employment system from a gender-specific angle. In 1970 (Tables 4.1.9 and 4.1.10), only one third of all wage-earners were female, while, in 2003, this percentage had increased to 46.2 per cent. The relative increase in female employment at the end of the 1990s is largely caused by the fact that between 1995 and 2003 1.2 million men lost their jobs, while, in the same period the absolute number of employed women rose by almost one million.

---

5   In the comparative analysis in Chapter Five, we will focus not so much on the question of why the percentage of industrial employment decreases but rather, why, in Germany, it is, in comparison to other countries, still relatively high.

Table 4.1.9   **Wage-earners by economic sector: men (%)**

	Year	Agriculture	Industry: manufacturing, mining, electricity & water, construction	Services I : wholesale and retail trade, transport, hotels and restaurants	Services II : financial operations	Services III : social services	N (1000)
West	1970	6.0	55.3	17.7	4.0	16.9	17004
West	1979	4.8	53.5	18.9	4.9	17.9	15855
West	1988	3.8	49.6	17.5	6.6	22.5	16759
Total	1995	1.8	50.3	19.5	7.1	21.3	18395
Total	2003	1.7	45.5	20.4	10.1	22.3	17225

Source: ILO, Yearbooks of International Labour Statistics; various volumes.

This finding must be interpreted against the background of the sectoral composition of dependent employment which, in the case of men, follows more closely those features that we have attributed to Fordism. In 1970, over 55 per cent of male wage-earners, as opposed to just 38.8 per cent of female wage-earners, were occupied in the industrial sector. In 2003, male industrial workers still amounted to 45.5 per cent, while the corresponding percentage for women was only 17.5. Hence, male employment is over-represented in sectors which are in decline, while female employment is over-represented in the service sectors (especially in the social service sector), the relative weight of which is increasing. The so-called feminization of paid employment correlates with its tertiarization.

Table 4.1.10   **Wage-earners by economic sector: women (%)**

	Year	Agriculture	Industry: manufacturing, mining, electricity & water, construction	Services I : wholesale and retail trade, transport, hotels and restaurants	Services II : financial operations	Services III : social services	N (1000)
West	1970	10.2	35.2	26.0	5.8	22.8	9489
West	1979	7.5	29.0	25.0	7.1	31.4	9661
West	1988	4.9	25.7	24.8	9.0	35.6	10607
Total	1995	1.5	21.0	25.1	11.3	41.2	13835
Total	2003	1.0	17.5	24.6	13.5	43.4	14818

Source: ILO, Yearbooks of International Labour Statistics; various volumes.

4.1.3.5 Annual hours worked, part-time employment, long-term unemployment, and labour market policy

Germany has until very recently followed a labour-intensive growth strategy. Between 1973 and 2003, the average number of annual hours worked has decreased by more than 400 hours.

Table 4.1.11   Average annual hours worked per person in employment

Year	1973	1983	1990	1999	2003
Hours worked per person	1868	1692	1541	1479	1446

*1979–83: West Germany; from 1990: unified Germany.

Source: OECD, 1997, and 2004.

This increase is due, above all, to collective reductions in working hours, and to the increase in part-time employment. Men are not only over-represented in self-employment and in traditional sectors of employment (manufacturing especially) they also seem to dominate 'standard employment contracts'. While just 5.9 per cent of men worked part-time in 2003, 36.3 per cent of women were in part-time employment. Many of the recently created jobs in the service sector that are considered to be typically 'female' appear to be part-time jobs.

Table 4.1.12   Part-time employment (as percentage of total employment)

	1990	**1994**	**1996**	**2000**	**2003**
Total	13.4	13.5	15.0	17.6	19.6
Men	2.3	2.7	3.3	4.8	5.9
Women	29.8	27.9	29.8	33.9	36.3

Source: OECD, 1997, and 2004.

As Table 4.1.13 indicates the loss of one's job does not necessarily mean total and final exclusion from the labour market. About one-third of the unemployed do find a new job without much trouble, that is, within six months. Two-thirds, however, face greater difficulty and are still unemployed after six months; and a rising proportion has not succeeded in finding a new job even after an entire year. If we disregard the temporal relief caused by the post-unification boom (1990–1994), there is a tendency towards prolongation of unemployment. While in 1983, 41.6 per cent of all unemployed persons had no job for more than a year, in 2003, this percentage was 50.0. This is the highest percentage by far among the five countries observed.

Table 4.1.13   Long-term unemployment (as percentage of total unemployment)

Year	1983		1990		1994		1996		2000		2003	
Period	Over 6 months	Over 12 months	Over 6 months	Over 12 months	Over 6 months	Over 12 months	Over 6 months	Over 12 months	Over 6 months	Over 12 months	Over 6 months	Over 12 months
Total	65.3	41.6	64.7	46.8	63.8	44.3	65.3	47.8	67.6	51.5	68.5	50.0
Men	66.5	42.8	65.2	49.1	60.4	41.2	61.8	44.5	65.9	50.1	67.2	48.3
Women	65.1	40.2	62.2	44.5	67.1	47.2	69.4	51.5	69.5	53.1	70.3	52.3

Source: OECD, 1997, and 2004.

Table 4.1.14   Public expenditure on labour market policies as percentage of GDP

Year	1991	1997	2002
Active measures	1.33	1.25	1.18
Public employment services and administration	0.22	0.21	0.23
Labour market training	0.47	0.36	0.32
Youth measures	0.05	0.07	0.10
Wage subsidies in private sector	0.06	0.05	0.03
Support of unemployed persons starting enterprises	–	0.03	0.05
Direct job creation (public or non-profit)	0.28	0.26	0.15
Vocational rehabilitation	0.5	0.13	0.13
Work for the disabled	0.10	0.14	0.17
Passive measures	1.80	2.54	2.13
Total	3.13	3.79	3.31

Source: OECD, 1996 and 2004.

In 1983, men were more affected by long-term unemployment than women. However, when interpreting this fact, one must consider that in 1983 the activity rate of women was about 50 per cent, and that it was only in the 1990s that it grew to levels beyond 60 per cent (Table 4.1.4). Long-term unemployment among women increased along with their economic activity, and from the 1990s, women were hit harder by long-term unemployment than men. While long-term unemployment increases among men, it does so much faster among women.

Germany spends over 2 per cent of its GDP on the financial support of the unemployed. A decreasing percentage of GDP (1.33 per cent in 1991; 1.18 per cent in 2002) is being spent on active employment creation measures. Due to the special conditions in East Germany, a particularly large number of persons were in direct job creation programmes. Towards the end of the 1990s, these schemes were cut – with the result that the total spending on active measures was below the level of 1991 in 2003. The SPD/Green government started special support schemes for youth and the disabled and these are reflected in the increasing expenditure.

4.1.3.6   Underemployment, income inequality, poverty, and the distribution of income

International unemployment statistics consider only a section of the population actually affected by underemployment and labour market marginality. The Institute for Employment Research of the Federal Employment Services (*Institut für*

Arbeitsmarkt- und Berufsforschung) approaches the actual extent of underemployment in the following way:

Table 4.1.15   The extent of underemployment in 2003

Registered unemployed (national definition)	4,233,000
Unemployed in public or communal training measures	1,258,000
Unemployed in early retirement schemes	1,077,000
Workers on short-time	75,000
Secret reserve	2,000,000
Total number of underemployed	8,643,000

Source: Wirtschaftswoche, No. 29, 08.07.04., p. 24.

If one relates the number of underemployed persons (8,643,000) to the number of economically active persons in 2002 (40,022,000, Table 4.1.2), then the underemployment rate amounts to 21.6 per cent. In relation to the population aged between 16 and 64 (55,228,000, Table 4.1.2), the underemployment rate is 15.6 per cent. Taking into consideration the complication that arises through the use of different sampling methods when comparing data from the ILO and the *Institut für Arbeitsmarkt- und Berufsforschung*, we can cautiously estimate that around every fifth German person is affected by underemployment.

As measured by the Gini coefficient, income inequality has remained constant overall. However, after a decrease between 1973 and 1989, income inequality rose to a level of 0.270 in 2002. In relation to relative poverty, since 1989 there has also been an upward tendency. Of particular interest is the great increase of the percentage below the 50 per cent line between 2000 and 2002. If we relate these percentages to the absolute number of the population in 2000 (82.16 million, Table 4.1.2) and in 2002 (82.46 million, Table 4.1.2), the absolute number of people earning less than 50 per cent of the median income increased from 6.74 million to 9.15 million. While the percentage of the 'total poor' (measured at 60 per cent of earnings) has remained almost constant during the same period, the percentage of those who fall under the 50 per cent line is growing fast. Finally, Table 4.1.16 informs about relative poverty by age groups. While in the 1970s and 1980s, the elderly were particularly affected by income poverty, in the 1990s, increasingly it was children who were exposed.

Further information is provided by the Federal Statistical Office (*Statistisches Bundesamt*, 2004, p. 632) of Germany. In 2002, 4.7 per cent of full-time workers were poor (below the 60 per cent line), compared to 14.7 per cent of part-time workers. As part-time work is concentrated among women (Table 4.1.12), we can conclude that there is a particularly German version of the working poor: the female part-time poor. Following *Statistisches Bundesamt* (2004, p. 632), poverty is further concentrated among the unemployed, whose poverty rate amounts to 37.9 per cent.

Table 4.1.16   Income inequality and relative poverty

Year	Gini coefficient	Relative poverty: total population		Relative poverty: children		Relative poverty: elderly	
		50 % line	60 % line	50 % line	60 % line	50 % line	60 % line
1973	0.271	6.7	12.2	4.4	9.9	17.8	28.5
1983	0.260	5.8	11.7	4.7	10.1	14.3	25.6
1989	0.257	5.8	11.4	4.1	10.6	11.3	22.4
1994	0.272	8.2	13.6	9.5	15.2	9.7	17.8
2000	0.264	8.3	13.2	9.0	14.3	10.1	18.3
2002	0.270	11.1	13.1	–	–	–	–

Source: Luxembourg Income Study:<www.lisproject.org/keyfigures/ineqtable.htm>; Statistisches Bundesamt, 2004.

If we remember that every second German unemployed is long-term unemployed (Table 4.1.13), these different statistical snapshots add up to a picture of a process of economic exclusion that not only leaves sizeable strata of the population outside full-time participation in the work process, which is itself often connected to poverty, but also that this exclusion and downgrading of the persons involved increasingly takes on a durable character. Finally, the likelihood of falling into poverty increases particularly in one-parent households with children (*Statistisches Bundesamt*, 2004, p. 633). This household group has a poverty rate of over 40 per cent and is in the vast majority of cases headed by a woman. Increasing poverty among children should hence be seen against the background of increasing part-time work and the increasing percentage of single-mother households.

Table 4.1.17 presents data from the German Institute for Economic Research (*Deutsches Institut für Wirtschaftsforschung*) in relation to the distribution of different types of income for 1960 and 1996. Income from dependent employment is still the most important source of income for households, but income from gains from capital and other assets and social transfers have increased their percentages of total disposable income.

Table 4.1.17   Disposable income of private households as percentage of different types of income

Year	1960	1996
Income from dependent employment	56	43
Gains from capital and assets	24	32
Social transfers	19	25

Source: Bischoff, 1999, p. 237.

Finally, Table 4.1.18 looks at the way the SPD/Green government's recent tax reforms affected the incomes of different groups. While, following the tax reform in 2000, all households pay less tax, the top income groups benefit from these reforms especially. This is mainly due to the reduction of the highest tax rate from 51 per cent in 2000 to 42 per cent in 2005. While, for example, a household with a gross income of 40,000 euro paid 1,293 euro less between 2000 and 2005, the increase in net income for a household earning 200,000 euro is 14,137 euro. Households whose income amounts to 500,000 or one million euro in 2000, pay 42,627 and 90,108 euro less income tax in 2005 than in 2000. Also in relative terms, the net income increases more in high income households than in low income households.

Table 4.1.18   Changes in income tax for different income groups (single wage-earner, no children) 2000–2005

Gross income (euro)	Net income in 2000 (euro)	Net income in 2005 (euro)	Absolute relief 2000–2005	Increase of net income 2000–2005 (in % of net income in 2000)
20,000	13,215	13,763	549	4
30,000	17,817	18,720	903	5
40,000	21,901	23,194	1,293	6
50,000	26,185	27,753	1,568	6
60,000	30,837	32,095	1,258	4
70,000	35,473	37,274	1,801	5
80,000	40,095	42,843	2,748	7
90,000	44,717	48,412	3,695	8
100,000	49,340	53,981	4,641	9
150,000	72,437	81,826	9,389	13
200,000	95,534	109,671	14,137	15
300,000	141,727	165,361	23,634	17
500,000	234,114	276,741	42,627	18
1,000,000	465,083	555,191	90,108	19

Source: Eicker-Wolf, 2004, p. 194.

4.1.4   Summary of the case study

The reforms in socio-economic regulation of the 1980s and 1990s in Germany led to a structural weakening of the position of employees within the corporate triangle of trade unions, employers and the government. At the level of industrial relations, this was carried out through a stealthy undermining of the collective agreements at sector level (_Flächentarifvertrag_). The traditional system of wage determination began to become cancelled out by the increased use of 'opening clauses'. During the Kohl era, socio-economic regulation was characterized by a somewhat surprising continuity. For a long time it seemed as if the reaction to the crisis would be a moderate one taking the form of minor adjustments without qualitative changes. This was the predominant view throughout the 1990s when Van Riel, for example, explained the emergence of mass unemployment by pointing to the 'particular distribution of power between the major political tendencies' that neutralized each other to a certain extent: 'On the defensive side, the labour movement has been strong enough to prevent the expansion of low-wage jobs. However, on the offensive side, the left has been too weak to push for a rapid expansion of public employment or active labour market policies' (Van Riel, 1995, p. 95). It was paradoxically a SPD/ Green government that ended the tradition of seeking consensus in labour market and welfare issues. The changes that have been implemented since 2003 almost one-sidedly followed capital interests and did not consider public employment policies and major strategic public investments as was the case in Sweden (4.2) or a reduction in working hours as in the Netherlands (4.5).

In the period of 1961 to 1973, the occupational and social structure in West Germany was characterized by high growth rates of both GDP and productivity, full employment and sizeable wage increases. Compared to this high extent of socio-economic inclusion, which accompanied Fordist prosperity, the labour market of the 1980s and 1990s was a great deal less inclusive. Slow economic growth rates and small income increases were the rule. The remaining growth did not lead to the creation of sufficient employment to absorb those persons – particularly women – who were entering the labour market for the first time. Rather, this growth was produced in a labour market characterized by increasing part-time work and unemployment. The rising percentage of long-term unemployment indicates that processes of labour market marginalization increasingly take the form of durable or even permanent exclusion. However, until recently, these processes of economic exclusion appear not to have led to increasing poverty among the German population. The fact that both Gini coefficient and the relative poverty rate largely remained constant between 1973 and 2002 leads one to conclude that Germany's traditional welfare system was quite capable of effectively dealing with the challenges it faced.[6]

However, with currently around 8.6 million under- and unemployed people, there is a new consensus across the main political parties of Germany that qualitative and extensive reforms in the economic and social system are necessary. Even though recent reforms in labour market regulation initiated by the SPD/Green government were implemented too late for this study to consider their impact on the labour market and social structure, we can hypothesize that the consequences of these reforms will be quite dramatic for certain social groups. First of all, many of the long-term unemployed, who were until recently covered by the non-means-tested

---

6   That is if we measure the efficiency of a welfare system not in financial terms in the first instance, but by its ability to compensate for extreme inequalities imposed by the market and to prevent people from living in poverty.

Table 4.1.19   Selected empirical results

	1961–1973	1974–1985	1986–1995	1996–2005
GDP growth (4.4.1)	4.3	1.7	2.7	1.3
Labour productivity growth (4.4.1)	4.0	1.9	1.8	1.0
Real wages per head (4.4.1)	5.5	1.4	1.9	0.2
Activity rate (4.4.2)	–	65.6 (1976–85)	71.1 (1985–94)	72.1 (1994–2003)
'Feminization' (Activity rate women) (4.1.4)	–	50.2 (1976–85)	59.0 (1985–94)	63.6
Self-employment as percentage of total employment (4.1.5)	15.9 (1970)	–	9.0 (1993)	11.4 (1997–2003)
(De)industrialization (4.1.8)	49.3 (1970)	44.2 (1979)	39.1 (1988-95)	32.6 (2003)
Tertiarization (4.1.8)	42.0 (1970)	50.5 (1979)	58.0 (1988-95)	66.1(2003)
Average hours worked per person (4.1.11)	1868 (1973)	1692 (1983)	1541 (1990)	1446 (2003)
Part-time employment (4.1.12)	–	–	13.5 (1994)	19.6 (2003)
Unemployment (4.1.1)	0.7	4.2	6.5	8.7
Long-term unemployment (over 12 months) (4.1.13)	–	41.6 (1983)	44.3 (1994)	49.8 (1996–2003)
Relative poverty (60 per cent line) (4.1.16)	12.2 (1973)	11.7 (1983)	12.5 (1989–94)	13.1 (2002)

Sources: Various materials from EUROSTAT, ILO, OECD, and Luxembourg Income Study.
Brackets after labour market issue indicate the Table that previously commented in detail, on this issue.

unemployment benefits (*Arbeitslosenhilfe*), lose some or all their benefits since all kinds of income, earnings and savings, not only their own, but also those of their closest relatives, are now considered when their entitlement for financial support is calculated. Particularly women in East Germany, who are overproportionally exposed to unemployment and used to be entitled to *Arbeitslosenhilfe* since they were usually economically active in the former GDR, are now expected to rely on the income of their partners/relatives. The tax reform does not appear to be at all 'balanced in social terms', as the Federal German Government claims, but relieves high-income households much more than low-income households. Taken together, the Agenda 2010 does not so much seem to 'secure Germany's future', but rather the financial future of a wealthy and influential minority. It is much better described as a programme of redistribution of social wealth from the bottom to the top: those who already have the largest share of disposable income receive even more tax relief, while those at the bottom of the income ladder – the long-term unemployed especially – are denied further state support, despite the fact that many of them contributed to the unemployment insurance schemes over decades; and are now expected to accept any available jobs, no matter what. The modest relief experienced by low-income households as a result of the tax reforms is in all likelihood overcompensated by the cuts in passive labour market and welfare policy. The 'unintended' consequences of AGENDA 2010 could include even weaker domestic demand and a widening of the hitherto low wage inequality. Relative poverty rates are likely to increase as a result.

From a more general perspective, one might raise the issue of whether the overall direction of Agenda 2010 will lead to a change of the German growth strategy, which has traditionally been a 'high-wage, high-productivity strategy' (Streeck, 1997). The new strategy appears to follow the British (and US American) way: 'making work pay' strategies through capital-oriented reforms in labour market policies substantially increased private service employment (Scharpf, 2000) and the establishment of a low-wage sector. Again, when applied to German circumstances this might trigger unintended consequences. As long as wage levels for unskilled full-time workers were usually over the reservation wage, which is determined by the social assistance level, it was 'unprofitable for employers to offer jobs yielding low productivity'. As a consequence, 'jobs for low-skilled workers have been largely squeezed out of the production process' (Hinrichs, 2002, p. 88). Agenda 2010 now targets this relationship by forcing many unemployed persons into new forms of (self-)employment and establishing a low-wage sector in the labour market, especially in the private service sector. It might turn out that what is won at the lower end of the labour market is going to be lost at the upper end: the more attractive it becomes for employers to employ cheap unskilled labourers the less their incentive to increase productivity – the traditional strength of the German 'export economy'. This possibility is all the more worrying as the measures taken so far are not supplemented by policies that upgrade industrial and technological capacity, which is the case, for example, in Sweden.

4.2   Sweden

4.2.1   Economic and social system

Until the 1980s, Sweden's economic and social system was based on central collective bargaining, which was designed to achieve wider normative goals such as full employment and wage equality. The wage determination process comprised of central wage negotiations between employers' organizations (SAF) and trade unions (LO), sector level bargaining on the application and adjustment of the central agreements, and company-level negotiations on any remaining details (Pestoff, 1995). The underlying notion that economic action should be carried out as part of social responsibility, however, was not always taken for granted even by Swedish standards. The first three decades of the 20th century especially, were characterized by severe conflicts between employers and workers. The frequency of strikes was in this period higher than in most other European countries (Benner, 1997, p. 42). In this situation, the state, represented by Social Democratic governments, played an active and engaged role in bringing about the 1938 Saltsjöbaden Agreement, the institutional basis of the new socio-economic model. Subsequently, governments could withdraw from the management of wage bargaining, which was increasingly carried out in the form of bipartite bargaining between strong unions and a highly centralized employer organization. As state intervention into wage determination procedures became increasingly unnecessary, governments supported the general growth strategy through complementary labour market and welfare policies. Active labour market polices stimulated, inter alia, geographical mobility and retraining, and were therefore always 'supply-oriented'. The universal and generous welfare regime complemented the trade unions' 'solidaristic' wage policies in bringing about full employment and a reduction in income inequalities.

   The 1956 agreement is seen as the crucial step during the post-war period in the manifestation of a mode of regulation based on central bargaining between the SAF and LO. The socio-economic background for this was a booming economy, which lead to maximum utilization of the workforce. Serious sectoral and regional inequalities, however, had remained and continued to generate wage competition within the companies organized by the SAF that was not in the interest of the employers as a whole. The trade unions, on their part, also wanted to avoid too great wage disparities at the company, regional and sector level and therefore favoured central bargaining with the paramount goal of a reduction of these inequalities (Åberg, 1994). Wage levels were not supposed to reflect the competitive situations of particular companies and sectors but rather the general balance of power between organized capital and labour. The label 'solidaristic' refers to the general goal of wage policies to gradually approximate incomes and to avoid labour market segmentation. This included state-wage subsidies for sectors and companies whose survival was under threat as a result of these wage policies. Any remaining wage differences were supposed to mainly reflect differences in skills. It can be seen as an implicit critique of the then hegemonic Keynesian economic policies that the state followed tight budgetary policies while expansive economic and financial policies were seen as resulting in inflation and the overheating of the economy.

In the period between 1950 and 1980, Swedish labour market policies were likewise more supply- than demand-oriented.[7] Shortages within the labour market were to be avoided by supporting the mobility of workers towards key industries and geographical regions in need of development. A further feature of the supply-oriented growth strategy was making unemployment benefit entitlement conditional to willingness to take up employment either in the formal or publicly subsidized labour market. Generally, full employment and social cohesion had top priority in labour market regulation. When, in 1977, for the first time since the war, there was a brief period of negative growth, the government went as far as to guarantee full employment by expanding both its role as employer and as supplier of subsidies to industries under threat. Since market processes were overlaid by social and labour market policies to such an extent that full employment was 'institutionalized', Esping-Andersen (1996) designated this era as the heyday of social democratic regulation.

The welfare system in Sweden has always been oriented towards the minimization of social inequality and the universalization of social citizenship rights. Regardless of one's socio-economic position, the whole population is insured against risks such as illness or old age. In addition there are benefits that are dependent on previous or current occupational status. The funding of the system is based on a combination of contributions paid by employers and employees and tax revenues. The pension system is based on three pillars; first, there is the state pension (*Folkspension*) which is independent on previous income; secondly, there is an additional pension (ATP) based on preceding salary; finally, there is the possibility of combining income from part-time work with pension payments for economically active citizens aged between 60 and 65. Unemployment insurance is administered by the trade unions. Unemployed persons who have been registered with an insurance scheme and who have worked and paid contributions for at least four months are entitled to benefits. Unemployed persons, who do not belong to any unemployment insurance, are entitled to state-run unemployment assistance (KAS), provided they worked for at least five months in the previous year. This form of support is limited to 150 days. Both forms of entitlements are oriented towards the previous wage and conditional on the incentive to taking employment or to starting a training programme. Long-term unemployed persons are entitled to social assistance.

4.2.2   Deregulation and re-regulation in Sweden

During the 1980s, Swedish corporate actors held on to the basic features of their 'solidaristic' development strategy. For example the Agreement on Efficiency and Trade in 1982, indicated the intention of combining the decentralization of decision-

---

7   See Harrysson and Petersson (2004) for the important difference between 'workfare' programmes and 'active labour market policies'.

making within companies with enhanced cooperation at sector and company level. Since the overall aim of labour market regulation – full employment – was not questioned by any of the corporate parties, unions actively participated in these debates (Koch, 2003, p. 124). Both wage determination and the role of the state appeared to change dramatically in the early 1990s, when a Conservative government came to power whose programme deprioritized the ideal of full employment in favour of other economic considerations such as price stability and the reduction of the budget deficit. Policy proposals focussed on strengthening the role of the company-level in wage determination and improving the competitive position of the employers.[8] Employers' taxes and contributions were reduced, fixed-term employment contracts were facilitated, and welfare entitlements were reduced (Pontusson and Swenson, 1996). The Swedish Employers Association (SAF) withdrew its representatives from tripartite boards in 1991 (Pontusson, 1997). However, the programme was not carried out in the way envisaged by the Conservative government of that time. In particular, currency instabilities leading to the massive flight of Swedish currency forced the government to cooperate with the Social Democrats and led to the eventual coupling of the national currency with the D-mark as the first step into the European Currency Union. As Garrett (1998, p. 142) shows, this happened at the worst possible point in time: the *Bundesbank* had just increased the base interest rate in reaction to Chancellor Kohl's economically questionable decisions to set the exchange rate for East German and West German marks at 1:1 and to transfer massive funds from West to East Germany. The high interest rate was passed on to other member states via the European Currency System, thereby hampering investments in the productive sector and deepening recession. An additional crisis factor was the fall of the Soviet Union and its allied countries, which affected a major sector of Swedish foreign trade.

Fears that the 'Swedish model' would collapse completely and would be replaced by one based on uncoordinated bargaining at company or individual level were not realized. In 1994, once again it was an engaged state that initiated the reorganization of the wage determination process and wider development strategy. After a brief period of uncoordinated decentralization of collective bargaining including the withdrawal of the employers from tripartite boards, both the trade unions and the Social Democratic government, which had been voted back into power, convinced the SAF to return to collective bargaining, which was now to take place mainly at sector level. The Central Bank, which was made formally independent in 1993, but which continued to be linked to the government's positions through its representatives on the board of the bank, supported sectoral wage developments from a more general perspective with a complementary interest rates policy. A further method supported by the government, which, if necessary, influenced the wage determination process, was the introduction of an 'arbitration institute', where all labour market parties were to be represented. This new institution was given the power to intervene in wage bargaining in the case of its outcome being assessed as

---

8   One of the most influential commissions was that led by the Economist Assar Lindbeck, which suggested no less than 113 policy proposals.

unfavourable for general socio-economic development. Its main function, however, was to create and enforce a common basis for negotiation before actual bargaining rounds began. Employers signed up for the new system of wage determination as they viewed it to be part of a wider strategy. The 'Alliance for Growth', in which the government had taken the initiative, was geared towards the technological upgrading of Swedish industry (Benner, 2003). Its main features included state support of sectoral innovation systems in existing areas of industrial specialization and research into promising technologies such as telecommunication, pharmaceuticals, biotechnology, and the information sector. Various policies for the upgrading of regional industrial and technological capacity were developed. At the same time, the institutional infrastructure was improved by establishing clusters that brought together regional actors and organizations. This was complemented by training and retraining programmes for staff and an expansion of the educational system. Some elements of this expansion were the increase of compulsory schooling age to 19, and the doubling of the number of students at university in comparison to the late 1980s.

The trade unions agreed to the new growth pact as the Social Democrats had reversed most of the Conservative reforms in labour market and welfare regulation. With regard to passive labour-market policy, the maximum unemployment benefit was reduced twice, from 90 per cent to 80 per cent in 1993 and from 80 per cent to 75 per cent in 1996 – a level that must still be considered generous in comparison to other countries. Active labour market policy was even expanded during the crisis, with 5 per cent of the labour force temporarily being employed in job creation programmes (Björklund, 2000, p. 157). Welfare reforms in general remained below the level of a paradigm change (Meidner, 1999). Gradual changes include a reduction in the generosity of the social insurance system (introduction of fees, individual contributions, waiting days as well as a general lowering of replacement rates), a reform of the pension system to control costs and to increase the supply of labour by basing pensions on life-long employment, and also savings in health and social service expenditure.

4.2.3   The transformation of the occupational and social structure

Sweden followed the development lines theoretically forecasted in Chapter Three quite directly. The 'Fordist' 1960s and early 1970s were characterized by considerable growth rates of both GDP and productivity and full employment. These elements formed the structural background for the successful practice of 'solidaristic' wage packages. Real wages per head could hence grow, on average, by 3.4 per cent annually.

4.2.3.1   Growth of GDP, productivity, wages, and unemployment
The example of the Swedish experience shows how critical regulation is for the maintenance of social inclusion in the labour market. First, it is obvious that Sweden was not untroubled by the Fordist crisis: since 1974 growth rates of GDP, productivity

Table 4.2.1   GDP growth, labour productivity growth, real unit labour costs, real wages per head, unemployment rate: 1961–2005

Year	GDP growth*	Labour productivity growth**	Real unit labour costs***	Real wages per head****	Unemployment rate*****
1961–1973	4.1	3.5	-0.2	3.5	1.9
1974–1985	1.8	1.0	-0.2	0.4	2.4
1986–1995	1.6	2.2	-0.6	1.2	4.6
1996–2005	2.6	2.0	0.4	2.4	6.7

*   *Gross domestic product at 1995 market prices; annual percentage change.*
**   *Gross domestic product at 1995 market prices per person employed, annual percentage change.*
***   *EUROSTAT definition; annual percentage change.*
****   *Real compensation per employee, deflator private consumption; national income; annual percentage change.*
***** *EUROSTAT definition.*

Source: European Economy, No. 73 and No. 4 (2004)

Table 4.2.2   GDP growth, labour productivity growth, unemployment rate: 1990–1995

Year	GDP growth*	Labour productivity growth**	Unemployment rate***
1990	1.4	0.4	1.7
1991	-1.1	0.4	3.1
1992	-1.4	3.2	5.6
1993	-2.2	3.2	9.1
1994	3.3	4.4	9.4
1995	3.9	2.4	8.8

*   *Gross domestic product at 1995 market prices; annual percentage change.*
**   *Gross domestic product at 1995 market prices per person employed, annual percentage change.*
****   *EUROSTAT definition.*

Source: European Economy, No. 73 .

and real wages were on a far lower level than between 1961–73. Equally noticeable is that full employment was maintained until 1990 (Table 4.2.2), that is, up to the point at which the collective actors gave priority to the maintenance of full employment.

After the U-turn from policies oriented towards full employment to policies oriented towards ensuring price stability and lowering the budget deficit had been announced, the situation on the labour market changed totally. The Swedish model, traditionally based on the goal of achieving as much labour market participation and social inclusion as possible, was temporarily defunct. A disintegration of the labour market resulted, which was above all expressed in the rapid increase of unemployment between 1991 and 1993: within just two years it reached the German level. However, after 1994, when unemployment peaked, the situation improved again. In the period of 1996 to 2005, Sweden enjoyed an annual GDP growth rate of 2.6 per cent and a rise in real wages of 2.4 per cent. While unemployment stood at 6.7 per cent in the overall period (1996-05), it diminished considerably in the most recent years: between 2001 and 2005 unemployment shrank to just 5.5 per cent.

4.2.3.2 *Population, economic activity, employment and unemployment*

Even though Sweden's accumulation regime had already become crisis-prone in the late 1970s and 1980s, the country held on to its political and economic mode of regulation until 1991. Corresponding with the U-turn in regulation, there was a reduction of both activity rate (VI) and employment rate (VIII) thereafter. In both cases the reversal point was in 1991. In absolute terms, 449,000 Swedes lost their jobs between 1991 and 1997 – a reduction of employment by 10 per cent (VIII). After 1997, however, there were indications of recovery; 312,000 jobs were created in the period between 1997 and 2003 with both activity rate and employment rate increasing. Even though both indicators are still way below the record levels of the late 1980s, the most recent data give reason for optimism: Sweden appears to be through the worst and on its way to (re-)defining a development path that combines growth with a high degree of labour market participation and inclusion.

Within comparative research, the high activity rate of Swedish women has always been remarkable (Table 4.2.5).[9] In 1976, it already stood at over 70 per cent; thereafter it rose to 81 per cent in 1991. As a result of the employment crisis of the 1990s, female activity rate fell to 74.5 per cent (1997) only to recover afterwards: by 2003, it had again risen to 76.2 per cent. By contrast, male activity rate showed a negative tendency throughout the period between 1976 and 1997 and fell from over 90 per cent to below 80 per cent (Table 4.2.4). This long-term trend only came to an end in 2000.

The fact that the labour market maintained its non-discriminatory character throughout the crisis is very positive. The reduction in employment by about 10 per cent between 1991 and 1997 does not exceed the corresponding decrease in male employment. Unlike in East Germany, where women, in the first instance, were expelled from the work process, in Sweden, the disintegration of the labour market was not accompanied by a reconstitution of traditional domination along gender lines.

---

9   It was, inter alia, this fact that brought Robert Boyer (1995) to label the Swedish model democratic Fordism.

Table 4.2.3 Population, economic activity, occupational system and unemployment

I Year	II Population (1000)	III Population 16–64 (1000)	IV Economically active population (1000)	V IV in II (%)	VI Activity rate (IV in III) (%)	VII Employed (1000)	VIII Employment rate (VII in III) (%)	IX Unemployed (1000)	X Unemployment rate (IX in IV) (%)
1970	8077	–	3913	48.4	–	3854	–	59	1.5
1976	8173	5157	4154	50.8	80.6	4088	79.3	66	1.6
1979	8294	–	4268	51.5	–	4180	–	88	2.3
1982	–	5250	4357	–	83.0	4219	80.4	138	3.2
1985	8416	5284	4423	52.6	83.6	4298	81.3	125	2.8
1988	–	5357	4418	–	82.5	4340	81.0	78	1.8
1991	8587	5409	4503	52.4	83.3	4371	80.8	132	2.9
1994	8838	5496	4267	48.3	77.6	3928	71.5	340	8.0
1997	8935	5549	4264	47.7	76.8	3922	70.7	342	8.0
2000	–	5601	4362	–	77.9	4156	74.2	203	4.7
2003	–	5700	4450	–	78.1	4234	74.3	217	4.9

Source: ILO, Yearbooks of Labour Statistics; various volumes.

Table 4.2.4   Population, economic activity, occupational system and unemployment: men

I Year	II Population (1000)	III Population 16–64 (1000)	IV Economically active population (1000)	V IV in II (%)	VI Activity rate (IV in III) (%)	VII Employed (1000)	VIII Employment rate (VII in III) (%)	IX Unemployed (1000)	X Unemployment rate (IX in IV) (%)
1976	4075	2607	2367	58.1	90.8	2337	89.6	30	1.3
1979	4113	–	2359	57.4	–	2315	–	44	1.9
1982	–	2655	2342	–	88.2	2272	85.6	70	3.0
1985	4157	2673	2341	56.3	87.6	2276	85.1	65	2.8
1988	–	2717	2295	–	84.5	2255	83.0	40	1.7
1991	4242	2746	2344	55.3	85.4	2267	82.6	77	3.3
1994	4366	2792	2218	50.8	79.4	2017	72.2	202	9.1
1997	4414	2819	2229	50.5	79.1	2042	72.4	187	8.4
2000	–	2846	2281	–	80.1	2167	76.1	114	5.0
2003	–	2896	2314	–	79.9	2191	75.7	123	5.3

Source: ILO, Yearbooks of Labour Statistics; various volumes.

Table 4.2.5   Population, economic activity, occupational system and unemployment: women

I Year	II Population (1000)	III Population 16–64 (1000)	IV Economically active population (1000)	V IV in II (%)	VI Activity rate (IV in III) (%)	VII Employed (1000)	VIII Employment rate (VII in III) (%)	IX Unemployed (1000)	X Unemployment rate (IX in IV) (%)
1976	4098	2549	1787	43.6	70.1	1751	68.7	36	2.0
1979	4181	–	1909	45.7	–	1865	–	44	2.3
1982	–	2595	2015	–	77.6	1947	75.0	68	3.4
1985	4259	2611	2082	48.9	79.7	2022	77.4	60	2.9
1988	–	2638	2123	–	80.5	2085	79.0	38	1.8
1991	4345	2664	2159	49.7	81.0	2104	79.0	55	2.5
1994	4472	2703	2049	45.8	75.8	1911	70.7	138	6.7
1997	4521	2730	2035	45.0	74.5	1880	68.9	155	7.6
2000	–	2755	2081	–	75.5	1992	72.3	89	4.3
2003	–	2804	2136	–	76.2	2043	72.9	94	4.4

Source: ILO, Yearbooks of Labour Statistics; various volumes.

4.2.3.3 Class-specific analysis of the economically active population

The percentage of the wage-earning class within the total employed was very large throughout the Fordist period. In 1970, over 92 per cent of the employed were dependent employees, while this percentage decreased to just below 89 per cent in 1994. Conversely, the percentage of the self-employed class grew during the employment crises, when alternatives in the sphere of dependent labour were rare. Since the absolute number of total employment hardly changed between 1970 and 1994 (Table 4.2.6), the size of companies as measured by the number of their employees must have decreased. Step by step, huge factories were replaced by smaller production units. The fact that small is beautiful appears to increasingly dominate self-employment, however, does not exclude the possibility that the diverse new small and medium-sized companies are connected to each other in chains and networks of production.

Table 4.2.6   Self-employment as percentage of total employment

Year	Employers (%)	Contributing family members (%)	All self-employed (%)	Total employment (1000)
1970	7.7	–	7.7	3913
1994	10.6	0.5	11.1	3928
2003	9.4	0.3	9.7	4234

Source: ILO, Yearbooks of Labour Statistics; various volumes.

In the last decade (1994–2003), the percentage of self-employment fell somewhat to a level below that of the peak of the employment crisis. However, it remained considerably above Fordist levels.

Throughout the period under observation, men were much more often self-employed than women; in 1970 especially, self-employment was a male domain. It was composed of 270,000 or 89.1 per cent men and just 33,0000 or 10.9 per cent women (Tables 4.1.7 and 4.1.8). By 2003, women had slightly increased their percentage within self-employment, when it was made up of 298,000 or 75.3 per cent men and of 98,000 or 24.7 per cent women.

Table 4.2.7   Self-employment as percentage of total employment: men

Year	Employers (%)	Contributing family members (%)	All self-employed (%)	Total employment (1000)
1970	12.3	–	12.3	2199
1994	15.3	0.4	15.7	2017
2003	13.6	0.3	13.9	2191

Source: ILO, Yearbooks of Labour Statistics; various volumes.

**Table 4.2.8   Self-employment as percentage of total employment:
women**

Year	Employers (%)	Contributing family members (%)	All self-employed (%)	Total employment (1000)
1970	2.7	–	2.7	1205
1994	5.8	0.6	6.4	1911
2003	4.8	0.2	5.0	2043

Source: ILO, Yearbooks of Labour Statistics; various volumes.

4.2.3.4   Wage-earners by economic sector
Overall, the development of occupation followed the lines forecasted on theoretical
grounds: the agricultural and industrial sector is in decline, while the service sectors
expands. The immense size of the social service sector reflects the Swedish strategy
of supplying key services by public means.

Table 4.2.9   Wage-earners by economic sector (%)*

Year	Agriculture	Industry: manufacturing, mining, electricity & water, construction	Services I: wholesale and retail trade, transport, hotels and restaurants	Services II: Financial operations	Services III: Social services	N (1000)
1970	8.1	38.4	21.4	5.0	27.1	3854
1976	6.2	35.4	21.2	5.9	31.2	4088
1987	1.6	30.7	21.0	8.1	38.6	3908
1994	1.4	25.8	20.6	10.2	42.0	3489
2003	0.9	23.0	20.9	14.3	40.9	3823

*1970–76: total employment by economic sector.
Source: ILO, Yearbooks of International Labour Statistics; various volumes.

While self-employment is dominated by men, Sweden is, within our comparison,
unique in that the number of female employees outnumbers that of their male
counterparts (Table 4.2.10 and 4.2.11). This development was facilitated through the
sectoral differences within the gendered distribution of work: while in 2003, six out
of ten women were employed in the expanding social services, this was true only for
22 per cent of male employees. Most men (36.4 per cent) were still employed in the
industrial sector which was overproportionally exposed to employment cuts.

Table 4.2.10   Wage-earners by economic sector: men (%)

Year	Agriculture	Industry: manufacturing, mining, electricity & water, construction	Services I: wholesale and retail trade, transport, hotels and restaurants	Services II: financial operations	Services III: social services	N (1000)
1976	8.1	48.5	20.9	5.5	17.0	2337
1987	2.5	46.7	22.7	8.2	19.9	1949
1994	2.2	40.8	23.2	11.5	22.4	1700
2003	1.3	36.4	24.2	16.1	22.0	1885

Source: ILO, Yearbooks of International Labour Statistics; various volumes.

Table 4.2.11   Wage-earners by economic sector: women (%)

Year	Agriculture	Industry: manufacturing, mining, electricity & water, construction	Services I: wholesale and retail trade, transport, hotels and restaurants	Services II: financial operations	Services III: social services	N (1000)
1976	3.7	18.1	21.6	6.5	50.2	1751
1987	0.7	14.8	19.3	8.0	57.2	1959
1994	0.7	11.6	18.1	9.1	60.6	1789
2003	0.4	10.0	17.8	12.6	59.2	1938

Source: ILO, Yearbooks of International Labour Statistics; various volumes.

4.2.3.5   Annual hours worked, part-time employment, long-term unemployment, and labour market policy

In Sweden, individual work loads hardly changed in thirty years; after reductions in working hours in the 1970s, when the country must appeared to be a paradise in terms of working hours, the trend has moved towards longer working hours since the early 1980s. After 1999, when the number of working hours peaked, they then decreased to roughly the same level as 1973. With 1564 hours worked per person in 2003, Sweden takes a middle position within the European Union.[10]

---

10 Unfortunately, our data do not allow for a measurement of the intensification of work that employees have had to deal with over time. A comparative inquiry into, for example, the amount of stress certain sections of employees were exposed to between 1973 and 2003 would be very interesting indeed.

Table 4.2.12 **Average annual hours worked per person in employment**

Year	1973	1983	1990	1999	2003
Hours worked per person	1557	1532	1561	1647	1564

Source: OECD, 1997, and 2004.

There is a comparatively low percentage of part-time employment; even during the employment crisis of the early 1990s. The part-time ratio remained almost constant at just over 14 per cent.

Table 4.2.13 **Part-time employment (as percentage of total employment)**

Year	1990	1994	2000	2003
Total	14.5	15.8	14.0	14.1
Men	5.3	7.1	7.3	7.9
Women	24.5	24.9	21.4	20.6

Source: OECD, 1997, and 2004.

Those few Swedes who were unemployed in the 1980s had a good chance of quickly finding a new job; only 10 per cent of the unemployed took more than a year to do so. Throughout the 1990s, unemployment took on a somewhat more durable character, so that by 2000, 26.4 per cent of the unemployed were affected by long-term unemployment. By 2003, however, the long-term unemployment ratio went down to approximately the same level as 1994. Men are more affected by long-term unemployment than women.

In 1997, Sweden spent 4.25 per cent of its GDP on labour market policies, which, from a comparative perspective, is sizeable. In the period between 1997 and 2002, this percentage decreased to 2.45 per cent. Two factors appear to explain this trend: on the one hand, unemployment decreased from 8.0 to 4.9 per cent between 1997 and 2003 so that there was less 'demand' for labour market programmes. The decrease in unemployment also helps to explain why, in 2002, direct job creation programmes were no longer funded with public money. On the other hand, unemployment benefits were reduced from 90 to 75 per cent of the last salary. By international standards, however, this is still very generous. Within active labour market policy, the considerable support of the disabled is noticeable. Further focal points of funding are labour market training and, increasingly, the support of unemployed persons starting enterprises.

Table 4.2.14   Long-term unemployment (as percentage of total unemployment)

Year	1983		1990		1994		2000		2003	
Period	Over 6 months	Over 12 months	Over 6 months	Over 12 months	Over 6 months	Over 12 months	Over 6 months	Over 12 months	Over 6 months	Over 12 months
Total	24.9	10.3	22.2	12.1	38.5	17.3	41.4	26.4	35.4	17.8
Men	25.9	10.8	22.2	12.3	40.5	19.4	44.3	29.3	38.4	19.6
Women	23.8	9.7	22.2	11.8	35.3	14.1	37.9	22.8	31.4	15.3

Source: OECD, 1997, and 2004.

Table 4.2.15   Public expenditure of labour market policies as percentage of GDP

Year	1991	1997	2002
Active measures	2.46	2.09	1.40
Public employment services and administration	0.21	0.26	0.37
Labour market training	1.01	0.43	0.29
Youth measures	0.14	0.02	0.02
Wage subsidies in private sector	0.09	0.20	0.21
Support of unemployed persons starting enterprises	0.02	0.08	0.17
Direct job creation (public or non-profit)	0.16	0.42	-
Vocational rehabilitation	0.11	0.08	0.03
Work for the disabled	0.72	0.56	0.47
Passive measures	1.65	2.16	1.05
Total	4.11	4.25	2.45

Source: OECD, 1996, 2004.

4.2.3.6   Income inequality and poverty

Income inequality remained stable for two decades. It was not until the period of 1995 to 2002 that the Gini coefficient increased from 0.221 to 0.252. Despite this increase, this is, along with the Netherlands, still the lowest level among the countries observed. The high degree of income equality is also reflected in the comparatively low level of relative poverty, which has remained constant throughout the whole period of observation. While children are slightly less affected by poverty, the elderly are more so.

4.2.4   Summary of the case study

Traditionally, the Swedish labour market was regulated through negotiations at the societal level in order to secure full employment in periods of economic recession. The trade unions' central and solidaristic wage polices were in this context just as important as the state's active labour market policies and the employers' willingness to cooperate. On this basis, the state supported the 'activation' of increasingly more people above all through training programmes and incentives to increase professional and geographical mobility. While the state's regulation of the economy was always supply-oriented, the main feature of social policy was its universal character that ensured each citizen the support of the welfare state. The latter is funded through comparably high and progressive taxation. Over many decades, the combination of 'solidaristic wage policies plus welfare state transfers' resulted in the intended

Table 4.2.16   Income inequality and relative poverty

Year	Gini coefficient	Relative poverty: total population		Relative poverty: children		Relative poverty: elderly	
		50 % line	60 % line	50 % line	60 % line	50 % line	60 % line
1975	0.215	6.5	12.5	2.4	5.0	13.9	35.0
1981	0.197	5.3	7.7	4.8	18.6	2.9	11.8
1987	0.218	7.5	12.5	3.5	6.3	7.2	20.6
1992	0.229	6.7	12.1	3.0	6.2	6.4	19.8
1995	0.221	6.6	10.0	2.6	5.5	2.7	7.8
2000	0.252	6.5	12.3	4.2	9.3	7.7	21.2

Source: Luxembourg Income Study:<www.lisproject.org/keyfigures/ineqtable.htm>.

reduction in inequality. Both social class and gender differences declined through the application of these policies. In relation to the gender-specific division of labour, there are differences in terms of the composition of dependent and independent work and in relation to economic sectors but not in relation to overall labour market participation. While men tend to dominate self-employment and industry, women are over-represented in dependent labour and in the service sector.

The intensified competition of international markets had its effect on the Swedish export industry. However, it is important to remember that the improvement of the determinants of competitiveness was first attempted in a way that did not disrupt the traditional regulatory framework. The Agreement on Efficiency and Participation (1982), especially, can be seen as evidence of the original intention of combining decentralization of decision making and increased cooperation at sector and company level. As the main goal of all labour market regulation, the maintenance of full employment, was not called into question, the trade unions participated in this process actively and constructively.

All this was to change temporarily with the break in labour market and welfare regulation in 1991, when the combat of inflation was suddenly prioritized. Employers' short-term interests now determined the state's economic and social policies rather than those of the trade unions, which favoured a continuation and expansion of active labour market policies. This temporary change in orientation of political and economic regulation was reflected in labour market and welfare state reforms in which the market gained ground at the expense of state and social forms of regulation. It also resulted in a weakening of the positions of both employees and the unemployed.

By 1994, however, the Social Democrats were voted back to power and decelerated or reversed many of the reforms initiated by the previous Conservative government. In the final analysis, the wage determination system of the old Swedish model did not survive; bipartite bargaining at national level was given up and replaced by sector-level bargaining. While strict and automatic forms of wage indexation were avoided, the state ensured – for example, through the new 'Arbitration Institute' – that the discussion of wage matters was to take place within the wider socio-economic context. After negative experiences with decentralized bargaining, collective actors (including the employers) again started to value the determination of wage norms related to productivity development and economic growth. Sweden's 'Alliance for Growth' combines a technological upgrading of industry with investment in training for employees, the expansion of the education system and the retention of the welfare state on a high quantitative level.

From a regulation theoretical perspective, the Swedish experience is particularly interesting as it indicates that alleged or real 'external shocks' such as, in the Swedish case, the loss of the Eastern European market, do not directly effect a given national regulatory set-up. On the contrary, the corporate triangle was capable of mediating this pressure in different ways. The 1960s and early 1970s were an almost ideal-typical example of Fordist prosperity: high growth rates of both GDP and productivity combined with full employment and rapidly increasing wages. In

Table 4.2.17   Selected empirical results

	1961–1973	1974–1985	1986–1995	1996–2005
GDP growth (4.1.1)	4.1	1.8	1.6	2.6
Labour productivity growth (4.2.1)	3.5	1.0	2.2	2.0
Real wages per head (4.2.1)	3.5	0.4	1.2	2.4
Activity rate (4.2.3)	–	82.4 (1976–85)	81.1 (1988–94)	77.6 (1997–2003)
'Feminization' (activity rate women) (4.2.5)	–	75.8 (1976–85)	79.1 (1988–94)	75.4 (1997–2003)
Self-employment as percentage in total employment (4.2.6)	7.7 (1970)	–	11.1 (1994)	9.7 (2003)
(De)industrialization (4.2.9)	38.4 (1970)	35.4 (1976)	28.3 (1987–94)	23.0 (2003)
Tertiarization (4.2.9)	53.5 (1970)	58.3 (1976)	70.3 (1987–94)	76.1 (2003)
Average hours worked per person (4.2.12)	1557 (1973)	1532 (1983)	1561 (1990)	1606 (1999–2003)
Part-time employment (13)	–	–	15.2 (1990–94)	14.1 (2000–03)
Unemployment (4.2.1)	1.9	2.4	4.6	6.7
Long-term unemployment (over 12 months) (4.2.14)	–	10.3 (1983)	14.7 (1990–94)	22.1 (2000–03)
Relative poverty (60 per cent line) (4.2.15)	–	10.1 (1975–81)	11.5 (1987–95)	12.3 (2000)

Sources: Various materials from EUROSTAT, ILO, OECD, and Luxembourg Income Study.
Brackets after labour market issue indicate the Table that previously commented in detail, on this issue.

the 1970s and 1980s, the accumulation regime went into crisis, while the collective actors held on to the full employment-oriented regulatory system. The public sector was used as an instrument to create employment and to absorb the labour force which was made redundant in the industrial sector. For the sake of solidarity, it was accepted that growth of GDP, productivity and real wages would slow down. We can therefore talk of a temporary primacy of politics (or of regulation) over the economy (or the accumulation regime).

The Swedish case equally clarifies just how incisively the structural transformation of the international economy can affect a nation-state if a national government amplifies the external pressure through its own economic and social policies. As argued above, in this regard there was a paradigm shift in 1991: in order to boost the business cycle, the sacred cow of full employment was slaughtered and social solidarity was sacrificed on the altar of competitiveness. The labour market was soon shaped by a drastic decrease of the economically active population and a quickly increasing unemployment rate (Table 4.2.17). Within this comparison, the speed of the partial breakdown of the Swedish labour market is only comparable with East Germany; the time frame was also roughly the same.

After 1994 however, the Swedish experience again points to the conclusion that decision-makers at the national level do have an alternative to following the neo-liberal mantra that postulates the competition of national locations against each other to undercut social and ecological standards. The Conservative reforms had led to a disintegration of labour market and society, which Swedes had previously only known from reports from foreign countries. But the renunciation of the ideal of solidarity in economic and social policy also provoked the development of a social movement that protested against the government. This protest was reflected, among other things, in gains of votes for the Left Party and the Greens, who formed a coalition with the Social Democrats in 1998. It is not least due to the influence of the latter political forces that, after balancing the budget deficit of 16 per cent, the ideal of full employment began to play a more important role again.

In what Rudolph Meidner (1999) calls a 'modernized Social Democratic' growth strategy, Sweden seems indeed to have 'responded successfully' (Benner, 2003, p. 142) to the challenges of the 1990s. Far from isolated cuts in welfare arrangements as in Germany, Sweden appears to have found a 'holistic' road out of the crisis that ranges from changes in wage-bargaining to qualitative amendments of the welfare state and the expansion of the education sector, to strategic investments in research and development. After the short and chaotic years of the Conservative government, this new growth path was negotiated and agreed by the collective actors. In the present political climate especially, it should be underlined that a supply-oriented growth strategy can be combined with a consideration of the ideal of full employment and low wage inequalities. Since the crisis of the early 1990s, unemployment has gone down to about 5.5 per cent (2001–05). But in contrast to the British path, this reduction did not go hand in hand with a large increase in wage inequality. Cross-national comparisons of earning and income inequality show that wage dispersion has remained stable. Low levels of the Gini coefficient (Table 4.2.16), especially, confirm earlier studies that concluded that Sweden is one of the four countries in the OECD with the highest income equality (Gottschalk and Smeeding, 1997).

4.3 Spain

Compared to the other countries observed, wage determination, industrial relations and socio-economic regulation developed differently as it was only with the political transition from Francoism to parliamentary democracy (late 1970s) and economic integration into the European Union (mid-1980s) that a 'modernization' of economy and society took place. The country was faced with the dual problem of not only having to transform a protected and inwardly focused economy into an open and competitive one, but also had to introduce institutions of labour market and welfare regulation at a time in which other European countries had already begun to deregulate and/or restructure them. Thus, in the strict sense of a predominating growth strategy of the post-war era, there was no Fordism in Spain. However, as similar institutions to those in other European countries were eventually established we could talk of a 'delayed' Fordism.

4.3.1 Economic and social system

The state has traditionally played a strong role in socio-economic regulation in Spain. During the Franco era, the development strategy was based on a kind of autarchy, which itself consisted of a 'rigorous' and a 'relaxed' phase. During the rigorous phase, which lasted from the end of the civil war to the end of the 1950s, the seclusion from the world market was extreme and led to migration from the cities towards the countryside. In the second half of Franco's regime, the economy began to be liberalized and Spain opened towards the world market. This integration into the international division of labour, increased and accelerated by the Europeanization process, was to present the Spanish economy with difficulties for the rest of the century. According to Antonio Zabalza (quoted in Boix, 1998, p. 111) the civil governments inherited a country which did 'not enjoy enough capital stock to employ all the available labour force'. Since, under the conditions of open markets, the traditional recipe of devaluing the peseta in order to increase the competitiveness of Spanish products was increasingly difficult to sustain; productivity and labour costs became the 'fundamental variables that determined the competitive edge of Spanish companies'. The Socialists who were voted to power in 1982 saw both the exaltation of the capital stock and the improvement of the level of skills of the labour force as the paramount task of the public sector.[11] Public investment projects were supposed to provide an impulse for the private sector and to contribute to a diminution of regional inequalities in socio-economic development.

---

11 Public expenditure, measured as a quotient of the GDP, increased by 7.7 per cent between 1982 and 1991 (Boix, 1998, p. 112).

In the first decades of the Franco era, the state determined industrial relations per decree. This applied especially to the regulation of wages and working conditions. While independent unions were illegal for a long time, employers and employees were amalgamated in the vertical *Organización Sindical Española* (OSE), in which any conflict of interests between capital and labour was negated. However, the vertical structure of the trade unions had already been penetrated in the late 1950s when the 'Workers Commissions' (*Comisiones Obreras*, CC. OO.) were founded in Asturias. In 1958 decentralized collective bargaining was legally permitted and elected employee councils were introduced. Marc van der Meer (1996, p. 314) assesses this development as significant, 'since it meant that the first forms of collective action and professional employee representation was being permitted. The system thus became "porous" and could be altered from inside'. In the post-Franco era (1977-86), the state initiated 'social concertation' (*concertación social*), a process of building a new industrial relations framework. The term refers to tripartite bargaining at the central level, starting with the *Pactos de la Moncloa* of 1977, which were followed by five additional agreements of which the 'Workers' Statute' (*Ley del Estatuto de los Trabajadores*, LET) of 1980 and the 'Organic Law on Freedom of Trade Union Organization' (*Ley Orgánica de Libertad* Sindical, LOLS) of 1984 were the most important. On the one hand, the LET aimed at adapting the industrial relations system to Western European standards. On the other hand, the state maintained crucial regulation power of intervening into the labour market (Sagardoy et al., 1995); for example, it retained the right to determine working hours.

The purpose of these agreements was to restrain wage demands, control inflation, which was at the time at a very high level, and to facilitate the recovery of business profits. In respect to wage determination, the government defined a wage margin based on the expected inflation rate within which bipartite bargaining on lower levels could take place. Taking the Fordist wage relation of other European countries as an example, this ensured a generalization of wage norms and, at the same time, the consideration of macro-economic parameters in social bargaining. Both the Workers' Statute and the Organic Law on Freedom of Trade Union Organization complemented the new industrial relations system by introducing a dual structure of employee representation in decision-making at company level. Works councils (*delegados de personal* in companies with between 11 and 49 employees and *comités de empresa* in companies with more than 50 employees) and trade unions (*sección sindical*) were given the right to participate in decision-making in issues such as employment contracts, health and safety, personnel policy and working hours and, above all, to call strikes (van der Meer, 1996).

As in the original Swedish model, it was agreed that collective bargaining would take place at different levels. Central agreements between government, employers and employees are reached at the national level. They are interpreted to give general guidelines by embedding wage bargaining into wider socio-economic developments and making it compatible with growth rates of productivity and GDP. These agreements are normally legally binding. The minimum wage, for example, is annually determined by the government after discussions with employers' organizations and trade unions. Once agreed, it legally covers all employees, regardless of their occupational status and whether their employment contract is permanent or temporary.[12] Sector-level bargaining between employers' organizations (*Confederación Estatal de Organizaciones Empresariales*, which represents over 90 per cent of employers, and *Confederación Española de Pequeñas and Medianas Empresas*) and trade unions (above all the originally communist *Comisiones Obreras* and the socialist *Unión General de Trabajadores*) result in applications and adjustments of collective agreements in relation to particular needs in different economic sectors. Finally, negotiations at company level between works councils and management determine any remaining details.

Crucial decisions in labour market policies are made in three institutions that are all connected to the Ministry for Labour and Social Affairs. The most important functions of the National Employment Institute (*Instituto Nacional de Empleo*, INEM) are the management of unemployment insurance, the organization of further training and education for unemployed persons, and, since 1986, the administration of the financial support Spain receives from the European Structural Fund as a result of the entry into the European Union. INEM is a tripartite institution, whereby the Ministry of Labour and Social Affairs designates the director, while employers' organizations and trade unions designate representatives. The second relevant administrative body is the *Unidades de Mediación Arbitraje y Conciliación* (MAC), which was introduced to facilitate the conciliation and settlement of industrial disputes. According to the Spanish law, these conflicts must be dealt with in the MAC in the first instance. Only in the event of failure of intermediation at this level, do labour courts start to deal with industrial disputes. With regard to redundancies, one of the most frequent causes of conflict, the 'success rate' of mutual agreements at MAC level is remarkably high; in the 1990s, 70 per cent of redundancy-related industrial disputes were settled in this way (Toharia, 1997, p. 123). The third labour-market institution has also legal status. The Labour Inspection, formally a Directorate General in the Ministry of Labour, plays a fundamental role in the settlement of collective redundancies. In these cases, it writes a report on the economic and financial situation of the company to be submitted to the administrative authority, which, on this basis, decides whether redundancies are to be regarded as 'necessary' or not. This, in turn, is decisive for the question of whether employees are entitled to compensation or whether they must be re-employed.

Unemployment insurance, created in 1961 and modernized in 1980 as a part of the *Ley Básica de Empleo*, is based on two pillars: one is related to contributions (*nivel contributivo*) and one is needs-based (*nivel asistencial*). The amount of the benefits of nivel contributivo is related to previous earnings. Entitlements to *nivel asistencial* are normally dependent on the expiring of entitlements from *nivel contributivo*. Persons without any work experience have no entitlement to any benefits whatsoever. The social insurance system, to which membership is compulsory, was introduced

---

12 The only exception are persons under the age of 18 whose minimum wage is allowed to be below the national level.

in 1974. As in other significant cases in labour market and welfare affairs in Spain, modifications in the social insurance system are dealt with in tripartite bargaining and normally result in corresponding agreements at the national level. Its benefits comprise above all sickness allowance, old age pension, which follows the *pay-as-you-go* principle, and child allowance. According to the child allowance law, parents have the right to take leave from work for up to three years. While the same job remains reserved during the first year, an equivalent position must be provided during the second. The third year is merely considered in terms of pension entitlements (without employment guarantee). If an employer employs an unemployed person who receives unemployment benefits during the period of parental leave of absence, he or she saves 95 per cent of social insurance contributions in the first year, 60 per cent in the second, and 50 per cent in the third year.

4.3.2   Deregulation and re-regulation in Spain

In a narrow sense, it is not accurate to refer to a 'deregulation' of the Spanish labour market and welfare institutions since their implementation took place at a time when institutions had already gone into crisis in other countries. The emergence and crisis of Fordist labour market institutions therefore did not take place at different times but coincided as they were 'delayed' (Tickel and Peck, 1995, p. 362) in comparison to the rest of Western Europe. The debate on reforms of the labour market and welfare system must be seen against the background of mass unemployment (4.3.3) and an occupational structure that had taken on a segregated form: on the one hand, those with permanent contracts were provided with high job protection and effective union representation and, on the other hand, those who were excluded from the labour market. Young people especially, entering the labour market for the first time, found it extremely difficult to join the formal economy.

In the period of 1986 to 1995 – Spain had joined the European Union and the economy was in a temporal upturn – industrial relations worsened. It was not possible to reach further central agreements, which could have served as a benchmark for bargaining rounds at lower levels. On the one hand, the Socialist government followed its 'rationalization' and restructuring policies, which included, above all, the facilitation of fixed-term contracts and the lowering of dismissal costs for employers in order to increase labour market flexibility. At the same time, both the government and the employers' organization intended to carry on with central-level bargaining since they hoped that this would be the best way to keep labour costs at relatively low levels (Marsden, 1992). In their view, given the high level of unemployment, the Spanish economy could not afford a considerable increase in wages. On the other hand, both major unions refused to participate in central negotiations because they thought they could bring about larger wage rises through decentralized bargaining. At the same time, they organized political protests against the government's policies culminating in three national general strikes between 1988 and 1994. As the bargaining system had temporarily broken down, the Socialist government's reforms of the 1980s and early 1990s were carried out against the resistance of the two major union confederations: by parliamentary legislation. Included in the bills enacted by the mid-1990s, were the removal of legal impediments of fixed-term contracts, the admission of private employment services, further liberalizations of dismissal law, and the increase of pressure on employees to be professionally and geographically mobile.

The most recent period (since 1996) brought a resurgence of national-level bargaining. This was somewhat surprising as it coincided with the victory of the conservative Partido Popular in the 1996 general election. Regulatory items that were dealt with at national level included a new system to resolve labour conflicts between employees and employers with the goal of avoiding these conflicts being dealt with in the labour courts, a reform of the pension system, which improved its financial basis and made it more equitable, and a new form of cooperation between unions and employers in the field of training and retraining of workers (Royo, 2002). Even more significant, as dismissal costs had been an extremely controversial issue between unions and employers' organizations, was the trade-off between lower redundancy costs in cases of unfair dismissal for the employers against the tightening of the use of fixed-term employment. A new type of permanent contract with lower dismissal costs was introduced, while, at the same time, entitlements to unemployment benefits for fixed-terms employees were improved (Golsch, 2003). Finally, and most significantly in the present context, the first central agreement on wage guidelines since 1984 was signed by the main trade unions and the employers' organization CEOE in December 2001, according to which wage demands had to move slightly above the expected rate of inflation. Most recent wage settlements reflected this strategy.

When discussing possible reasons for this new compromise, it has to be considered that while the government and the employers had always been in favour of central agreements, the positions of the unions in decentralized bargaining was not as strong after the breakdown of social concertation as the unions originally had hoped. Bargaining turned out to be difficult as the unions were concentrated in declining industries and so their importance was diminished (Royo, 2002). The bargaining power of the unions was further weakened through the frequent use of fixed-term contracts, which led to a segmentation of the labour market into roughly two-thirds of the workforce with permanent contracts, who were well represented by trade unions, and one-third with temporary contracts, who were largely without representation. Finally, the introduction of the Economic and Social Council in 1991, where representatives from the government, trade unions, and the employers discuss socio-economic issues, is generally seen as having contributed to a better atmosphere within the corporate triangle. While it was not provided with formal regulation power, it nevertheless helped to bring the political and economic positions of the labour market parties closer together. The re-emergence of central agreements can hence be seen as the result of a learning process which included the establishment of a new labour market institution.

4.3.3   The transformation of the occupational and social structure

After attempts of establishing a kind of economic autarchy in the 1940s and 1950s, Franco followed a development strategy that could be described as not only delayed but also as authoritarian Fordism. As in many Latin American countries, the aim was to promote a sort of industrial import substitution in the hitherto agriculturally dominated country. Inwardly, industrial relations were regulated through coercion in order to keep labour costs down. Outwardly, the domestic industry was protected by high tariff walls against foreign competition. On this basis, in the period of 1961 to 1973, socio-economic prosperity was achieved in similar ways as in the other European countries: high growth rates of both GDP and productivity were accompanied by low levels of unemployment and rising real wages (Table 4.3.1). The growth of real wages per head and the low level of unemployment between 1961 and 1973 should be seen, however, against the background of two particular developments. First, the base level of wages was in 1960 much below Spain's north-eastern neighbours. Secondly, an important contributing factor to the low level of unemployment was the fact that Spain partially 'exported' its employment problems: on the one hand, many workers left the country as wage levels – despite the increases in Spain – were much higher in other European countries; on the other hand, political repression forced thousands of Spaniards into exile. Unfortunately, there are no reliable data to measure the impact of emigration on the unemployment rate.

4.3.3.1   Growth of GDP, productivity, wages, and unemployment
In the 1970s and early 1980s, which were shaped by the transition from authoritarian towards democratic rule, it had already become clear that Franco's development strategy had failed in the sense that it had not led to the emergence of an industrial structure that would have been competitive in an open and less protected economy (Fina, 1996; Marimon, 1996). With Spain's increasing integration into the European economic space, many companies, whose survival had largely depended on the supply of a cheap and powerless workforce as well as on state support, went bankrupt. In addition, especially in 1975 and 1976 when increases in real wages amounted to 6 per cent (Koch, 2003, p. 161), the trade unions proved to be particularly strong and capable of attaining wage increases that exceeded productivity growth.

The 1980s and most part of the 1990s were characterized by the adjustment problems of an underdeveloped and peripheral economy having to integrate in an itself crisis-ridden European political and economic space. While growth in GDP recovered after 1985, growth in labour productivity continued to decline. This was accompanied by a rapid disintegration of the labour market. In the mid-1990s, the unemployment rate exceeded 22 per cent (Koch, 2003, p. 162): a level reached among the countries observed only regionally, in East Germany. Mass unemployment had repercussions for the bargaining position of the trade unions which, as a consequence, could not prevent the decline of the growth of real wages per head. Wage restraint on the part of the trade unions facilitated an extensive utilization of the labour force, and this, in turn, was a crucial requirement for the economic recovery of the period

Table 4.3.1   **GDP growth, labour productivity growth, real unit labour costs, real wages per head, unemployment rate: 1961–2005**

Year	GDP growth*	Labour productivity growth**	Real unit labour costs***	Real wages per head ****	Unemployment rate*****
1961–1973	7.2	6.5	0.5	7.6	0.8
1974–1985	1.8	3.2	-0.6	2.4	8.2
1986–1995	3.0	1.4	-0.1	1.6	16.6
1996–2005	3.2	0.6	-0.6	0.6	12.9

*   *Gross domestic product at 1995 market prices; annual percentage change.*
**   *Gross domestic product at 1995 market prices per person employed, annual percentage change.*
***   *EUROSTAT definition; annual percentage change.*
****   *Real compensation per employee, deflator private consumption; national income; annual percentage change.*
*****   *EUROSTAT definition.*

Source: European Economy, No. 73 and No. 4 (2004).

of 1996 to 2005. In the new growth strategy, a low productivity route is united with a massive growth in employment (Table 4.3.2).

4.3.3.2   Population, economic activity, employment and unemployment
The demographic trend has been beneficial for the financing of public funds (Table 4.3.2). While, in 1976, the share of those aged 16 to 64 (III) in the total population (II) was 62.3 per cent, it rose to 67.4 per cent by 2003. However, this ratio is only advantageous to society as long as the potentially employable workforce is really in demand on the labour market. This, however, was not the case in Spain for a long period of time.

The Spanish labour market went through a long and painful period of decomposition and recomposition. In a first phase, 1976-93, the activity rate (VI) hardly increased, while the employment rate (VIII) stagnated: in the mid-1990s, not even every second employable Spaniard was in gainful employment.[13] At the same time, the unemployment rate (X) skyrocketed from 4.9 to 22.7 per cent. In a second phase, between 1993 and 2003, both activity and employment rate rose to 68.8 and 61.1 per cent respectively, and the unemployment rate reduced by half.

The labour market has traditionally been extremely gendered (Tables 4.3.3 and 4.3.4). Both male activity and employment rate follow the logic of de- and recomposition with 2003 levels still below that of 1976. However, an activity rate

---

13 In 1997, there was still a huge gap between Spain and Germany, the country with the second lowest employment rate of 68 per cent (Table 4.1.2).

Table 4.3.2   Population, economic activity, occupational system and unemployment

I Year	II Population (1000)	III Population 16–64 (1000)	IV Economically active population (1000)	V IV in II (%)	VI Activity rate (IV in III) (%)	VII Employed (1000)	VIII Employment rate (VII in III) (%)	IX Unemployed (1000)	X Unemployment rate (IX in IV) (%)
1976	35433	22064	12840	36.2	58.2	12208	53.3	632	4.9
1979	37242	23493	12822	34.4	54.6	11587	49.3	1235	9.6
1982	37683	23096	12998	34.5	56.3	10764	46.6	2234	17.2
1985	–	23167	13575	–	58.6	10641	45.9	2934	21.6
1988	38887	24351	14624	37.6	60.1	11773	48.3	2851	19.5
1991	38817	25171	15074	38.8	59.9	12610	50.1	2464	16.3
1993	38873	25172	15318	39.5	60.9	11837	47.0	3481	22.7
1997	39069	25874	16122	41.3	62.3	12765	49.3	3357	20.8
2000	39212	25758	16844	43.0	65.4	14357	55.7	2487	14.8
2003	40555	27332	18815	46.4	68.8	16687	61.1	2128	11.3

Source: ILO, Yearbooks of Labour Statistics; various volumes.

Table 4.3.3   Population, economic activity, occupational system and unemployment: men

I Year	II Population (1000)	III Population 16–64 (1000)	IV Economically active population (1000)	V IV in II (%)	VI Activity rate (IV in III) (%)	VII Employed (1000)	VIII Employment rate (VII in III) (%)	IX Unemployed (1000)	X Unemployment rate (IX in IV) (%)
1976	17309	10827	9123	52,7	84.3	8681	80.1	442	4.8
1979	18273	11665	9101	49,8	78.0	8273	70.9	828	9.1
1982	18491	11444	8455	45,7	73.9	7627	66.6	1433	16.9
1985	–	11534	9427	–	81.7	7553	65.5	1874	19.9
1988	19821	12140	9623	48,5	79.3	8157	67.2	1466	15.2
1991	18937	12545	9723	51,3	77.5	8531	68.0	1192	12.3
1993	18953	12515	9687	51,1	77.4	7850	62.7	1837	19.0
1997	19101	12870	9849	51,6	76.5	8267	64.2	1582	16.1
2000	19082	12739	10067	52,8	79.0	9034	70.9	1033	10.3
2003	19896	13720	11194	56,3	81.6	10279	74.9	915	8.2

Source: ILO, Yearbooks of Labour Statistics; various volumes.

of 81.6 per cent, an employment rate of 74.9 per cent, and an unemployment rate of 8.2 per cent are about the European mean. While in the mid-1980s four in five men were economically active (VI), this applied to only every third woman. This appears to be a late effect of the Franco regime, in which gender discrimination was carried to extremes. The fact that women had to serve men was seen as the word of God and had legal status until 1978; both sexes have been equal before the law only since this time and women are, for example, now allowed to have their own bank account. After the abolition of such obstructions from economic activity, there was a steady rise in the female activity rate. However, in the period of 1979 to 1997 a great number of the economically active women were unemployed and the employment rate stagnated. It was only in 1993 that the female employment rate returned to the comparatively low level of 1976. Unemployment rates of almost 30 per cent are a negative record level for Western Europe. Again, as for men, the period between 1997 and 2003 indicates recovery. The employment rate of women increased especially quickly while unemployment decreased from over 28 to just under 16 per cent.

4.3.3.3   Class-specific analysis of the economically active population

The percentage of the self-employed in total employment stood at over 25 per cent in 1970. This by far the biggest percentage within our comparison points to the delayed nature of socio-economic development in Spain. While the percentage of self-employment in the other countries observed decreased with the expansion of the Fordist accumulation regime and, subsequently, increased as a result of the crisis of this production and accumulation context and the development of Post-Fordist growth strategies, we do not find this logic of decomposition and recomposition in Spain. Instead, the Spanish employment system is characterized by a slow decrease in self-employment throughout the entire period of observation. A sector-specific study of Spanish self-employment (Koch, 2003, p. 166) shows that, in the 1970s, it consisted mainly of employers and contributing family members in agriculture; 56.4 per cent of all self-employed persons worked in this economic sector. However, with the reduction of protective tariffs on agricultural products and increasing international competition, the number of agricultural businesses decreased. In the 1990s, the number of agricultural employers and their contributing family members had decreased by 820,000. Their percentage within all enterprises fell to 26.1 per cent.

In 1970, the self-employed class was male-dominated. It consisted of 2,497,000 or 83.8 per cent men and 481,000 or 16.2 per cent women. While almost half of the self-employed women worked as 'contributing family members' – with no or few controlling assets in the work process – this only applied to about every fifth man. Men, therefore, not only quantitatively predominated in the self-employed class, they also tended to occupy senior and executive positions.

By 2003, women had improved their position within self-employment considerably. While the absolute number of female self-employed increased to 942,000, their relative percentage in total self-employment rose to 38.4 per cent.

Table 4.3.4   Population, economic activity, occupational system and unemployment: women

I Year	II Population (1000)	III Population 16–64 (1000)	IV Economically active population (1000)	V IV in II (%)	VI Activity rate (IV in III) (%)	VII Employed (1000)	VIII Employment rate (VII in III) (%)	IX Unemployed (1000)	X Unemployment rate (IX in IV) (%)
1976	18124	11237	3717	20.5	33.1	3527	31.3	190	5.1
1979	18969	11855	3757	19.8	31.7	3350	28.3	407	10.8
1982	19192	11653	3938	20.5	33.8	3137	26.9	801	20.3
1985	–	11634	4148	–	35.7	3088	26.5	1060	25.6
1988	19067	12207	5001	26.2	41.0	3616	29.6	1385	27.7
1991	19879	12625	5351	26.9	42.4	4079	32.3	1272	23.8
1993	19920	12656	5631	28.3	44.5	3987	31.5	1644	29.2
1997	19967	13004	6273	31.3	48.2	4498	34.6	1775	28.3
2000	20130	13019	6777	33.7	52.1	5323	40.9	1454	21.5
2003	20659	13612	7621	36.9	56.0	6408	47.1	1213	15.9

Source: ILO, Yearbooks of Labour Statistics; various volumes.

Table 4.3.5　Self-employment as percentage of total employment

Year	Employers (%)	Contributing family members (%)	Own account workers (%)	Members of producers' cooperatives (%)	All self-employed (%)	Total employment (1000)
1970	19.2	6.4	–	–	25.6	11600
1991	4.0	5.0	15.5	0.8	25.3	12610
2003	5.5	1.6	10.8	0.6	18.3	16694

Source: ILO, Yearbooks of Labour Statistics; various volumes.

Table 4.3.6　Self-employment as percentage of total employment: men

Year	Employers (%)	Contributing family members (%)	Own account workers (%)	Members of producers' cooperatives (%)	All self-employed (%)	Total employment (1000)
1970	21.2	5.5	–	–	26.7	9353
1991	5.1	2.8	16.6	0.9	25.4	8531
2003	7.0	0.9	12.3	0.6	20.8	10284

Source: ILO, Yearbooks of Labour Statistics; various volumes.

In relation to the quality of self-employment ('employers' versus 'contributing family members'), the situation for women equally improved. The percentage of contributing family members in all female self-employment fell to 18.4 per cent.

Table 4.3.7　Self-employment as percentage of total employment: women

Year	Employers (%)	Contributing family members (%)	Own account workers (%)	Members of producers' cooperatives (%)	All self-employed (%)	Total employment (1000)
1970	11.0	10.4	–	–	21.4	2247
1991	1.8	9.6	13.1	0.6	25.1	4079
2003	3.0	2.7	8.5	0.5	14.7	6410

Source: ILO, Yearbooks of Labour Statistics; various volumes.

4.3.3.4 Wage-earners by economic sector

Spain's economy transformed from a protected and domestically oriented one into an economy integrated in the world market: a transformation that left its mark in the employment system (Table 4.3.8). In 1973, over 60 per cent of all wage-earners were in agriculture or industry. The fact that almost every fourth Spaniard worked in the agricultural context is unique within this comparison. By 2003, however, nearly two-thirds of wage-earners were employed in the three service sectors with financial operations increasing its percentage in employment fivefold and services I and III also expanding. While the percentage of agricultural occupation decreased by over 20 per cent, the relatively strong position of industrial employment is remarkable. Spanish industry seems to have survived recent changes and has even increased the absolute number of employees. While, in 1995, there were 3,111,000 industrial wage-earners, by 2003 this number had risen to 4,365,000. This recovery of the Spanish labour market does, hence, not only rely on employment growth in the service sectors, but is also built on a strong industrial basis.

Table 4.3.8   Wage-earners by economic sector (%)*

Year	Agriculture	Industry: manufacturing, mining, electricity & water, construction	Services I: wholesale and retail trade, transport, hotels and restaurants	Services II: financial operations	Services III: social services	N (1000)
1973	24.3	36.7	18.3	1.9	18.8	12838
1979	19.6	36.7	25.1	3.4	15.2	11587
1988	14.4	32.5	25.6	5.0	22.5	11773
1995	3.9	33.3	24.5	8.9	29.4	9343
2003	3.1	32.1	25.2	10.7	28.9	13598

*1973–88: Total employment by economic sector.

Source: ILO, Yearbooks of International Labour Statistics; various volumes.

In relation to gender-specific differences, there is great continuity in male employment. All remaining sectors benefited from the agricultural sector's loss in relative weight. It is a particular feature of the Spanish labour market that the percentage of industrial employment among male wage-earners was higher in 2003 than in 1973. While industry is still the sector with the highest employment among men (44.1 per cent), nearly 85 per cent of women work in the service sector. Financial operations and social services have the most spectacular growth rates.

Table 4.3.9   Wage-earners by economic sector: men (%)

Year	Agriculture	Industry: manufacturing, mining, electricity & water, construction	Services I: wholesale and retail trade, transport, hotels and restaurants	Services II: financial operations	Services III: social services	N (1000)
1976	22.0	42.6	23.1	3.5	8.7	8681
1979	19.8	42.5	24.6	3.8	9.3	8237
1988	15.3	39.3	23.1	4.5	15.5	7553
1995	5.0	42.9	24.5	7.7	19.9	6073
2003	3.9	44.1	23.7	9.0	19.2	8136

Source: ILO, Yearbooks of International Labour Statistics; various volumes.

Table 4.3.10   Wage-earners by economic sector: women (%)

Year	Agriculture	Industry: manufacturing, mining, electricity & water, construction	Services I: wholesale and retail trade, transport, hotels and restaurants	Services II: financial operations	Services III: social services	N (1000)
1976	21.0	24.6	25.6	2.3	26.5	3527
1979	18.9	22.4	26.5	2.5	29.7	3350
1988	12.4	17.1	28.6	4.4	37.5	3616
1995	2.0	15.6	24.6	11.0	46.8	3270
2003	1.9	14.2	27.5	13.1	43.3	5462

Source: ILO, Yearbooks of International Labour Statistics; various volumes.

*4.3.3.5   Annual hours worked, part-time employment, long-term unemployment,
            and labour market policy*

Table 4.3.11 shows that reductions in individual working hours could indeed contribute to a further reduction of unemployment. Average hours worked per person and year has gone down since 1979, but, especially since 1990, this reduction has been very slow indeed. Within our comparison and throughout the whole period of observation, Spain is the country with the most hours worked per person per year.

It was only in the mid-1990s that Spanish trade unions began to address the reduction of working hours as a possible way of fighting unemployment. However, the focus here was on making moonlighting and overtime as difficult as possible, not

Table 4.3.11   Average annual hours worked per person in employment

Year	1979	1983	1990	1999	2003
Hours worked per person	2022	1912	1824	1816	1800

Source: OECD, 1997, and 2004.

on the reduction of the statutory working week. Part-time work is rare and plays a role among women only (Table 4.3.12).

Table 4.3.12   Part-time employment (as percentage of total employment)

Year	1990	1994	2000	2003
Total	4.6	6.3	7.7	7.8
Men	1.4	2.0	2.6	2.5
Women	11.5	14.4	16.5	16.5

Source: OECD, 1997, and 2004.

Long-term unemployment (over 12 months) has been an issue for a long time, especially in the 1980s and 1990s when it exceeded the 50 per cent mark. For Spain, the ILO provides data that define those persons as long-term unemployed who are unemployed longer than three years separately (<http: //laborsta.ilo.org/ cgi-bin/brokerv8.exe>). We could refer to this group as the extremely long-term unemployed. In 1988 their absolute number was as high as 481,000 corresponding to 17.0 per cent of all unemployed. By 1997 this number had risen to 734,000 or 20.9 per cent (Koch, 2003, p. 173). However, between 1997 and 2003 the number of the extremely long-term unemployed shrank to 256,000 or 12.0 per cent. It follows that the tendency towards the 'persistence' of long-term unemployment that I diagnosed on the basis of the 1997 data (Koch, 2003, p. 178) was fortunately reversed. The OECD data also indicate a decrease in long-term unemployment (over 12 months) since 2000. In 2003, the level of long-term unemployment in Spain was 10 per cent below the level of Germany. Throughout the entire period of observation, women were more affected by long-term unemployment than men. Since 2000, however, female long-term unemployment appears to be shrinking more rapidly than male long-term unemployment.

The cuts in public expenditure on passive labour market policy (Table 4.3.14) by over a third can be explained through the decreasing unemployment rate. Active labour market policies slightly expanded reaching a level below Germany but well above the UK. Funds appear to have been especially concentrated on labour market training and wage subsidies.

Table 4.3.13   Long–term unemployment (as percentage of total unemployment)

Year	1983		1990		1994		2000		2003	
Period	Over 6 months	Over 12 months	Over 6 months	Over 12 months	Over 6 months	Over 12 months	Over 6 months	Over 12 months	Over 6 months	Over 12 months
Total	72.8	52.4	70.2	54.0	73.4	56.1	64.8	47.6	59.6	39.8
Men	69.9	48.9	63.2	45.6	68.6	49.6	58.5	41.0	54.5	34.3
Women	77.7	58.5	76.5	61.5	78.4	62.9	69.3	52.2	63.4	43.9

Source: OECD, 1997, and 2004.

Table 4.3.14 Public expenditure on labour market policies as percentage of GDP

Year	1991	1997	2002
Active measures	0.76	0.50	0.83
Public employment services and administration	0.12	0.08	0.09
Labour market training	0.18	0.14	0.22
Youth measures	0.05	0.07	0.06
Wage subsidies in private sector	0.12	0.11	0.28
Support of unemployed persons starting enterprises	0.20	0.03	0.06
Direct job creation (public or non-profit)	0.08	0.06	0.09
Vocational rehabilitation	–	–	–
Work for the disabled	0.01	0.02	0.03
Passive measures	2.85	1.87	1.55
Total	3.60	2.37	2.38

Source: OECD, 1996, and 2004.

4.3.3.6 Income inequality and poverty

Unfortunately, the Luxemburg Income Study provides data in relation to income inequality and relative poverty for the years 1980 and 1990 only. I have therefore added data from *Encuestas de Prosupuestos Familiares* and *Encuestas Continuas de Presupuestos Familares* for the years 1974 and 2001.[14] In 1974 in Spain, the Gini coefficient was at the highest level within the five countries compared. By 1990, income inequality had decreased, leaving the UK with the most unequal income distribution. In 2001, income inequality in Spain (0.325) had risen again, almost to the level of the UK (Table 4.4.15). Therefore it seems that first, income inequality was very high under Franco and during the transition towards democracy; that, secondly, it decreased in the 1980s only to increase again in the 1990s. Toharia and Malo (2000, p. 319) interpret the relatively stable wage inequalities of the 1980s and early 1990s 'as a result of across-the-board application of the nation-wide agreements'. More recently, however, wage inequalities 'have tended to widen as the lack of such agreements has given a certain leeway to higher wage dispersion'. Of special interest is the fact that income inequality has increased in the most recent period (1990–2001), which brought economic recovery and many jobs. As in the UK (4.4) the creation of employment and the decrease in unemployment coincided with even larger wage inequalities.

---

14 Without the help of Olga Salido Cortés from the Universidad Complutense de Madrid I would not have been able to access these data.

Roads to Post-Fordism

Table 4.3.15   Income inequality and relative poverty

Year	Gini coefficient	Relative poverty: total population		Relative poverty: children		Relative poverty: elderly	
		50 % line	60 % line	50 % line	60 % line	50 % line	60 % line
1974	0.340	–	–	–	–	–	–
1980	0.318	12.2	19.5	12.7	20.4	18.8	30.7
1990	0.303	10.1	17.3	12.2	20.1	11.3	24.2
1997	–	14.0	20.0	–	–	–	–
2001	0.325	–	–	–	–	–	–

Source: Luxembourg Income Study: <www.lisproject.org/keyfigures/ineqtable.htm> (1980, 1990);
Encuestas de Presupuestos Familiares (1973–74); Encuestas Continuas de Presupuestos; Familiares (2001); EUROSTAT, 2002 (1997).

Poverty rates also appear to be in the range of the UK. In 1997, every fifth Spaniard lived below the 60 per cent poverty line. The issue of relative poverty is in the Spanish case aggravated by the fact that the country 'has the third lowest median income level' across the European Union (EUROSTAT, 2002, p. 137). Relative poverty is therefore often accompanied by a comparatively low standard of living in absolute terms. In the 1990s, the elderly were overproportionally affected by poverty.

4.3.4   Summary of the case study

After the 'autarchic' phase, Franco's development strategy aimed at building an industrial structure that would – in the future – be able to survive in international competition.[15] Outwardly, Spanish industry was protected by high tariff walls, and inwardly the growth strategy was supported by an authoritarian factory regime in which the influence of the trade unions' was negligible. After Franco's death, the country was faced with the dual problem of not only having to transform a protected and inwardly focused economy into an open and competitive one, but also had to implement institutions of labour market and welfare regulation at a time in which other European countries had already begun to deregulate them. In doing so, however, governments now cooperated with both trade unions and employers' organizations. Tripartite bargaining on the societal or national level maintained its crucial significance within decision-making in socio-economic regulation until the mid-1980s. After a temporary breakdown of tripartite bargaining at the national level and a period of decentralized bargaining, collective agreements were resumed

---

15 Had Franco not clung onto autarchy for so long, the economy would have presumably started to take on 'modernized' features earlier: the agricultural sector would have been smaller and the adaptation to Western Europe would have been easier.

Table 4.3.16   Selected empirical results

	1961–1973	1974–1985	1986–1995	1996–2005
GDP growth (4.3.1)	7.2	1.8	3.0	3.2
Labour productivity growth (4.3.1)	6.5	3.2	1.4	0.6
Real wages per head (4.3.1)	7.6	2.4	1.6	0.6
Activity rate (4.3.2)	–	56.9 (1976–85)	60.3 (1988–93)	65.5 (1997–2003)
'Feminization' (activity rate women) (4.4.4)	–	33.6 (1976–85)	42.6 (1988–93)	52.1 (1997–2003)
Self-employment as percentage in total employment (4.4.5)	25.6 (1970)		25.3 (1991)	18.3 (2003)
(De)industrialization (4.4.8)	36.7 (1973)	36.7 (1979)	32.9 (1988–95)	32.1 (2003)
Tertiarization (4.4.8)	39.0 (1973)	51.0 (1979)	58.0 (1988–95)	64.8 (2003)
Average hours worked per person (4.4.11)	–	1967 (1979–83)	1824 (1990)	1808 (1999–2003)
Part-Time Employment (4.4.12)	–	–	5.5 (1990–94)	7.8 (2000–03)
Unemployment (4.4.1)	0.8	8.2	16.6	12.9
Long-term unemployment (over 12 months) (4.4.13)	–	52.4 (1983)	55.1 (1990–94)	43.7 (2000–03)
Relative poverty (60 per cent line) (4.4.15)	–	19.5 (1980)	17.3 (1990)	20.0 (1997)

Sources: Various materials from EUROSTAT, ILO, OECD, and Luxembourg Income Study.
Brackets after labour market issue indicate the Table that previously commented in detail, on this issue.

after 1996. Somewhat surprisingly, it was during the Aznar government that wage matters, for example, were again discussed in wider socio-economic contexts. After rather negative experiences with decentralized bargaining, collective actors (including employers) again started to value a determination of wage norms related to productivity development and economic growth. In a compromise in labour market regulation between both the interests of trade unions and employers' organizations, dismissal costs for employers were reduced, while the conditions for the use of fixed-term employment were tightened, and the entitlements to unemployment benefits for fixed-term employees were improved. The Spanish state, which had basically monopolized regulation power under Franco, dispensed parts of this competence to the labour market parties. Governments became increasingly 'moderating' in their attempts to reach central agreements. The opening of the road towards the recent compromise was due to the trade unions, who had reviewed their priorities. With the opening of the economy it became clear that Franco's development strategy had not been very successful after all. Many companies were not able to cope with the new situation and went bankrupt. Labour market and social structure proved to be in the focus of a transition from a protected and domestically oriented economy towards an open and world-market oriented one.

The particular social space that corresponded with the old development strategy went into a long decline. The most striking features of this was the decrease in agricultural occupation which was, in this first development stage, not compensated by the creation of additional employment in the service sectors. While the activity rate stagnated at a comparatively low level until the mid-1990s, unemployment skyrocketed to ever higher record levels. In the most recent period, however, this decline was reversed: with the exception of agriculture, employment was created in virtually all sectors (including the industrial sector), unemployment decreased considerably, and the activity rate also rose. The decomposition of the old 'Francist' social structure was followed by its recomposition along Post-Fordist lines. There are clear indications that these lines follow a labour extensive rather than a high productivity road, which accepts rising wage inequalities. Indicators for this are, above all, the decreasing growth in productivity, very long working hours, a diminishing growth in real wages and a rising Gini coefficient. Growth in both GDP and employment have come at the price of increased polarization within the workforce and increased poverty.

4.4   United Kingdom

Among the countries compared, the UK occupies a position closest to the ideal-type of a capital-oriented growth strategy. Collective bargaining traditionally takes place on the company level, whereby the previous strong position of the trade unions has been severely weakened over the years.

4.4.1   Economic and social system

David Soskice (1990, 1994) has called the form of institutional embedding of British capitalism a 'deregulated open market system'. While its regulation is carried out by market forces in the first instance, capital–labour relations are dealt with on the individual and/or company level. According to Soskice, since early industrialization these relations have been characterized by distrust and their short-term nature. This is reflected in the division of labour that has traditionally consisted of a great number of horizontal and vertical segmentations between occupational groups and departments according to skills and tasks. The precise divisions of these segmentations tended to be reproduced in an industrial relations system that has been described as 'adversarial' as it proliferated into hundreds of bargaining units (Lane, 1994). A 'strong but decentralized, craft-based union movement and a weakly organized employer class' effectively neutralized each other and 'impeded consensus on incomes, industrial organization, and technical change' (Rhodes, 2000, p. 24). As a result, the implementation of Taylorist organization principles at plant level were exacerbated (Heidenreich, 1997, p. 321). The potential for increased productivity, normally associated with these methods, was inhibited. The consequence was that the UK gradually lost its technological and economic lead that had originated in the Industrial Revolution. This decline also affected the level of consumption: in 1960 per capita income in Britain was 23 per cent above the European Union average, and fell to three per cent by 1970. A decade later (1980) per capita income in Britain was three per cent below the EU average (Klodt, 1998, p. 282). Far from imposing itself automatically by reason of its superior technology, British Fordism was 'flawed' (Boyer, 1995).

The blockade of the Fordist accumulation regime was supplemented by a rudimentary wage determination system. Unlike other European countries, where agreements at the national or sector level tended to cover a wide range of substantive issues – wages, in particular – and thereby established a generalization of wage norms in correspondence with productivity gains, in Britain, the tradition of bargaining and regulating at company level turned out to be difficult to overcome. Post-war governments, which were oriented towards the maintenance of full employment, tended to apply policies of Keynesian demand management and to seek more wage coordination and regulation of the labour market in general (Crouch, 2003). However, as is exemplified by Beardwell (1996), a whole range of government initiatives and Acts fell victim to the weakly organized industrial relations system. An integral part of the latter was the relatively strong and legally supported position of the trade unions at company level. For example, the law allowed for 'closed shops'[16] and provided immunity to trade unions in industrial action, especially in the case of secondary action.

---

16 'Closed shops' are companies in which only union members can be employed. A closed shop is the extreme case of the insider-outsider model outlined by Lindbeck and Snower (1986), since the competition between union 'insiders' and 'outsiders' is ruled out via mutual agreement between employers and employees.

Within Western Europe, the British welfare state comes closest to the liberal ideal-type (Esping-Andersen, 1990). In this model, the state supports and supplements market regulation rather than contributing to processes of 'de-commodification' and the limitation of market forces. State support of the market is carried out both passively – through the provision of minimal entitlements and actively through the subsidizing of private services. Examples for this include the three main pillars of the British welfare state: the pension system, unemployment entitlements, and the National Health Service. Every citizen is entitled to a state pension, which, however, does not normally provide recipients with an income level that is above the poverty threshold. Private pension schemes are therefore encouraged and supported via taxation. Primary health care provided by the National Health Service is practically free, while additional services must be paid for privately. The unemployment entitlement system is designed to increase the 'incentive to work' of the unemployed: entitlements are not related to previous salary but fixed at the minimum necessary to make ends meet. Generally, the quantitative level of transfer payments is low by international standards (Table 4.4.14).

4.4.2 Deregulation and re-regulation in the UK

The labour market and welfare state reforms of the Conservative governments (1979–97) have been characterized by 'the virtual absence of legal minimum standards, the replacement of collective employment rights with individual ones, and the decentralization of bargaining at the plant and individual level' (Samek Lodovici, 2000, p. 49). While the role of the state in pre-1979 socio-economic regulation was weak, it became an influential actor in the 1980s and 1990s. Not only were previous attempts to achieve more coordination in wage determination and labour market regulation terminated, the Conservative governments used their majority to 'liberate' market forces and this meant to carry out supply-oriented reforms to improve the competitiveness of British capital while the priority of maintaining full-employment, to which all previous post-war governments had been committed, was rejected. Unemployment was now seen as 'the consequence of irresponsible collective bargaining or of misguided government interference in the market, or both' (Hyman, 2003, p. 53). The state intervened into industrial relations and the regulatory system with the aim of bringing about 'pure' market regulation and, hence, making itself redundant. As a result of the corresponding reforms, the wage determination system was at least as uncoordinated as before, while changes in industrial relations clearly favoured the interests of employers.

The most important cornerstones of the new economic and political edifice can be summarized in five measures. The first was the undermining of the power of the unions, especially at company level. The various Employment Acts of the 1980s abolished statutory recognition procedures, extended the grounds for refusing to join a union, limited picketing, and made the establishment of a 'closed shop' conditional upon an 80 per cent majority in a ballot (Blanchflower and Freeman, 1994, p. 56). Unions were made liable for a wide range of industrial action conducted by local union representatives. Employers were given the right to pay non-union employees more than others (Purcell, 1995, p. 104). Second, collective institutions of wage determination were dismantled: the wage councils and consequently the minimum wage were abolished (Sakowsky, 1992; Blanchflower and Freeman, 1994, p. 56). Third, the reduction of public expenditure, particularly through the privatization of state companies and the diminishment of public employment. In addition, and despite vehement trade union resistance, unprofitable companies, in which the state had stakes or which were subsidized by the state, were closed, particularly in the mining and manufacturing sector. Fourth, reforms of the welfare system included various reductions of the replacement ratio for unemployment benefits, and a tighter link between benefit entitlements and the willingness to take up work or training (Rhodes, 2000, p. 46). Fifth, the partial refusal of the Europeanization process. Even though 50 per cent of the UK's foreign trade was carried out with continental EU countries, the Conservative governments under Thatcher and Major followed a sceptical line towards the EU. Some steps in the Europeanization process were taken grudgingly, while others such as the underwriting of the EU Social Charter not at all. Above all, it was decided not to belong to the core countries that have constituted the eurozone since 1999 (Klodt, 1998).

The New Labour government, in power since 1997, has made no qualitative change to the inherited capital-oriented growth strategy. Likewise, the attempts of earlier Labour governments to establish tripartism and labour market institutionalization have not been repeated, nor has the regulatory role of the state, weakened as a result of Conservative policies, been much enhanced. In the area of passive labour market policy, the inherited orientation was intensified further. The new deal (Making Work Pay) aimed at moving the longer-term unemployed into paid employment by linking unemployment and other benefits even more closely to participation in work or training programmes than under the Conservatives. Otherwise, reforms were passed which were designed to gradually improve the position of employees at company level and to arrest the enormous increase in income inequality and societal disintegration that had emerged under the Conservative governments (4.4.3). A degree of re-recognition of trade unions was expressed in the fact that workers in firms with more than twenty employees were now legally entitled to union representation if at least 40 per cent of the staff voted for it, while in firms where at least 50 per cent of workers were already union members, recognition was awarded as of right. Protection against dismissal was extended to all employees after twelve months of employment (Rhodes, 2000, p. 60–61). With regard to social inequality, the most important measures were the re-introduction of the minimum wage, and the signing of the European Social Charter. However, the sceptical line towards the euro has been maintained during the first two Labour governments. Expectations that a referendum on UK joining the eurozone will be held during Labour's third term, which began in the summer of 2005, are low. The reform of the pensions system added a new second and third tier to the existing flat-rate contributory pension, however, without restoring the link between pensions and earnings. The new Working Family Tax Credit was decided to be more generous than the preceding Family Credit and was therefore designed to allow families with children to live above the poverty threshold. The new taxation system was also intended to be redistributive as it tends to favour less well-off persons more than the better-off.

4.4.3   The transformation of the occupational and social structure

In the first half of the 20th century, the UK gradually lost its economic advantage that originated in the Industrial Revolution (Heidenreich, 1997). This decline was to be continued thereafter as labour productivity growth was just 2.9 per cent between 1961 and 1973 (Table 4.4.1). From a comparative perspective, this is a rather modest increase. While most European countries arrived at the peak of Fordist productivity in the late 1960s and early 1970s, during this period UK productivity growth was already declining. This development deteriorated between 1974 and 1985 when growth in both GDP and productivity sank to their respective lows and grew more slowly than real wages. Unemployment increased by nearly 5 per cent to 6.8 per cent between 1961 and 1973 and 1974 and 1985.

4.4.3.1   Growth of GDP, productivity, wages, and unemployment
Growth in GDP and in productivity recovered in the period of 1986 to 1995 and unemployment continued to increase. Between 1996 and 2005, however, unemployment went down considerably and GDP growth increased. The fact that productivity growth decreased between 1986 and 1995 and 1996 and 2005 leads to the assumption that the UK is following a labour extensive course. The fall in unemployment appears to be thanks to a development strategy in which profits are not in the first instance created as a result of reinvestments into the technological basis of the production process but rather due to an extensive and flexible use of the labour force.

4.4.3.2   Population, economic activity, employment and unemployment
The demographic development, if viewed separately, suits both the labour market and the financial situation of public funds: the percentage of the population aged 16 to 64 (Table 4.4.2, III) of the total population (II) increased from 62.7 per cent in 1973 to 63.8 per cent in 1997, and the percentage of the economically active population (IV) in the total population grew from 45.5 per cent in 1973 to 50.1 per cent in 2003. The actual financial burden of every single economic actor, however, is defined by the percentage of the employed (VII) in the total population. This percentage rose from 44.3 per cent in 1973 to 47.7 per cent in 2003.

The Conservative governments, in particular, reduced state subsidies for industry and mining or abolished them altogether. Unprofitable state companies were privatized, and during the clashes that ineluctably accompanied these processes, the government favoured a conflict rather than consensus-oriented approach. Such policies added to those tendencies of decomposition of the social structure that already accompanied the crisis of Fordism. During the period 1979 to 1981 alone, unemployment doubled. The employment crisis turned out to be persistent and

Table 4.4.1 GDP growth, labour productivity growth, real unit labour costs, real wages per head, unemployment rate: 1961–2005

Year	GDP growth*	Labour productivity growth**	Real unit labour costs***	Real wages per head****	Unemployment rate*****
1961–1973	3.3	2.9	0.1	3.3	1.9
1974–1985	1.4	1.5	- 0.2	1.7	6.8
1986–1995	2.5	2.1	- 0.2	1.8	9.0
1996–2005	2.7	1.7	0.2	2.6	5.8

*　　　*Gross domestic product at 1995 market prices; annual percentage change.*
**　　*Gross domestic product at 1995 market prices per person employed, annual percentage change.*
***　*EUROSTAT definition; annual percentage change.*
****　*Real compensation per employee, deflator private consumption; national income; annual percentage change.*
***** *EUROSTAT defintion.*

Source: European Economy, No. 73 and No. 4 (2004).

resulted in an unemployment rate that oscillated around 10 per cent in the following 13 years. From the second half of the 1990s, indications of recovery began to outweigh the negative trends. In 1997, the employment rate was above the level of 1973 for the first time, and, in 2003, unemployment stood at just 4.8 per cent; the lowest level since 1973.

The processes of decomposition and recomposition of labour market and social structure were gendered. Between 1977 and 1993, the number of employed men fell by 849,000 in two cycles. After a first recovery in 1991, when this number had risen to the level of 1977 again, there was a second reduction in employment between 1991 and 1993. From the second half of the 1990s, the number of employed men rose again. However, in 2003, there were only 89,000 more men employed than in 1977. Those economic sectors especially affected by deregulation – mining, manufacturing – were male domains, so that mass dismissals almost exclusively influenced male employment (see also Table 4.4.9).

With regard to women, the results are quite different. Both employment and activity rate grew quickly and, in 1997, stood at a level which is, within this comparison of countries, only exceeded by Sweden. Unemployment levels remained below the male equivalent throughout the period under observation. The sector-specific perspective shows that women are over-represented in those economic sectors that benefited from structural changes (see also Table 4.4.10).

Table 4.4.2 Population, economic activity, occupational system and unemployment

I Year	II Population (1000)	III Population 16–64 (1000)	IV Economically active population (1000)	V IV in II (%)	VI Activity rate (IV in III) (%)	VII Employed (1000)	VIII Employment rate (VII in III) (%)	IX Unemployed (1000)	X Unemployment rate (IX in IV) (%)
1973	55515	34821	25244	45.5	72.5	24609	70.7	635	2.5
1977	56427	35162	26104	46.3	74.2	24523	69.7	1581	6.1
1979	55946	–	26534	47.4	–	25061	–	1473	5.6
1981	55039	35450	26808	48.7	75.6	23988	67.7	2820	10.5
1985	56763	37192	27615	48.9	74.2	24539	66.0	3076	11.1
1988	57065	37421	28343	49.7	75.7	25860	69.1	2483	8.8
1991	57649	37516	28811	50.0	76.8	26399	70.4	2412	8.4
1993	57232	36516	28447	49.7	77.9	25511	69.9	2936	10.3
1997	58105	37086	28716	49.4	77.4	26682	71.9	2034	7.1
2000	58650	–	29411	50.1	–	27793	–	1619	5.5
2003	58337	–	29235	50.1	–	27820	–	1414	4.8

Source: ILO, Yearbooks of Labour Statistics; various volumes.

Table 4.4.3   Population, economic activity, occupational system and unemployment: men

I Year	II Population (1000)	III Population 16–64 (1000)	IV Economically active population (1000)	V IV in II (%)	VI Activity rate (IV in III) (%)	VII Employed (1000)	VIII Employment rate (VII in III) (%)	IX Unemployed (1000)	X Unemployment rate (IX in IV) (%)
1977	27476	17547	16003	58.2	91.2	14884	84.8	1119	7.0
1979	27265	–	16037	58.8	–	15028	–	1009	6.3
1981	26779	17692	16225	60.6	91.7	14245	80.5	1980	12.2
1985	27647	18677	16151	58.4	86.5	14289	76.5	1862	11.5
1988	27813	18767	16298	58.6	86.8	14824	79.0	1474	9.0
1991	28132	18807	16400	58.3	87.2	14887	79.2	1513	9.2
1993	27994	18280	16021	57.2	87.6	14035	76.8	1986	12.4
1997	28604	18735	16024	56.0	85.5	14720	78.6	1304	8.1
2000	28942	–	16327	56.4	–	15336	–	991	6.1
2003	28337	–	15840	55.7	–	14973	–	866	5.5

Source: ILO, Yearbooks of Labour Statistics; various volumes.

Table 4.4.4 Population, economic activity, occupational system and unemployment: women

I Year	II Population (1000)	III Population 16–64 (1000)	IV Economically active population (1000)	V IV in II (%)	VI Activity rate (IV in III) (%)	VII Employed (1000)	VIII Employment rate (VII in III) (%)	IX Unemployed (1000)	X Unemployment rate (IX in IV) (%)
1977	28951	17615	10101	34.9	57.3	9639	54.7	462	4.6
1979	28681	–	10497	36.6	–	10033	–	464	4.6
1981	28260	17759	10583	37.4	59.6	9743	54.9	840	7.9
1985	29116	18605	11464	39.5	61.6	10250	55.1	1214	10.6
1988	29252	18644	12045	41.2	64.6	11036	59.3	1009	9.1
1991	29518	18709	12411	42.0	66.3	11512	61.5	899	7.2
1993	29238	18238	12426	42.5	68.1	11476	62.9	950	7.6
1997	29501	18352	12692	43.0	69.2	11962	65.2	730	5.8
2000	29708	–	13084	44.0	–	12457	–	628	4.8
2003	29910	–	13395	44.8	–	12847	–	548	4.1

Source: ILO, Yearbooks of Labour Statistics; various volumes.

4.4.3.3   Class-specific analysis of the economically active population

The percentage of the self-employed in total employment rose from 7.3 per cent in 1971 to 12.5 per cent in 1992 and has since remained at that level. The size of companies as measured by the number of employees has, on average, decreased since the growth of total employment was much slower than the employers' percentage in total employment (Table 4.4.5). Against the background of the theoretical hypothesis of a growing percentage of self-employment in Post-Fordist employment systems, the UK turns out to be the most advanced case since the relative reduction of dependent employment already began in the 1980s. The recomposition of the social structure with its increasing percentage of self-employment was earlier initiated in the UK than elsewhere.

Table 4.4.5   Self-employment as percentage of total employment

Year	Employers (%)	Contributing family members (%)	All self-employed (%)	Total employment (1000)
1971	7.3	–	7.3	25244
1992	12.5	0.7	13.2	25812
2003	12.5	0.3	12.8	27820

Source: ILO, Yearbooks of Labour Statistics; various volumes.

Mass unemployment was only one result of Margaret Thatcher's re-adjustment policies that accelerated the transformation towards capital-oriented labour markets and social structures. The closure of the large corporations of the Fordist era appears to have been accompanied by an hitherto unprecedented start-up boom of small and medium-sized companies.

Table 4.4.6   Self-employment as percentage of total employment: men

Year	Employers (%)	Contributing family members (%)	All self-employed (%)	Total employment (1000)
1971	9.8	–	9.8	14947
1992	17.0	0.4	17.4	14321
2003	16.9	0.2	17.1	14973

Source: ILO, Yearbooks of Labour Statistics; various volumes.

The gender-specific perspective reveals that the trend towards self-employment was much greater among men than among women. Since men were particularly affected by unemployment (Table 4.4.3), one is tempted to assume that this was one of the main reasons for their turning towards self-employment. Presumably, a good part of today's self-employed did not set up their own company due to a sudden spread of entrepreneurial spirit, but, more profanely, due to a simple lack of promising alternatives in the sphere of wage labour. Alongside a new elite of 'modern' entrepreneurs in the financial and communication sectors, there is a stratum within the self-employed class that was previously only recorded in the countries of the developing world: entrepreneurship due to desperation.

Table 4.4.7   Self-employment as percentage of total employment: women

Year	Employers (%)	Contributing family members (%)	All self-employed (%)	Total employment (1000)
1971	4.3	–	4.3	8608
1992	6.9	1.1	8.0	11491
2003	7.4	0.4	7.8	12847

Source: ILO, Yearbooks of Labour Statistics; different volumes.

4.4.3.4 Wage-earners by economic sector
We have already seen at the example of productivity growth (Table 4.4.1), and from both the advanced percentage and decentralization of self-employment (Table 4.4.5) that the decline of the British social structure, which corresponded to the crisis of Fordist accumulation, was initiated earlier than elsewhere. Table 4.4.8 shows that Britain had already passed its industrial employment peak in the 1960s, by which time, the minimization of the agricultural sector was also advanced. In Germany, by contrast, industrial employment began to diminish only in the 1970s, while the percentage of agricultural employment was 8.6 per cent in 1970.

What followed was a rapid de-industrialization. Between 1967 and 2003, the percentage of industrial workers decreased from 45.6 per cent to 18.6 per cent. At the same time, the growth of the financial sector was tremendous. Benefiting especially from economic restructuring, this sector rose from 3.5 per cent in 1967 to 19.4 per cent in 2003. While the increase of the mostly private service sector I is remarkable, the percentage of the social services remained constant.

The gender-specific division of labour largely follows the patterns already known from the other country studies: the agricultural and industrial sector is male-dominated, while the influx of female wage earners is concentrated in the three service sectors.

Table 4.4.8   Wage-earners by economic sector (%)*

Year	Agriculture	Industry: manufacturing, mining, electricity & water, construction	Services I: wholesale and retail trade, transport, hotels and restaurants	Services II: financial operations	Services III: social services	N (1000)
1967	3.6	45.6	20.1	3.5	27.2	24570
1973	2.9	42.6	19.5	4.5	30.5	24609
1979	2.6	38.7	25.1	7.0	26.5	25061
1988	2.3	33.0	26.8	11.2	26.6	25860
1995	1.1	22.5	29.5	17.3	29.6	23304
2003	0.9	18.6	30.3	19.4	30.8	26000

*1967–88: Total employment by economic sector.

Source: ILO, Yearbooks of International Labour Statistics; various volumes.

Table 4.4.9   Wage-earners by economic sector: men (%)

Year	Agriculture	Industry: manufacturing, mining, electricity & water, construction	Services I: wholesale and retail trade, transport, hotels and restaurants	Services II: financial operations	Services III: social services	N (1000)
1979	3.5	48.8	23.6	6.5	17.7	15028
1985	3.6	41.7	25.0	9.0	20.8	14289
1995	1.8	32.6	30.2	17.0	18.3	11530
2003	1.3	28.0	31.0	20.3	19.5	13142

Source: ILO, Yearbooks of International Labour Statistics; various volumes.

Table 4.4.10   Wage-earners by economic sector: women (%)

Year	Agriculture	Industry: manufacturing, mining, electricity & water, construction	Services I: wholesale and retail trade, transport, hotels and restaurants	Services II: financial operations	Services III: social services	N (1000)
1979	1.3	23.7	27.4	7.9	39.6	10033
1985	1.2	18.0	27.7	10.5	42.7	10250
1995	0.5	12.5	28.7	17.6	40.6	11774
2003	0.5	9.0	29.6	18.6	42.3	12858

Source: ILO, *Yearbooks of International Labour Statistics; various volumes.*

4.4.3.5   Annual hours worked, part-time employment, long-term unemployment, and labour market policy

The UK has been following a labour extensive development strategy. After reductions of working hours in the 1970s, the volume of work per person and year remained around 1700 hours. A comparison with Germany is in this case of interest since, in 1983, the average number of annual hours worked was almost equal in both countries. Thereafter, however, the two countries started to follow different directions: while in Germany the number of hours worked had decreased to 1446 by 2003, in the UK, this number had only slightly diminished to 1673.

Table 4.4.11   Average annual hours worked per person in employment

Year	1973	1983	1990	1999	2003
Hours worked per person	1929	1719	1771	1719	1673

Source: *OECD, 1997, and 2004.*

Heavy workloads were accompanied by additional part-time work. With part-time work increasing, however, the overall volume of work per person can remain constant only if, at the same time, other people work excessive hours (over 40 hours per week). In the UK, individual working hours had to adjust more directly to the changeable conditions of companies' competitiveness than elsewhere. Tony Blair's signing of the European Social Charter can be seen as a softening of this capital-oriented course although this Charter merely has the character of recommendation: working hours of over 48 hours per week are supposed to be avoided. It remains to be seen, whether the deregulation of working hours – sometimes referred to as hyper-flexibility – will be limited by means of this instrument.

Table 4.4.12   Part-time employment (as percentage of total employment)

Year	1983	1990	1994	2000	2003
Total	18.4	20.8	22.6	23.0	23.3
Men	3.3	4.8	6.3	8.6	9.6
Women	40.1	39.3	40.4	40.8	40.1

Source: OECD, 1997, and 2004.

Women's part-time ratio is especially high – about twice as high as in Sweden. By contrast to negotiated labour market regimes, in the UK, the problem of harmonizing private and professional life is largely a 'private matter'. The government's refusal to politically regulate the work–life balance might help to bring the budget deficit under control; but the lack in public provisions for care of both children and the elderly also means the essential reproduction of the traditional division of labour between the sexes. While, in Fordism, women were largely reduced to their role as housewives and men held full-time jobs, men now tend to keep these jobs and work excessive hours with 40 per cent of women occupying the less privileged part-time jobs. This, however, occurs in addition to women's duties in the households since men do not appear to spend much time as 'househusbands'.

Table 4.4.13   Long-term unemployment (as percentage of total unemployment)

Year	1983		1990		1994		2000		2003	
Period	Over 6 months	Over 12 months	Over 6 months	Over 12 months	Over 6 months	Over 12 months	Over 6 months	Over 12 months	Over 6 months	Over 12 months
Total	66.4	45.6	50.3	34.4	63.4	45.4	43.2	28.0	37.3	23.0
Men	70.7	51.2	56.8	41.8	68.6	51.2	48.1	33.7	40.8	26.5
Women	58.6	35.5	40.8	23.7	53.3	33.9	35.6	19.0	31.4	17.1

Source: OECD, 1997, and 2004.

Between 1983 and 2003, long-term unemployment halved, whereby men were more affected than women throughout the whole period. The reduction in long-term unemployment can be seen as a success of a labour market policy oriented at increasing the spatial and occupational mobility and flexibility of the workforce. This strategy, aimed at increasing the 'employability' of people at all costs, seems to work. However, low long-term unemployment rates should also be interpreted against the background of the state's lack of involvement in economic and employment affairs. The fact that between 1991 and 2002 the level of public expenditure for active labour market policy as a percentage of GDP decreased from the already comparatively low level of 1.41 per cent to 0.37 per cent, indicates that British governments abstained from playing a major role in employment affairs. This assessment appears to be justified as there is less money spent on the maintenance of every single unemployed person: while unemployment decreased by 41.4 per cent between 1991 and 2003 (Table 4.4.2), public expenditures as percentage of GDP was reduced by 73.8 per cent (Table 4.4.14). It is not least by spending less money on unemployment benefits and making a life 'on the dole' as unattractive as possible that the government increases the 'incentive' of the unemployed to accept virtually any job.

Table 4.4.14   Public expenditure on labour market policies as percentage of GDP

Year	1991	1997	2002/3
Active measures	0.57	0.42	0.37
Public employment services and administration	0.20	0.18	0.17
Labour market training	0.15	0.09	0.02
Youth measures	0.17	0.13	0.13
Wage subsidies in private sector	–	–	0.02
Support of unemployed persons starting enterprises	0.02	–	–
Direct job creation (public or non-profit)	–	–	0.01
Vocational rehabilitation	–	–	0.01
Work for the disabled	0.02	0.02	0.01
Passive measures	1.41	1.05	0.37
Total	1.98	1.47	0.75

Source: OECD, 1996, 2004.

4.4.3.6   *Income inequality and poverty*
Previous studies have pointed out that as a result of Conservative economic and social policies, in the UK labour costs have decreased, and wages have been made more dependent on the competitive situation of the respective company and on the individual performance of the employee. 'Numerical and pay flexibilities have both been increased and part-time, temporary, and self-employment all grew' (Rhodes, 2000, p. 52). Other studies report a growing divide between a 'core' of

secure professionals and a 'periphery' of non-professional staff, which lead to rising wage dispersal and increasing numbers of the working poor. According to Piachaud (1998), by 1997 there were 14 million officially classified as poor, a good part of whom were working poor (Walker and Walker, 1997). This corresponded to almost a fifth of the population.

Table 4.4.15   Income inequality and relative poverty

Year	Gini coefficient	Relative poverty: total population		Relative poverty: children		Relative poverty: elderly	
		50 % line	60 % line	50 % line	60 % line	50 % line	60 % line
1969	0.267	5.5	12.4	6.0	13.0	15.3	35.6
1974	0.267	9.1	15.4	8.0	14.2	29.7	47.2
1979	0.270	9.2	17.3	9.0	15.3	21.6	49.5
1991	0.336	14.6	22.8	18.5	26.9	23.9	43.5
1994	0.339	10.8	20.0	13.9	26.6	15.1	29.4
1999	0.345	12.5	21.3	15.4	27.0	20.9	34.9

Source: Luxembourg Income Study: <www.lisproject.org/keyfigures/ineqtable.htm>.

By and large, Table 4.4.15 confirms the results of these studies. Between 1979 and 1999, the Gini coefficient significantly increased from 0.270 to 0.345, the highest level within the five countries compared.[17] In relation to relative poverty, the percentage of people below the 50 per cent line increased from 5.5 per cent in 1969 to 12.5 per cent in 1999. With respect to the 60 per cent line, the percentage of 'poor' people increased from 12.4 per cent in 1969 to 21.3 per cent in 1999. Against the number of the total population in 2000 (58,650,000, Table 4.4.2), this corresponds to 12.5 million persons. If we compare this number to the number of the poor given by Piachaud (1998), there is a decrease of 1.5 million since 1997, which is, however, still the highest level within the countries compared in this study. Both children and the elderly are overproportionally exposed to poverty, with children in poverty having faster growth rates.

4.4.4   Summary of the case study

In the course of the 20th century, the British economy fell behind that of other European countries. The previous headstart in terms of productivity, which had been achieved during the 18th and 19th centuries, had turned into relative 'backwardness' in relation to the application of Fordist management principles, the full productivity

---

17 According to Brewer et al. (2004, p. 15), the Gini coefficient still stood at 0.345 in 2002/03 so that apparently, it did not rise any further in the period 1999–2002/03.

potential of which the UK has never been able to retrieve. In order to overcome this gap in development, since 1979, the country followed a growth strategy close to the capital-oriented ideal-type. The core elements of this strategy were wage determination processes at the individual or company level and reforms in the general mode of regulation, which can be understood as having served the interests of employers in the first instance. Our country study confirms an assessment by the German Institute for Economic Research (*Deutsches Institut für Wirtschaftsforschung*) according to which the company level is the 'main level of bargaining between employers and employees. Multi-employer contracts amount to less than a quarter of all contracts' (*DIW-Wochenbericht* 44/97, p. 862, my translation). Earlier attempts to establish a greater degree of wage coordination were terminated by post-1979 governments.

In the 1980s and 1990s especially, the Conservative governments directly intervened in the industrial relations system with the aim of re-establishing the profitability of UK companies. However, this was largely identified with the structural debilitation of the trade unions, the termination of industrial policies and the privatization of public property. Attempts to navigate the wider socio-economic development using Keynesian concepts were also abandoned in other areas such as monetary and wage policies, and replaced by neo-liberal policies. Capital and financial markets were 'liberated' through programmes of privatization and deregulation. Social contributions were brought to a lower level by removing the connection between income earned, pension payments and contributions to unemployment schemes. The welfare state was redesigned with the aim, above all, of increasing the incentives to work.

If British Fordism was flawed (Robert Boyer) in the sense that the productivity potential arising from Taylor's 'scientific' management principles could not be established in the same way as in other European countries, the Conservative policies of 'modernization' had a catalytic effect on the emergence of a Post-Fordist labour market within a capital-oriented growth strategy. The governments of Margaret Thatcher, in particular, supported de-industrialization (by de facto abolishing subsidies for the manufacturing and mining sector) and by supporting (via deregulation) the expanding financial sector. On this basis, a highly flexible labour market and a corresponding social structure rapidly emerged as a result.

On the one hand, the significant decline in unemployment, both since 1996 and in comparison to other European countries, is impressive: unemployment decreased from 9.0 per cent between 1986 and 1995 to 5.8 per cent between 1996 and 2005. On the other hand, this decline in unemployment appears not to have been accomplished through the creation of highly skilled jobs in the first instance. Both the increase of service sector I (Table 4.4.8) and the accompanying reduction in labour productivity growth indicate that a relevant part of the new employment is actually 'bad jobs' in the private service sector. There appears to be a growing division between well-paid and professional employment (the 'core') and poorly paid, non-professional employment ('periphery') which is reflected in comparatively high income inequality and poverty levels. The new growth strategy is also labour extensive as is indicated by the number of hours annually worked per person.

Table 4.4.16   Selected empirical results

	1961–1973	1974–1985	1986–1995	1996–2005
GDP Growth (4.4.1)	3.3	1.4	2.5	2.7
Labour productivity growth (4.4.1)	2.9	1.5	2.1	1.7
Real wages per head (4.4.1)	3.3	1.7	1.8	2.6
Activity rate (4.4.2)	72.5 (1973)	74.7 (1977–85)	76.8 (1988–93)	77.4 (1997)
'Feminization' (activity rate women) (4.4.4)	–	59.5 (1977–85)	66.3 (1988–93)	69.2 (1997)
Self-employment as percentage in total employment (4.4.5)	7.3 (1971)	–	13.2 (1992)	12.8 (2003)
(De)industrialization (4.4.8)	44.1 (1967-73)	38.7 (1979)	22.5 (1995)	18.6 (2003)
Tertiarization (4.4.8)	52.7 (1967-73)	58.6 (1979)	76.4 (1995)	80.5 (2003)
Average hours worked per person (4.4.11)	1929 (1973)	1719 (1983)	1771 (1990)	1695 (1999–2003)
Part-time employment (4.4.12)	–	18.4 (1983)	21.7 (1990)	23.2 (2000–03)
Unemployment (4.4.1)	1.9	6.8	9.0	5.8
Long-term unemployment (over 12 months) (4.4.13)	–	45.6 (1983)	39.9 (1990-94)	25.5 (2000–03)
Relative poverty (60 per cent line) (4.4.15)	5.5 (1969)	14.8 (1974–79)	21.4 (1991–94)	21.3 (1999)

Sources: Various materials from EUROSTAT, ILO, OECD, and Luxembourg Income Study.
Brackets after labour market issue indicate the Table that previously commented in detail, on this issue.

Over the last quarter of a century, unemployment has mainly been seen as a problem of inflated price expectations on the part of those who supply labour power. If the government only ensured, so the mainstream view, that the 'price of labour' is adjusted to the changeable necessities of the market, then nothing is in the way of an increase of employment. However, our country study suggests that not even a return to full employment would necessarily stop the advanced disintegration of the labour market and the social structure. Rather it characterizes the British experience that reduction in unemployment and the simultaneous price reduction of labour power within the lower spectrum of the labour force coincides with high rates of relative poverty. Rising economic participation and inclusion go hand in hand with high levels of wage dispersal and the working poor. Far from eradicating poverty as a paramount social issue, poverty itself appears to have changed its face with the transition towards a capital-oriented Post-Fordist growth strategy.

While in the 1980s, poverty was mostly a consequence of unemployment, since the 1990s, it has increasingly been accompanied by economic inclusion. This fact is neither a feature of capitalism nor of Post-Fordism in general, but is typical for a development strategy that is based on wage bargaining at the individual or company level. Here, poverty does not so much result from economic exclusion but from the integration of increasingly more social groups in the dynamic of an accumulation process that produces, alongside a sizeable group of 'winners' (above all in the financial sector), a great number of 'losers', who are employed in occupational positions that do not require high skills (above all in the private service sector) and, less so, in manufacturing. People who are occupied in the lower regions of the occupational spectrum often have to make ends meet on the basis of the minimum wage. It is likely that a relevant number of the new self-employed have become so due to a lack of other opportunities as 'wage-earners'. Further research into the social structure of British employers could – in addition to bringing to light the specific background of their entrepreneurial aims by means of qualitative methods – find out how many of these new companies are actually one-person firms whose incomes barely exceed subsistence level.

Overall, the transformation from a Fordist-Keynesian towards a Post-Fordist and capital-oriented development strategy largely attained the goal of overcoming the gap in the UK's GDP growth to the other leading capitalist countries and to improve the competitive environment of the UK as a 'national location' in general. The price for the return to economic growth and the creation of millions of new jobs was the dispersion of poverty, the loss of social solidarity and an increasingly divided and polarized society.[18]

---

18 The data available do not allow for an assessment of the measures taken by the New Labour government. The introduction of a minimum wage and the tax reforms, especially, appear to support low-income groups so that income inequality might be somewhat reduced.

4.5 The Netherlands

In the Netherlands, the regulation of the labour market and welfare system is traditionally carried out in tripartite bargaining at societal level; the translation into socio-political practice, however, takes place at lower levels. Historically, the state often initiated thorough changes in the regulatory system and the overall growth strategy.

4.5.1 Economic and social system

Due to its relatively small size in terms of both geography and population, the Netherlands are extremely vulnerable to external influences. Unlike Spain, protectionism has never been an option, since the internal market is severely limited in small countries. Hence due to the extra pressure to perform well on the world market, it became necessary to develop effective corporate relations. To a greater extent than in large countries, the corporatist relations of small countries are characterized by an 'ideology of partnership, expressed at the national level; a relatively centralized and concentrated system of interest groups; and voluntary and informal coordination of conflicting objectives through continuing bargaining between interest groups, state bureaucracy and political parties' (Katzenstein, 1985, p. 32). Given this emphasis on informal communication and trust within the Dutch corporate triangle of employers' organizations, trade unions and the state, I suggest it is appropriate to label the corresponding type of Fordism as corporate.

Developing the ideas of Katzenstein, Visser and Hemerijck (1997, p. 92) distinguish between two types of corporatism: in its social democratic variant, its basic features are defined by socialist or social democratic parties as in Sweden, for example, while the Netherlands is an example of the liberal variant of corporatism. The latter is characterized by a rather weak and divided workers' movement and relatively strong and well-organized employers' organizations and conservative political parties. Indeed, union density is at a relatively low level of about 30 per cent (Ebbinghaus and Visser, 1997, p. 352), and, furthermore, the trade union movement is itself ideologically divided and split along these political lines: while the Confederation of Dutch Trade Unions (FNV), historically linked to the Socialist party, organized 1,200,000 employees in 1996, the Christian National Union Confederation (CNV) had 380,000 members. The latter is traditionally associated with the Christian Democrats and has largely Protestant members. Among the smaller trade unions, the Union of White Collar and Senior Staff Associations (VHP) should be mentioned; it organizes mainly white collar workers and had 170,000 members in 1996. Also in line with the ideal-type of a liberal corporatism, is the fact that Dutch employers have a high organization rate: 60 to 70 per cent of all private enterprises belong to one of the employers' organizations – a membership rate in the order of magnitude of Germany and the Scandinavian countries. Almost every company with more than 50 employees is a member of the Federation of Dutch Industry (VNO) which organizes larger and medium-sized companies. Companies with up to 50 employees tend to be represented by the MKB-Nederland. Both organizations are united under the umbrella of the Council of Central Business Organizations (RCO). The main function of the latter is the representation of the employers in national-level bargaining with the trade unions and the government concerning general issues beyond the sphere of interest of single companies or sectors.

Post-war industrial relations in the Netherlands were organized in the communal belief that a high degree of cooperation and centralized bargaining were indispensable. General orientations of political economy and major reforms in labour market and welfare state were normally negotiated in the two tripartite bodies at the national level, *Stichting van de Arbeid* (STAR) and *Sociaal Economische Raad* (SER). STAR, founded in 1945 as a private foundation, was made the primary body of wage negotiations and employment conditions. Government memoranda and/or macro-economic proposals by the Central Planning Agency (CBP) are normally the foundation for the consultations in STAR, which, if successful, lead to a central agreement (*Ceentraal Akkoord*, CA). On the basis of these agreements, the actual collective bargaining rounds take place. Proceeding decentrally on the sector and company level, these are oriented towards the central agreement but, beyond that, consider regional and sectoral particularities. Dutch labour market regulation is therefore a specific mix of central and decentral elements. Consisting of representatives of the corporate triangle, labour market experts, the President of the Central Bank and the Director of the Central Planning Agency, the SER focuses more on general and longer-term concerns. Until 1995 the government was legally bound to consult the SER in all important economic and social affairs. Meanwhile this obligation has been changed to a mere advisory function, but, nevertheless, the SER is still the most relevant body for providing general guidelines on labour market and welfare policies.

Wage determination had a particular form since public sector wages were indexed to private wage development. The latter, in turn, was automatically adjusted to cost-of-living developments (Hemerijck, 1995, p. 207). The state was of crucial importance to wage determination and general socio-economic regulation. For example, the government retained the right to approve or reject wage provisions resulting from collective agreements. Further possibilities for the government to keep wage developments within certain limits existed in the right to impose a 'wage freeze' in the case of 'serious disturbance in the national economy' and in the right to set the minimum wage (Hemerijck, 1995). Most governments, normally led by Christian Democrats, followed a growth strategy based on wage restraint. The particular Dutch Fordist compromise consisted in a trade-off between the government and the trade unions to establish a 'low-cost' zone' in exchange for the recognition of the trade unions in overall socio-economic policies. Full employment and relative income equality via wage indexation were generally recognized as regulatory goals.

These objectives were also reflected in the creation of a comprehensive social security system. The latter is of the 'continental' type (Esping-Andersen, 1990), albeit with 'universal' elements, and rests on three pillars. The first pillar is pension insurance, to which all Dutch citizens are entitled and which is financed by tax revenues. The second pillar is the unemployment and health insurance, funded by contributions from both employers and employees. Of special relevance in the Dutch case is the disability insurance, which, in 1976, was expanded to civil servants, professionals and freelancers. The third pillar is social assistance, which covers those persons who are not already insured according to the first two pillars of the welfare state – for example unemployed persons whose entitlements have expired. Since 1974, the level of social assistance is, for a single person, legally fixed at 70 per cent of the minimum wage.

When having to cope with unemployment, in particular, 'continental' welfare states appear to either complicate the access to the labour market for particular occupational groups and/or to facilitate their leaving the labour market. Different continental regimes thereby apply different methods. The Netherlands, like Germany, favoured early retirement as an exit strategy from economic activity. In addition, in the 1980s, there was a generous interpretation of the sickness and disability legislation, according to which 980 in 10,000 older employees received a disability pension, while, in Germany, only 262 did so (Prins, 1991 quoted in Visser and Hemerijck, 1997, p. 138). This strategy, to exclude older employees from economic activity, was supported by all relevant labour market parties. On the one hand, it was in the interest of the government and the trade unions to keep the unemployment rate within certain limits. On the other hand, the employers could rationalize their companies, inter alia, by getting rid of older employees without having to consider dismissal legislation and the resistance of the trade unions. Thus, a rejuvenation of the workforce was achieved without jeopardizing the consensus within industrial relations.

4.5.2   Deregulation and re-regulation in the Netherlands

Especially vulnerable to external shocks due to its relatively small size, the Netherlands suffered heavily from the economic crisis of 1974–75. Growth rates of GDP and productivity fell, accompanied by a crisis affecting both the labour market and the welfare state. Industrial relations deteriorated when the practice of central wage determination to achieve wage restraint was temporarily questioned by both employers and organized labour. The public budget became increasingly imbalanced as a result of growing unemployment and the practice of index-linking wages in the public sector to the private sector (Visser and Hemerijck, 1997). Unemployment rose, while the vicious circle of welfare without work intensified. For example, the number of people depending on income transfers doubled between 1970 and 1985 from 1.6 million to 3.2 million (Visser and Hemerijck, 1997, p. 138). Furthermore, 300,000 workers were on sick leave.

After the experience of poor capital–labour relations and industrial conflicts in the 1970s and early 1980s, it was once again the state – in the form of the first Lubbers administration – that in 1982 took the initiative of introducing a new strategy. It was based around the balancing of the public budget, improved business competitiveness by way of tax reductions and wage moderation, and the restoration of full employment via the reduction of individual working hours. Among these three goals, the recovery of the public sector clearly had first priority. This was then supplemented to accommodate the interests of both employers and employees. The first measure was the abolishment of the wage indexation system in 1982. It was re-established in 1989 – on the condition that wage increases would not exceed the expected growth in GDP and that the number of social benefit recipients would not increase in relative terms to the working population – but excluded public sector workers for whom separate collective bargaining mechanisms were established.

The second measure was the double strategy of wage moderation plus reduction in working hours, which was above all carried out in the form of an expansion of part-time work (Visser, 2002, p. 25). Unions and employers negotiated lower wage demands against a reduction of the working week. This reduction led to a 5 per cent drop in wage earners' real wages between 1979 and 1994 (Gorter, 2000). However, this wage cut was partially compensated by lower taxes, lower social contributions and wage subsidies. Labour market reforms included the increase of 'flexible employment' such as fixed-term employment, casual labour and employment contracts with a variable number of working hours, but did not lead to pure 'deregulation' since in 2001 81 per cent of part-time jobs (and 91 percent of full-time jobs) were covered by collective agreements (Visser, 2002, p. 33). The search for more flexibility in working hours to improve competitiveness of Dutch companies was complemented by improvements in the work-life balance as individual workers in companies of ten and more employees were given the right to adjust working hours (Visser, 2002, p. 32). The social security of part-time workers was increased. Pro rata social insurance contributions were now usually paid in exchange for pro rata entitlements. As a result, a trade-off between labour market flexibility in exchange for more security for workers with 'flexible' contracts emerged ('flexicurity').

The final measure concerned welfare state reforms. The quantitative goal of reducing the public budget deficit was accompanied by the qualitative renovation of welfare state entitlements, in which the corporatist actors agreed to move from a labour-substituting paradigm towards a participating paradigm. The public budget imbalance had risen to as much as 10 per cent in 1982. In subsequent steps, which encompassed a small decline in public employment, a pay freeze of public service salaries, and cuts in unemployment benefits, in 1996 the EMU target rate of 3 per cent was reached. Social expenditures were kept under control 'by lowering the duration and level of insurance benefits and by "freezing" the level of assistance and state pension' (van Oorschot, 2002, p. 403). As a result, for those with shorter work records, especially, it became 'more difficult to get benefits for more than half a year' (van Oorschot, 2002, p. 408). However, there were also reforms in the interests of the employees. The 'compromise' character of the changes as a whole is expressed by two elements; first, the possibility of receiving temporary or permanent wage subsidies for employees who accept a job at a lower wage level than their previous job. Such combined wage policies, in connection with a mandatory minimum wage, tend to narrow wage inequalities, and, in particular, 'the differences between part-time and full-time employment' (Visser, 2002, p. 35). The second element was state expenditure for labour market and welfare policies in general, which continued on comparatively high levels (4.5.3.5).

4.5.3 The transformation of the occupational and social structure

4.5.3.1 Growth of GDP, productivity, wages, and unemployment

In the 1950s, wage restraint policies had resulted in wage gaps when compared to neighbouring countries such as Germany and Belgium. Since many Dutch employees looked for work abroad, this facilitated the achievement of full employment in the Netherlands. In the 1960s, low unemployment rates were connected with high growth rates in both GDP and productivity. Real wages increased as a result. Faced with the improved competitiveness of Dutch companies and with low unemployment rates, the trade unions no longer followed STAR's wage guidelines and achieved pay rises of 6.3 per cent on average in the period of 1961 to 1973. This was, in practical terms, the end of the first era of low-wage strategies.

Table 4.5.1 **GDP growth, labour productivity growth, real unit labour costs, real wages per head, unemployment rate: 1961–2005**

Year	GDP growth*	Labour productivity growth**	Real unit labour costs***	Real wages per head****	Unemployment rate *****
1961–1973	4.8	3.9	1.1	6.3	1.1
1974–1985	1.9	2.0	-0.7	1.1	6.9
1986–1995	2.8	1.3	-0.2	1.0	6.6
1996–2005	2.2	0.9	0.0	1.1	4.1

*	*Gross domestic product at 1995 market prices; annual percentage hange.*
**	*Gross domestic product at 1995 market prices per person employed, annual percentage change.*
***	*EUROSTAT definition; annual percentage change.*
****	*Real compensation per employee, deflator private consumption; national income; annual percentage change.*
*****	*EUROSTAT definition.*

Source: European Economy, No. 73 and No. 4 (2004).

The high-wage phase ceased with the crisis of 1974/75 when GDP growth tended towards zero and unemployment increased to 5.5 per cent (Koch, 2003, p. 226). In subsequent years until 1982, growth of GDP, productivity, and real wages remained on low levels, while unemployment rose to almost 12 per cent. In the Wassenaar Agreement, wage restraint again was used with the aim of initiating a new period of prosperity. And indeed, negative trends in GDP growth and employment were reversed. The validity however of the popular hypothesis that this success was due to wage restraint in the first place must be investigated.

Supporters of the 'wage-restraint-creates-employment-thesis' argue that low wages lead to greater profits, which, in turn, allow for larger investments and, eventually, additional employment. This is usually countered by critics of low-wage strategies who stress the demand side: low wages also mean diminished purchasing power, hence fewer sales and, finally, fewer investments and less employment. Further more, the advocates of a strictly supply-oriented policy approach appear to underestimate repercussions on the international division of labour. Torsten Schulte (1999, p. 40) reminds us that within internationally interwoven economies connected by a fixed exchange rate, gaps in demand caused by low wages can only be compensated for through increased exports. Wage restraint then becomes nothing but a 'beggar–my–neighbour–policy'. The introduction of the European Monetary Union eliminated the risk of forfeiting advantages won through wage restraint through currency appreciations.[19] Since that introduction wage restraint has had a direct advantage for a country's competitive situation, therefore the incentive to even further increase wage restraint is likely – and hence the likelihood of a destructive downward spiral of wages in Europe.

In the Dutch case, there is a parallel between wage restraint and the fall in unemployment. The question of why this is so, however, is far from clear. Our comparison has shown that strategies of wage restraint were followed practically everywhere in Europe – but with quite different results in relation to the creation of employment and the fight against unemployment. Since wage restraint coincides in some cases with positive employment trends but in other cases not (Germany, for example), the Dutch employment 'miracle' should not exclusively be ascribed to the consensual establishment of a low-wage paradise. Other factors such as the redistribution of working hours must also be considered (4.5.3.5).

Furthermore, the often implied inter-relation between wage restraint and employment growth can easily act in the opposite manner. The fact that productivity growth continued to diminish even during the 'successful' 1990s leads to the assumption that the relative price reduction of labour power contributed to a deceleration of companies' rationalization processes. Less substitution of labour through capital took place than in other, comparable, countries, and this could result in a pitfall for further development: should wage restraint policies continue to arrest rationalization, then the innovative ability of the Dutch economy could be weakened in the long term. This would no doubt be accompanied by a worsening of the competitive situation and could result in employment losses.

---

19 This was the case in the Netherlands in the early 1980s – before the connection of the Dutch florin with the D-mark.

Table 4.5.2 Population, economic activity, occupational system and unemployment

I Year	II Population (1000)	III Population 16–64 (1000)	IV Economically active population (1000)	V IV in II (%)	VI Activity rate (IV in III) (%)	VII Employed (1000)	VIII Employment rate (VII in III) (%)	IX Unemployed (1000)	X Unemployment rate (IX in IV) (%)
1970	13060	8165	4600	35.2	56.3	4554	55.8	46	1.0
1976	13578	8648	4853	35.7	56.1	4643	53.7	210	4.3
1979	14091	9292	5031	35.7	54.1	4821	51.9	210	5.2
1982	14286	9543	5552	38.9	58.2	5010	52.5	542	9.8
1985	14572	9960	5905	40.5	59.3	5144	51.6	761	12.9
1988	14665	10175	6641	45.3	65.3	6032	59.3	609	9.2
1991	15010	10371	7011	46.7	67.6	6521	62.9	490	7.0
1994	15239	10473	7184	47.1	68.6	6692	63.9	492	6.8
1997	15558	10563	7616	49.0	72.1	7194	68.1	422	5.5
2000	–	10719	8060	–	75.2	7731	72.1	262	3.3
2003	–	10920	8371	–	76.7	7935	72.7	356	4.3

Source: ILO, Yearbooks of Labour Statistics; various volumes.

4.5.3.2 Population, economic activity, employment and unemployment
The percentage of the population aged between 16 and 64 (III) in overall population
(II) increased from 62.5 to 67.9 per cent between 1970 and 1997. The quotient
total population/number of employed people (VIII), crucial for every single labour
market participant's tax burden, took a positive development: from 2.9:1 in 1970,
and 2.8:1 in 1985, to 2.2:1 in 1997. Until 1985, labour market and social structure
were characterized by decomposition: Despite an increasing activity rate (VI) the
employment rate (VIII) fell from 55.8 per cent in 1970 to 51.6 per cent in 1985. In the
same year, the unemployment rate (X) peaked at 12.9 per cent. Thereafter tendencies
of recomposition became dominant: since 1988, both activity and employment rate
have increased in a parallel manner, while the unemployment rate has sunk to just
above four per cent.

The quotient population aged between 16 and 64 (III) and employed persons
(VII) was 1.9:1 in 1985. In a society in which there were almost two economically
passive persons for every single employed person, it is not surprising that
fundamental issues of social solidarity were raised. While the Scandinavian countries
traditionally followed development strategies that aimed at bringing as many people
in employment as possible, countries such as the Netherlands, Germany, France,
Belgium, Italy, and Spain preferred a course that subsidized the exit of the elderly
from the labour market and made the access of women to the labour market difficult.
The Netherlands, especially, became a prime example of what Esping-Andersen
(1996) refers to as welfare without work.

Welfare without work takes the form of a vicious circle. The starting point is
the fact that companies in countries with high wage levels can only survive as long
as they are able to increase productivity growth to an even greater extent. This is
normally achieved through the substitution of labour by capital: the least productive
units within the work process are replaced through the upgrading of its technological
basis. The least productive employees are then often made redundant. At the other
end, increasing economic passivity leads to increasing taxation of labour and
contributions to unemployment and social insurance schemes. This increases wage
costs and creates additional pressure to increase productivity levels of those still
active in the work process. Further dismissals often follow. The vicious circle of
comparably high wage-costs, relatively low net-incomes, the exclusion of less
productive employees, and rising contributions to passive labour market policy
schemes results in a further round in welfare without work. This particular parallel
of a growing number of economically passive citizens, who receive income from
public funds, and a decreasing number of citizens in the formal employment system,
undermines the solvency of the welfare state and, as a consequence, its social
legitimacy. Consequently, the reforms of the Lubbers government (4.5.2) aimed to
end this vicious circle. As a result, the quotient population 16–64/employed persons
improved considerably: the percentage of the employed in the population aged 16 to
64, which was 51.6 in 1985, increased to 68.1 in 2003 (Table 4.5.2).

If we consider the issue of gender, the opposite tendency in the rates of activity
and employment in the 1970s and early 1980s can be discerned. In the 1970s,

Table 4.5.3 Population, economic activity, occupational system and unemployment: men

I Year	II Population (1000)	III Population 16–64 (1000)	IV Economically active population (1000)	V IV in II (%)	VI Activity rate (IV in III) (%)	VII Employed (1000)	VIII Employment rate (VII in III) (%)	IX Unemployed (1000)	X Unemployment rate (IX in IV) (%)
1976	6785	4369	3502	51.6	80.2	3342	76.5	160	4.6
1979	6994	4699	3531	50.5	75.1	3399	72.3	132	3.7
1982	7082	4830	3746	52.9	77.6	3370	69.8	376	10.0
1985	7228	5042	3912	53.7	77.6	3414	67.7	498	12.7
1988	7274	5161	4100	56.4	79.4	3809	73.8	291	7.1
1991	7445	5267	4230	56.8	80.3	4004	76.0	226	5.3
1994	7559	5316	4233	56.0	79.6	3979	74.8	254	6.0
1997	7717	5353	4390	56.9	82.0	4194	78.3	196	4.5
2000	–	5429	4584	–	84.4	4420	81.4	118	2.6
2003	–	5525	4682	–	84.7	4432	80.2	194	4.1

Source: ILO, Yearbooks of Labour Statistics; various volumes.

there was no other Western European country – with the exception of Spain, where womens' participation in the labour market was partially illegal – where the activity rate was as low as in the Netherlands. The fact that in 1979 not even a third of the Dutch female population of working age was economically active (Table 4.5.4) points to the assumption that the traditional gender-specific division of labour that legitimized gainful employment of women merely until marriage and motherhood – if at all – was especially pronounced.

The increase in the activity rate (Table 4.5.2) is mainly due to the economic activity of women increasing in the 1980s and 1990s (Table 4.5.4). Between 1976 and 2003, the activity rate of women more than doubled from 31.6 to 68.4 per cent, whereby it reached European levels. Among men, the activity rate increased slightly from 80.2 to 84.7 per cent overall, while the employment rate largely followed the direction forecast in the hypothesis of the decomposition and recomposition of the social structure (Table 4.5.3): despite a considerable increase in the absolute number of economically active men (IV), between 1976 and 1985 the number of employed men (VII) remained largely constant. Only thereafter did the activity rate and employment rate begin to advance in a parallel manner.

In the second half of the 1970s and first half of the 1980s, the numbers of the economically active, employed and unemployed women all rose. Unlike the male case, both the activity and employment rate grew in a parallel manner. It is only the development of the unemployment rate of women that follows the same pattern as that of men: until the mid-1980s, unemployment of both sexes rose to about 13 per cent, declining thereafter.

4.5.3.3 Class-specific analysis of the economically active population
The long-term trend of a decline in the percentage of self-employed persons within the employment system appears to have come to an end. While there was a further reduction of self-employment within total employment between 1971 to 1995, this percentage has since remained stable.

While male self-employment largely follows this general trend (Table 4.5.6), female entrepreneurship has more than doubled. Women, whose position within self-employment, in 1971, was mostly that of contributing family member, were more often in the responsible position of employers (Table 4.5.7) in 2003.

4.5.3.4 Wage-earners by economic sector
In 1970, about 46 per cent of dependent employment was concentrated in industry and agriculture. Thereafter, these sectors declined, while service sectors expanded. Since 1995, three-quarters of wage-earners have been occupied in the three service sectors within which financial operations have had the fastest growth rate. The size of the social services sector has remained nearly constant since the 1980s.

Men are over-represented in the industrial sector, while women predominate in social services. Every second employed women works in this sector, and this is despite the fact that the absolute number of women in dependent employment increased almost threefold between 1970 and 2003.

Table 4.5.4   Population, economic activity, occupational system and unemployment: women

I Year	II Population (1000)	III Population 16–64 (1000)	IV Economically active population (1000)	V IV in II (%)	VI Activity rate (IV in III) (%)	VII Employed (1000)	VIII Employment rate (VII in III) (%)	IX Unemployed (1000)	X Unemployment rate (IX in IV) (%)
1976	6813	4278	1352	19.8	31.6	1301	30.4	51	3.8
1979	7097	4557	1500	21.1	32.9	1422	31.2	78	5.2
1982	7204	4714	1806	25.1	38.3	1640	34.8	166	9.2
1985	7344	4918	1993	27.1	40.5	1730	35.2	263	13.2
1988	7391	5016	2541	34.4	50.7	2223	44.3	318	12.6
1991	7565	5104	2781	36.8	54.5	2517	49.3	264	9.5
1994	7680	5155	2952	38.4	57.3	2713	52.6	239	8.1
1997	7841	5209	3227	41.2	62.0	3000	57.6	227	7.0
2000	–	5290	3476	–	65.7	3311	62.6	144	4.1
2003	–	5395	3689	–	68.4	3503	64.9	162	4.4

Source: ILO, Yearbooks of Labour Statistics; various volumes.

Table 4.5.5   Self-employment as percentage of total employment

Year	Employers (%)	Contributing family members (%)	All self-employed (%)	Total employment (1000)
1971	11.7	2.8	14.5	4389
1995	10.7	1.3	12.0	6835
2003	10.7	0.5	13.2	7935

Source: ILO, Yearbooks of Labour Statistics; various volumes.

Table 4.5.6   Self-employment as percentage of total employment: men

Year	Employers (%)	Contributing family members (%)	All self-employed (%)	Total employment (1000)
1971	13.3	0.9	14.2	3524
1995	12.5	0.4	12.9	4047
2003	13.0	0.2	13.2	4432

Source: ILO, Yearbooks of Labour Statistics; various volumes.

Table 4.5.7   Self-employment as percentage of total employment: women

Year	Employers (%)	Contributing family members (%)	All self-employed (%)	Total employment (1000)
1971	3.5	7.4	10.9	1238
1995	7.9	2.5	10.4	2787
2003	7.9	1.0	8.9	3503

Source: ILO, Yearbooks of Labour Statistics; different volumes.

Table 4.5.8   Wage-earners by economic sector (%)*

Year	Agriculture	Industry: manufacturing, mining, electricity and water, construction	Services I: wholesale and retail trade, transport, hotels and restaurants	Services II: Financial operations	Services III: Social services	N (1000)
1970	7.2	38.9	24.9	5.7	23.3	4554
1976	5.6	33.6	23.3	7.6	29.9	4643
1982	5.0	28.7	23.7	9.3	33.3	5010
1988	4.5	25.4	23.8	10.5	35.7	6521
1995	1.9	24.5	26.0	13.0	34.5	5866
2002	1.6	21.5	26.0	15.8	35.0	6943

*1973–88: Total employment by economic sector.

Source: ILO, Yearbooks of International Labour Statistics; various volumes.

Table 4.5.9   Wage-earners by economic sector: men (%)

Year	Agriculture	Industry: manufacturing, mining, electricity and water, construction	Services I: wholesale and retail trade, transport, hotels and restaurants	Services II: financial operations	Services III: social services	N (1000)
1976	6.6	41.0	23.1	7.2	22.1	3342
1982	6.0	36.8	23.6	8.9	24.7	3370
1988	5.5	34.7	22.5	9.8	27.5	3809
1995	2.3	34.5	26.1	12.4	24.6	3456
2002	2.1	31.7	26.7	16.0	23.5	3841

Source: ILO, Yearbooks of International Labour Statistics; various volumes.

Table 4.5.10   Wage-earners by economic sector: women (%)

Year	Agriculture	Industry: manufacturing, mining, electricity & water, construction	Services I: wholesale and retail trade, transport, hotels and restaurants	Services II: financial operations	Services III: social services	N (1000)
1976	3.1	14.6	23.8	8.7	49.8	1301
1982	2.8	12.1	24.0	10.2	50.9	1640
1988	3.4	11.2	23.6	10.0	51.8	2223
1995	1.3	10.2	25.9	13.8	48.7	2410
2002	1.1	8.9	25.1	15.5	49.4	3102

Source: *ILO, Yearbooks of International Labour Statistics; various volumes.*

4.5.3.5   Annual hours worked, part-time employment, long-term unemployment, and labour market policy

After the economic crisis of 1974/75, the Netherlands, like Germany, promoted reductions in working hours in order to distribute employment more evenly across the economically active. In 2003, the average annual hours worked was 1323, this is by far the lightest workload among the countries compared.

Table 4.5.11   Average annual hours worked per person in employment

Year	1973	1979	1983	1990	1999	2003
Hours worked per person	1724	1591	1530	1433	1343	1323

Source: *OECD, 2004.*

In contrast to Germany, however, collective cuts in working hours did not dominate, rather emphasis was placed on expanding part-time work: 'three-quarters of the two million new jobs since 1983 have been part-time jobs' (Visser, 2002, p. 25).

No other OECD country has such a high part-time ratio as the Netherlands; almost 60 per cent of female employees work part-time. Günther Schmid (1996) observes in this context that most part-time employment contracts are agreed on voluntarily, that two-thirds of part-time employees are well qualified, and that part-time work is generally better regulated than, for example, in Germany. Furthermore,

Table 4.5.12   Part-time employment (as percentage of total employment)

Year	1983	1990	2000	2003
Total	18.5	28.2	32.1	34.5
Men	5.6	13.4	13.4	14.8
Women	44.7	52.5	57.2	59.6

Source: OECD, 1997 and 2004.

men make use of part-time work more often than in comparable other countries (Table 4.5.12).[20] Critically, Schmid (1996. p. 13) points to the fact that 35 per cent of the part-time employed (43 per cent among men, 32 per cent among women) are of little account, that is, they work less than ten hours per week. He concludes that due to such small numbers of working hours and the low wages resulting from these jobs, a great number of persons receiving these wages must have other ways of making ends meet.

If we relate the OECD part-time ratio of women to the overall number of female employment in 2003 (Table 4.5.4), we find that from 3,503,000 female employees 2,087,779 worked part-time. Of these, we might estimate on the basis of Schmid's analysis, 668.089 worked less than ten hours per week and earned correspondingly small incomes. This of course relativizes the 'employment miracle' – especially in relation to female employment – as often all kinds of part-time work are counted as regular employment. The enormous expansion of part-time employment also contributed to the fact that, despite increasing 'employment' as such, the overall volume of work diminished in the 1980s. According to Schmid (1996, p. 13), the 1970s level was not again reached until as late as 1993. For the remainder of the 1990s, however, the volume of work increased (Stille, 1998, p. 298). Taking the low unemployment rate of around 4.3 per cent in 2003 (Table 4.5.2) into consideration, it is likely that the demand for employment exceeding ten hours per week will continue to rise.

Despite declining unemployment rates it is striking that long-term unemployment remained at a constantly high level until the end of the 1990s. While in 1997, unemployment stood at just 5.5 per cent (Table 4.5.2), almost every second unemployed person was still unemployed after one year. It was only in 2003 that a noticeable reduction of long-term unemployment was achieved.

Even though the Netherlands has practically re-attained full employment, it continues to spend a considerable percentage of its GDP on labour market policies. Since 1997, this expenditure exceeds even that of social democratic Sweden. In 2003, it was almost five times the level of the UK. As the level of unemployment

---

20 Within our comparison of five countries, male part-time rates in 2003 oscillated between 2.5 per cent in Spain and 9.7 per cent in the UK.

Table 4.5.13   Long-term unemployment (as percentage of total unemployment)

Year	1983		1990		1994		1997		2003	
Period	Over 6 months	Over 12 months	Over 6 months	Over 12 months	Over 6 months	Over 12 months	Over 6 months	Over 12 months	Over 6 months	Over 12 months
Total	70.7	48.8	63.6	49.3	77.5	49.4	80.4	49.1	49.2	29.2
Men	68.4	42.3	65.6	55.2	74.3	50.0	76.6	49.9	30.7	15.5
Women	74.1	49.9	62.0	44.6	80.9	48.7	83.4	48.5	48.4	28.1

Source: OECD, 1997 and 2004.

Table 4.5.14   Public expenditure on labour market policies as percentage of GDP

Year	1991	1997	2002
Active measures	1.09	1.53	1.84
Public employment services and administration	0.14	0.35	0.28
Labour market Training	0.22	0.13	0.60
Youth measures	0.06	0.10	0.04
Wage subsidies in private sector	0.03	0.23	0.04
Support of unemployed persons starting enterprises	–	–	–
Direct job creation (public or non-profit)	0.02	0.19	0.29
Vocational rehabilitation	–	–	–
Work for the disabled	0.62	0.54	0.59
Passive measures	2.49	3.33	1.72
Total	3.58	4.86	3.56

Source: OECD, 1996 and 2004.

diminished, more funding was made available for active measures. The emphasis is here on work for the disabled, direct job creation, and, especially in recent years, labour market training.

4.5.3.6   Income inequality and poverty
Overall income inequality, as measured by the Gini coefficient, remained constant in the 1980s, and diminished slightly in the 1990s. The level is about the same as in Sweden, slightly below Germany and well below the UK and Spain.

Even so, there was an increase in relative poverty. In the 1990s, there were more people below the 50 per cent and 60 per cent threshold than in the 1980s. However,

Table 4.5.15   Income inequality and relative poverty

Year	Gini coefficient	Relative poverty: total population		Relative poverty: children		Relative poverty: elderly	
		50 % line	60 % line	50 % line	60 % line	50 % line	60 % line
1983	0.260	3.9	7.6	2.7	6.9	–	–
1987	0.256	4.7	8.2	5.2	9.8	–	–
1991	0.266	6.3	12.2	8.1	13.8	3.2	19.5
1994	0.253	7.2	13.3	7.9	12.8	5.3	22.7
1999	0.248	7.3	12.7	7.5	14.8	2.4	12.8

Source: Luxembourg Income Study: <www.lisproject.org/keyfigures/ineqtable.htm>; EUROSTAT, 2002.

the 12.7 per cent below the 60 per cent line was just slightly more than in Sweden, slightly below Germany and considerably below the UK. Neither children nor the elderly were considerably over-represented in this poorest strata of the population.

4.5.4   Summary of the case study

In the 1950s, Dutch corporate actors were already following a development strategy based on wage restraint. This allowed the country to easily incorporate itself into the international division of labour and to achieve fast growth rates of GDP and productivity throughout the 1960s. With economic expansion however the demand for labour grew. The unions no longer committed themselves to the low-wage strategy, and, as a consequence, wage differentials to the neighbouring countries gradually diminished. By the 1970s, the Netherlands belonged to those European countries with relatively high wages.

As the Netherlands has always been especially dependent on export, it was seriously affected by the economic crisis of 1974/75. Growth rates of GDP and productivity fell, and this was accompanied by a crisis of the economic and social system, and corresponding changes in the occupational and social structure. Features of the decomposition of the post-war social structure were unemployment, which rose to levels above 10 per cent, de-industrialization, a fall in the volume of work, and the deterioration of the vicious circle of welfare without work.

The trajectories of Sweden, the Netherlands, and Spain have in common the fact that, after a temporary breakdown in wage determination processes at the national level and a period of decentralized bargaining, wage coordination was resumed in some form. In the Netherlands, supply-oriented policies to facilitate labour market flexibility were complemented with more security for 'flexible workers', while the welfare state was renovated but not downsized. The government took the initiative of carrying out modifications of the regulatory systems, while employers and trade

Table 4.5.16   Selected empirical results

	1961–1973	1974–1985	1986–1995	1996–2005
GDP growth (4.5.1)	4.8	1.9	2.8	2.2
Labour productivity growth (4.5.1)	3.9	2.0	1.3	0.9
Real wages per head (4.5.1)	6.3	1.1	1.0	1.1
Activity rate (4.5.2)	56.3 (1970)	56.9 (1976–85)	67.2 (1988–94)	74.7 (1997–2003)
'Feminization' (activity rate women) (4.5.4)	–	35.8 (1976–85)	54.2 (1988–94)	65.4 (1997–2003)
Self-employment as percentage in total employment (4.5.5)	14.5 (1971)	–	12.0 (1995)	13.2 (2003)
(De)industrialization (4.5.8)	38.9 (1970)	31.2 (1982–86)	25.0 (1988–95)	21.5 (2002)
Tertiarization (4.5.8)	53.9 (1970)	63.6 (1982–86)	71.8 (1988–95)	76.8 (2002)
Average hours worked per person (4.5.11)	1724 (1973)	1561 (1979–83)	1433 (1990)	1333 (1999–2003)
Part-time employment (4.5.12)	–	18.5 (1983)	28.2 (1990)	33.3 (2000–03)
Unemployment (4.5.1)	1.1	6.9	6.6	4.1
Long-term unemployment (over 12 months) (4.5.13)	–	48.8 (1983)	49.4 (1990–94)	39.2 (1997–2003)
Relative poverty (60 per cent line) (4.5.15)	–	7.6 (1983)	11.2 (1987–94)	12.7 (1999)

Sources: Various materials from EUROSTAT, ILO, OECD, and Luxembourg Income Study.
Brackets after labour market issue indicate the Table that previously commented in detail, on this issue.

unions played rather passive roles. The state was crucial in finding ways out of the crisis, and remains active in current socio-economic governance today. It generally played a more inclusive role in combining supply-oriented growth strategies with reforms in the interest of employees. The answer to the crisis was twofold: on the one hand, as was the case 30 years previously, wage restraint was agreed, and, on the other hand, this was accompanied by individual reductions in working hours. The Wassenaar Agreement was completed with measures to reduce the public deficit and by reductions in tax to improve the competitive situation of Dutch companies.[21] Equally crucial within the process of reorganization of industrial relations was the strengthening of the middle- and micro-level as well as the increasing importance of local actors.

Social policy reforms can be understood as a paradigm change away from labour substitution towards participation: the old paradigm involved relatively generous levels of public transfers, which allowed for a reasonably decent standard of living for those who were not part of the employment system, and reacted to unemployment by reducing the supply of male labour power and even excluding women from access to the labour market altogether. The new paradigm, however, aims at bringing as many people into employment as possible with women mostly into part-time employment. The Netherlands therefore stands for a regulated and socially agreed strategy of a redistribution of labour especially through part-time work and job-sharing (Detje, 1998).

In the final analysis, this strategy has turned out to be quite successful. When summarizing the different economic and social trends (Table 4.5.16) we arrive at the picture of a recomposed social structure that corresponds with the negotiated strategy of growth and flexibility. The measures taken have helped to bring the public budget back under control and to ease the problem of unemployment. Full employment has been re-achieved, and this was established on the basis of a massive reduction in working hours which only temporarily lead to a decline of the volume of work; since the early 1990, it has been rising. The creation of employment was therefore substantial and not merely a redistribution of already existing employment (Stille, 1998, p. 298).

Social structure indicators equally confirm the closeness of the Dutch road out of the crisis to what we ideal-typically labelled a negotiated growth strategy. While more people have part-time and flexible contracts, Remery et al. (2002, p. 48) could not find any evidence 'of an emerging dichotomy between temporary and permanent workers in the labour market'. Not only do flexible workers not constitute 'a new kind of underclass' ('once flexible-always flexible'), almost 50 per cent of workers with flexible contracts had permanent contracts two years later. The authors relate

---

21 Hinrichs (2002, p. 85) shows that this development was not a 'well-ordered and deliberate sequence of politically motivated actions' but constructed 'ex-post'. 'At the end of the 1980s the declining generosity of the welfare state was regarded as simple retrenchment, not different from what was going on elsewhere ...'. See also, for a similar argument, Becker (2001).

this finding to the legal measures by the Dutch government, especially the Law on Flexibility and Security ('Flexicurity'). The authors go so far as to claim that 'labour market flexibility has been introduced in the Netherlands without generating real "losers"' (Remery et al., 2002, p. 50).

Despite the fact that the moderate wage policy pursued since the early 1980s led to a stagnation in real wages, our analysis of data from the Luxembourg Income Study (Table 4.5.15) confirms earlier studies that reported that 'wage inequality did not increase to any significant extent' in the 1980s and 1990s (Ter Weel, 2003, p. 361). There is indeed a 'relatively stable Dutch wage structure (and labour market) in which the worldwide increase in (skill-based) technological change and the subsequent increase in the demand for skill has not been increasing wage inequality to any significant extent' (Ter Weel, 2003, p. 363). This finding is very much in line with our theoretical assumption that the 'flexibilization' of welfare and labour market regimes in order to restore the competitiveness of nation-states does not necessarily lead to growing income inequality, social exclusion, and poverty. The Dutch experience points to the conclusion that the latter phenomena can be avoided, if the necessary institutional infrastructure is provided. In the Netherlands, minimum wage, state pension, and social assistance have proven to be useful tools to keep income inequalities within certain limits. The comparatively high levels of public expenditure for labour market and welfare state purposes (Table 4.5.14) also serve this aim.

In a nutshell, the Dutch growth strategy is a positive example, how maximum social integration can be achieved in a period of socio-economic transition. Although the adjustment problems that come with the transition from Fordism to Post-Fordism are solved comparatively well, in one important aspect the Dutch road differs from the ideal-type of a negotiated growth strategy. The weak productivity growth (only 0.9 per cent between 1996 and 2005, Table 4.5.16) marks a significant difference to Sweden – the country that comes closest to the negotiated ideal-type – and raises questions about the sustainability of the growth model. The favouring of cheap labour following the philosophy of beggar-my-neighbour appears to have contributed to a slowdown of rationalization processes of Dutch companies. In the long run, this could hamper their innovative ability and endanger the competitive position of the entire economy. One can only hope that the relaxed labour market will bring the trade unions in a stronger bargaining position so that they are able to achieve higher wages. This would, in turn, stimulate employers' motivation for rationalization and innovation and, eventually, lead to increases in productivity growth. This hope is encouraged by Spithoven (2002, p. 361), who argues that, due to recent labour shortages, the strategy of distributing work among larger number of persons is 'no longer' practicable. As firms are unlikely to be able to reap the competitive sales advantages of low wages for much longer, a 'fast catching-up process' will indeed be required.

Chapter 5

Summary of the Empirical Results in Comparative Perspective

In Chapter Four, a range of empirical investigations were carried out in order to scrutinize those hypotheses relating to changes in labour markets and social structures in the transition from Fordist to Post-Fordist growth strategies that were raised in Section 3.2. In what follows I will interpret the most relevant results from a comparative perspective. Are those changes that we postulated on the basis of the theoretical discussion in Chapter Three indeed a matter of general trends in the sense that they remain empirically identifiable even after the influences that arise from particularly national trajectories have been scrutinized? What are the main differences between the national roads to Post-Fordism?

The point of departure is a comparison of the emergence and development of the regulatory institutions in the labour market and welfare systems of the five countries after World War II (5.1). Special emphasis will be attached to the procedures and contents of wage determination, the political and social processes through which wage norms are generalized in a national economy. The second focus will be on the role of the state as an institutional form in these processes of regulation. Thereafter, we will scrutinize the thesis of a development of Fordist labour markets and social structures' (5.2). Section 5.3 serves to validate the related hypothesis of the decomposition of the social structure following the crisis of Fordism. In Section 5.4, again with a special focus on processes of wage determination and the role of the state, we will compare the labour market and welfare reforms against the background of the ideal-typical Post-Fordist development paths that were suggested in Section 3.1. Finally, in Section 5.5, we will ask, if and to what extent a recomposition of labour markets and social structures that is dependent on the particular Post-Fordist growth strategy a country follows has taken place.

5.1   Fordism in the five countries

As suggested in Section 2.2, economic and social affairs in all five countries were characterized by attempts to institutionalize them either shortly before or after World War II. Different interests of the collective actors involved were compatibilized into common national projects of growth and prosperity. In comparative research, however, we should not be surprised to find that the concrete historical manifestations of the Fordist growth model varied significantly from country to country. These differences range from the levels of collective bargaining, via the point in time of the implementation of regulatory institutions to the extent to which the state intervened in the economy and labour market. Furthermore, we are faced with different types of welfare states and different roles of trade unions ('bellicose' versus 'consensus-oriented' trade unions).

Table 5.1   Fordism from a comparative perspective

Country	Type of Fordism	Characteristics
USA	*Genuine*	Taylorist organization of work. Lifestyle and consumption norms highly commodified.
UK	*Flawed*	Company level bargaining. Weak state whose attempts to establish more wage coordination failed. Low productivity due to the fragmented division of labour in which specific boundaries of skills and stratification were defended at times by archaic class politics.
Sweden	*Democratic*	Early attempts to replace Taylorism. National level bargaining initiated by the state. Full employment policy. High level of indirect wages and welfare. High geographical labour mobility. High economic activity of women.
Germany	*Flexible*	Professional and craft labour markets rather than Taylorism. Wage determination at sector level. Decentralized federal state that 'moderates' rather than intervenes in economy and labour market. Heterogeneity of regulatory institutions. Conservative welfare state.
Spain	*Delayed*	Under Franco: cheap labour. State intervention to support industrialization. Low activity rate of women in formal economy. *Pactos de Moncloa* provided wage determination at national level. Legislation of special importance in labour market regulation.
The Netherlands	*Corporate*	Tripartite collective bargaining at central level. Development strategies often initiated by the state. Corporate relations based on mutual trust. Low activity rate of women.

Sources: Developed from Tickel and Peck (1995, p. 362); Boyer (1995, pp. 28–32); Koch (2004b, p. 16).

Though not specifically observed in this study, the USA is seen as the classic or *genuine* case of Fordism by regulationists due to the fact that the work process followed Taylorist principles quite directly (Aglietta, 1987). Divisions between blue- and white-collar workers and between engineers and manual workers were common, whereas the levers of control were concentrated in the hands of managers. A further feature of American Fordism was the advanced commodification of private consumption and lifestyles. The British case, in contrast, showed that Fordism was not inevitable and did not impose itself automatically by reason of its superior efficiency. On the contrary, the strong British labour movement was able to defend specific divisions within the working class according to skills, tasks and job rules (4.4.1). Wage determination processes continued to take place at the company level, and attempts to establish more wage coordination were largely unsuccessful. The potential for increased productivity, normally associated with Taylorist methods, was inhibited, and Britain's Fordism was hence *flawed* (Boyer, 1995, p. 29). The consequence was that the UK gradually lost its technological and economic lead that had originated in the Industrial Revolution.

In countries such as Sweden and Germany, the Fordist principle of the maximum division of labour and the deskilling of blue-collar work was moderated by continuing craftsmanship and professional labour markets. Whereas the leading principle of Taylor's 'scientific management' sought to remove skills from the shop floor, in these countries the employers increased shop floor skills and invested in the shop floor workers. The differences between Sweden and Germany lie mainly in the form of collective bargaining, the role of the state and in the orientation of employment policy. Until the early 1990s, the main aim of Swedish labour market regulation, which was decided by tripartite talks at the national or societal level, was the maintenance of full employment (4.2.1). To achieve this goal, the trade unions' 'solidaristic' wage policies were as important as the state's active labour market policies, which stimulated geographical and occupational mobility. Hence, state regulation of economic reproduction and accumulation was always supply-oriented. Over the decades, these elements, together with a universal and Social Democratic welfare state, brought about a lessening of income inequalities: not only between social classes but also between the employed and unemployed. A final peculiarity of Swedish labour market regulation, which may have led Boyer (1995) to label this type of Fordism as *democratic*, was the high proportion of women in the economically active population. In striking contrast to the predominant male-breadwinner model of other industrial societies, gender-specific differences with respect to participation in the labour market were lessened (Swensson, 2003). Gender was still important in the allocation of women to specific economic sectors and branches but not to the degree of the overall participation in the labour market (4.2.3.4).

In contrast to Sweden, labour market regulation in Germany has always been more decentralized. Collective bargaining took place mainly at the sector level and a range of regulatory functions was delegated to independent institutions. General goals such as currency stability and free competition were therefore partially de-politicized. The right to free collective bargaining had a similar effect in that it excluded the state from the regulation of wages and working conditions. Consensual conflict resolutions were further expressed in collective and individual work legislation. Federalism, the independence of the *Bundesbank* and the constitutionally guaranteed autonomy of collective bargaining made reforms of the institutional setting comparatively difficult. Neither the manufacturing industries nor the educational and vocational system ever tried to implement 'scientific methods' in a rigorous manner at company level. Rather, managers often embraced workers' involvement: especially the incorporation of those with high skills. As a result, German commodities were always more differentiated than the Fordist philosophy suggests. Collective agreements and bargaining within industries and companies partially integrated new technologies and new ways of organizing work. Wage levels were more closely linked to actual performance than in most other countries. Faced with this heterogeneity of regulatory institutions, Boyer (1995) suggested the term 'Flex-Fordism'. A final peculiarity was the decentralized federal state and the conservative welfare state system.

Tickel and Peck (1995) have described Spanish Fordism as *delayed*, because it was only with the political transition from Francoism to parliamentary democracy (late 1970s) and economic integration into the European Union (mid-1980s) that the previously protected and agriculturally dominated economy began to be exposed to international competition (4.3.1). This resulted in a sharp increase in unemployment, and inflation (15.2 per cent by 1981; European Commission, 2001). Franco's development strategy had been largely based on cheap labour and was increasingly oriented towards industrialization. After his death, the country was hence faced with the dual problem of not only having to transform a protected and inwardly focused economy into an open and competitive one, but also with the necessity of implementing labour market and welfare institutions at a time when other European countries had already begun to deregulate them. Under these circumstances, the *Pactos de la Moncloa* of 1977, which were followed by five additional agreements, were signed by all the labour market parties: business, unions, and the government. The purpose of these agreements was to define a new industrial relations setting that could restrain wage demands, control inflation, foster the recovery of business profits, and contain labour militancy. These agreements expressed a social bargaining process in which macro-economic considerations were taken into account for the first time. The labour market parties agreed to create corporatist relations, in which the legislatory level was to become more important than collective agreements. Legislation was normally the outcome of tripartite bargaining between trade unions, employers' organizations and the government, thereby considering the recommendations of the main institutions of labour market policy, brought together by the ministry for labour, in which the labour market parties were likewise equally represented: *Instituto Nacional de Empleo*, and *Unidades de Mediacion Arbitraje y Concilación*.

As in the cases of Spain and Sweden, the societal level was the most important stage in Dutch tripartite bargaining (4.5.1). Reforms in the labour market and welfare system were normally based on previous agreements in the two labour market bodies *Stichting von de Arbeid* and *Sociaal Economische Raad*, while the translation of these general guidelines into concrete practice was carried out at lower levels. Historically, the state often initiated extensive changes in the overall political and economic strategy. The Netherlands was extremely vulnerable to external influences due to its relatively small size in terms of both geography and population. In contrast to Spain, protectionism was never an option, since the internal market of a small country like the Netherlands is severely limited. Hence, due to the extra pressure to perform well on the world market, it became necessary to develop effective corporate relations. Given this emphasis on informal communication and trust within the Dutch triangle of employers' organizations, trade unions and the state the corresponding type of Fordism was given the label *corporate*. Finally, up until the 1980s, both countries, Spain and the Netherlands, were characterized by extremely low rates of female economic activity.

5.2   Labour markets and social structures during the growth period of Fordism

The hypothesis raised in Section 3.2 postulated that a social structure emerged in correspondence with the growth period of Fordism. This Fordist social structure was defined as having, above all, high growth rates of both GDP and productivity, full employment with maximum use of the male workforce, industrialization, and a rising percentage of dependent employment within economic activity. The stability of the demand for mass-produced goods was said to be ensured by rising real wages. My preference for using the concept of Fordism as an ideal-typical point of departure for the long-term restructuring of Western European countries after World War II does not mean, however, that those real-typical particularities of national trajectories identified by comparative analysis should be neglected. Specific national development trends were doubtlessly important, but on the whole, as the following summary of the main features of labour market and social structure during the growth period of Fordism shows, were of less significance than the 'grand' economic and political trends we referred to in theoretical terms (3.2).

Between 1961 and 1973 – the heyday of Fordism – Sweden, Germany, and the Netherlands displayed this particular combination of high growth rates of both GDP and productivity rates, on the one hand; and full employment and rising real wages, on the other, that we postulated to be typical for a Fordist social structure in Section 3.2.[1] In these three countries, growth rates of GDP oscillated between 4.1 and 4.8 per cent and productivity growth increased between 3.5 and 4.0 per cent, while real wages rose between 3.5 and 6.3 per cent. Further common features include high percentages of industrial employment between 38 per cent in the Netherlands and Sweden and 49 per cent in Germany, and a decrease in self-employment. In the early 1970s, the rate of self-employment stood at 7.7 per cent in Sweden, 14.5 per cent in the Netherlands, and 15.9 per cent in Germany.[2] However, there were also

---

1   See Tables 4.1.19, 4.2.17 and 4.5.16 (Selected empirical results).
2   Percentages for Germany and the Netherlands include contributing family members.

differences across these countries, most significantly with respect to the ways by which full employment was established, and here, more specifically, with respect to the extent to which women participated in the labour market. In 1976, female activity rates stood at 31.6 per cent in the Netherlands, 49.4 per cent in Germany, but at 70.1 per cent in Sweden.[3] As a consequence of this comparatively high level of female labour market participation, Sweden also had the highest overall activity rate: 80.6 per cent in 1976, while the corresponding values for Germany were 65.8 per cent, and for the Netherlands 56.1 per cent.[4] Sweden not only had the highest rate of economic activity in the early 1970s, but also the comparatively shortest annual working hours. The Swedes worked 1557 hours in 1973 compared to the Dutch, who worked 1724 hours, and the Germans, who worked 1868 hours per year.[5] Hence, in Sweden, full employment was achieved against the background of the most fair distribution of work. In contrast to the Swedish inclusive model, 'full employment' in the Netherlands existed only on paper, that is, in the statistics, since in 1976, over two-thirds of women were not economically active. The relatively low unemployment figures were to a significant degree due to the economic exclusion of Dutch women, albeit in combination with relatively short annual working hours. Germany was characterized by the longest working hours per year with more women in employment than in the Netherlands, but much less than in Sweden.

The label of 'flawed' British Fordism appears to be justified in the face of the slow growth of GDP and productivity in the 1960s and early 1970s. Though the general pattern of Fordist growth is clearly identifiable – a parallel rise of growth in GDP, productivity, and real wages plus full employment – growth rates remained significantly below the levels of the three countries analysed above: between 1961 and 1973, the average annual growth of GDP was 3.3 per cent, that of productivity 2.9 per cent, and that of real wages 3.3 per cent. British workers also had to work longer hours (1929 hours in 1973) than in the three countries mentioned above, as if, by working longer, they had to make up for the slower productivity growth of their industry in order to remain competitive. Other indicators do not show huge deviations from the general trend. With 44.1 per cent industrial employment in the period of 1967 to 1973, Britain took second place after Germany. Due to the relatively early industrialization of the 'birthplace' of capitalism, the agricultural sector had already ceased to play a crucial role by the 1960s. The low self-employment rate of 7.3 per cent in 1971 indicates that capital was concentrated in relatively few companies. Unemployment remained below two per cent until 1973, while the activity rate stood at 72.5 per cent.[6] Furthermore, if we consider that Britain had the second highest

---

3   See Tables 4.1.4, 4.2.5 and 4.5.4 (Population, economic activity, occupational system and unemployment: women).

4   See Tables 4.1.2, 4.2.3 and 4.5.2 (Population, economic activity, occupational system and unemployment).

5   See Tables 4.1.19, 4.2.17 and 4.5.16 (Selected empirical results).

6   All values used in this paragraph so far refer to Table 4.4.16 (Selected empirical results).

activity rate of women within our comparison (57.3 per cent in 1977),[7] it appears reasonable to speak of a relatively large overall labour market participation and a comparatively inclusive society up until the mid-1970s.

Nothing could better express Spain's peripheral position and a certain 'backwardness' within Europe than the fact that in the early 1970s one-quarter of the economically active were self-employed or a contributing family member, while, at the same time, nearly 25 per cent of wage earners were employed in the agricultural sector.[8] Comparison with the UK, the pioneer in this development, makes clear that the long-term process of the concentration of the economically active population in industrial companies, which peaked in Fordism, was all but complete in Spain. The fast growth rates in both GDP and productivity for the period of 1961 to 73 (7.2 and 6.5 per cent, respectively) must be relativized by interpreting them against the background of the very modest point of departure of the 1950s. Likewise, the unemployment rate of 0.8 per cent[9] is partly to do with comparatively low wages and political repression, which meant that many Spaniards tried to find work elsewhere. A further factor that crucially contributed to statistical 'full employment' was the low rate of economic activity of just 58.2 per cent in 1976.[10] This, in turn, was largely due to the exclusion of women since only one-third of all women aged between 16 and 64 were economically active.[11] The low use of the potential workforce in the formal economy and the low productivity level of a country that had yet to progress to the industrial era, was mirrored in overexploitation: with 2022 annual hours worked per person in 1979, Spain was characterized by the longest annual working hours within the five countries compared.

5.3   Social structures during the decline: The crisis of Fordism

According to a further requirement of regulation theory, from the mid-1970s, the Fordist development strategy came under pressure both from the demand and the supply side. In relation to the social structure, we hypothesized in Section 3.2 that those labour markets and social structures that had developed in the growth period of Fordism were decomposed in the subsequent crisis. It was claimed that disintegration of labour market and society could be recognized empirically through shrinking growth rates of GDP and productivity, a slowdown or stagnation of real

---

7   See Table 4.4.4 (Population, economic activity, occupational system and unemployment: women).

8   See Tables 4.3.5 (Self employment as percentage of total employment) and 4.3.8 (Wage-earners by economic sectors).

9   See Table 4.3.16 (Selected empirical results).

10 See Tabe 4.3.2 (Population, economic activity, occupational system and unemployment).

11 See Table 4.3.4 (Population, economic activity, occupational system and unemployment: women).

wages, de-industrialization, and increasing labour market marginality, especially through unemployment.

The hypothesis of the decomposition of the Fordist social structure is largely validated by the data analysed. If we compare the periods of 1961 to 1973 and 1974 to 1985, growth rates of GDP and productivity decreased significantly in all five countries.[12] If we momentarily ignore the specific Spanish case, to which we will return below, between 1974 and 1985, GDP growth oscillated between 1.4 per cent (UK) and 1.9 per cent (the Netherlands), while productivity growth varied between 1.0 (Sweden) and 2.0 per cent (the Netherlands). Equally, the presumed increase in unemployment and the deceleration of real wages are largely confirmed. Furthermore, changes in national employment systems indeed brought about a general trend towards deindustrialization and tertiarization. Initially, the crisis of the Fordist labour market was aggravated by the increasing economic activity of women.

Again, while the case studies generally confirm the postulated trend towards the decomposition of the Fordist social structure, they equally point to significant differences at the level of specific national trajectories. First, although de-industrialization shaped employment systems in each country, in Germany, the percentage of industrial employment still stood at 44.2 per cent in the late 1970s, while the corresponding values for the other countries oscillated between 31.2 per cent (the Netherlands) and 38.7 per cent (UK). The fact that Germany could basically maintain its industrial core well into the 1980s supports Alain Lipietz's hypothesis of an economic centre–periphery structure in Europe based around Germany (Lipietz, 1998).

Second, while unemployment remained on relatively low levels in the period of 1974 to 85 in Sweden (2.4 per cent) and Germany (4.2 per cent), in the Netherlands and the UK, it increased to 6.9 per cent and 6.8 per cent respectively. This finding appears to be reflected in different points in time when paradigm shifts in policy approaches were implemented (see Section 5.4 below): while in the Netherlands and in the UK far-reaching changes in the regulation of labour market and welfare system had already been introduced by the early 1980s – albeit with very different aims and directions that corresponded with different levels of relative poverty (7.6 per cent in the Netherlands versus 14.8 per cent in the UK) – in Germany and Sweden, the labour market parties continued within the old paradigms. In Sweden, especially, the consensus of maintaining full employment remained in place up until the early 1990s. The priority of sustaining employment in times of increased foreign competition was politically defended even at the cost of practically stagnating real wages (0.4 per cent growth for the period of 1974 to 1985). The unemployment crisis only started in the 1990s when preference was given to stability parameters rather than to the ideal of full employment.

Third, in Spain's delayed Fordism, labour market institutions were only introduced after the signing of the *Pactos de la Moncloa* in 1977; at a time, when the

---

12 See Tables 4.1.19, 4.2.17, 4.3.16, 4.4.16 and 4.5.16 (Selected empirical results).

other countries under observation had already started to feel the crisis of Fordism. Even though, in relation to Spain, one can hardly talk of a crisis of Fordist regulation in the narrow sense, the country was far from unharmed by the general decline in Western Europe. Between 1961 and 1973 and 1974 and 1985, growth in GDP and productivity slowed down from 7.2 to 1.8 per cent and from 6.5 to 3.3 per cent respectively. Growth in real wages per head decelerated from 7.6 to 2.4 per cent, while unemployment skyrocketed from 2.6 to 8.2 per cent. 52.4 per cent of the unemployed were so over one year. One fifth of the population lived in relative poverty. Spain therefore displayed the hallmarks of a country with a still high agricultural focus having to integrate in a European economic and social community that itself had begun to struggle with a socio-economic crisis.

5.4   Deregulation and re-regulation: The five countries compared

Fordism was based on an accumulation regime, in which the demand and supply of mass-produced commodities mutually re-enforced each other. However, the set-up of institutions of labour market and welfare regulation, which crucially contributed both to the generalization of wage norms within a national economic space and to the enhancement of the social acceptance of the new socio-economic model, was equally important in making the interests of the corporate triangle of employers, employees and the state compatible. Forms of social insurance against risks such as old age, sickness, and unemployment emerged virtually everywhere in Western Europe and provided those social groups who were transitionally or totally economically inactive with a decent standard of living. The extraordinary high popularity of these institutions was not least due to the fact that – somewhat in an act of social solidarity – both employers and employees contributed to their financing. By achieving the commitment of opposing interests of social classes and groups to the common project of welfare capitalism, an unprecedented extent of social and system integration was accomplished. While this development is to be welcomed from a moral or ethical angle, the regulation theory perspective makes apparent that the pacification of social antagonisms in Fordism was not due to moral reasoning in the first instance, but due to the fact that the set-up of labour market and welfare institutions had an economic foundation. The stabilization of the demand structures for mass-produced goods was a requirement for the turnover of fixed capital that itself was a relatively slow process as the investments into the elements necessary for mass production (factory buildings, machinery, etc.) were enormous and, hence, could only be written off over a long period of time.

The further discussion showed that the Fordist production and consumption paradigm that had a long-term perspective was replaced by one oriented at the short-term perspective and that followed the logic of flexibility and the *just-in-time* principle. Instead of treating the demand side as a given and organizing the production process towards the greatest possible output of uniform products over a long period of time, tendentially the production process itself became the dependent variable as it was increasingly adjusted to ever more individual and flexible demand structures. At the company level, crucial decisions on both quality and quantity of products were increasingly made according to the needs of sales departments (2.3). These transitions were themselves a reflection of the far-reaching deregulation of the previously relatively stable international system, which had helped to stabilize the Fordist regime of accumulation.

The transformation from Fordist to Post-Fordist growth strategies was analysed within a paradigm that postulated two ideal-typical scenarios. The capital-oriented approach, on the one hand, abolishes the Fordist class compromise, favours the employers' short-term competitive interests, and is mainly aimed at lowering labour costs. Wages are de-indexed, and trade unions are weakened. In company-level bargaining or in individual negotiations with their employers, employees find it increasingly difficult to combine professional and private life. The role of the state is weak and largely reduced to carrying out reforms that are exclusively in the short-term interest of capital owners (for example, by attracting international capital through low labour costs and reduced taxes and contributions, while demoting previous goals of state regulation such as full employment and the avoidance of greater income inequalities). Once these reforms are carried out, the state withdraws from any active role in regulation and leaves it to 'market forces'. On the other hand, negotiated growth strategies, usually agreed at the sectoral or societal level, actively embrace the participation of workers in re-organizing the work process. These strategies do not depend on 'cheap labour' and the (over-)exploitation of workers but rather on their active integration and skills. These strategies are based not on conflict but on consensus, since the employers' interest in optimal competitiveness is not divorced from the employees' interest in long-term employment contracts, training, etc. The role of the state remains strong or is strengthened where supply-oriented policies are combined with the maintenance of employment rights. Such an 'engaged state' is generally oriented towards rationalization rather than the downsizing of the labour market and the welfare state, and continues to invest in key technologies, infrastructure and/or in active labour market policy.

Not surprisingly, the study of de- and re-regulation of wage determination processes, socio-economic standards, and the role of the state in these processes over time and across countries has brought to light deviations from the theoretically constructed Post-Fordist development paths. Like their Fordist predecessors, recent Western European growth strategies must be understood as the results of negotiations and struggles between different classes and social groups, with concrete outcomes varying from country to country. 'Globalizers', as Paul Hirst and Graham Thompson have labelled extreme globalization theorists, have a point in that there is generally a tendency towards strengthening the position of employers within the corporate triangle, which can be traced to increasing international competition. But this should not be confused with the proposal that a virtually unstoppable wave of neo-liberalism has become universal. In most European countries, the 'recommendations' of the diverse 'deregulation commissions' that have tried to convince national governments to follow capital-oriented strategies virtually everywhere, were not put into practice without substantial concessions being made to the trade unions[13] – a fact, which marks a decisive difference from the neo-liberal reshaping of many countries in Asia and Latin America.

Our theoretical position – which allows for the heterogeneity of national trajectories between the ideal-typical extremes of capital-oriented and negotiated growth strategies – is empirically supported by the comparative perspective taken in this study. In Figure 5.1, national trajectories are reconstructed along the two criteria theoretically discussed in Section 3.1. The first axis is the development of the wage determination process and the issue of whether it moved towards a model in which capital interests predominate – typically achieved through a lack of wage coordination and bargaining at company (C) or individual level (I) – or towards a new form of compromise in which not only the short-term interests of employers but also the long-term interests of employees are expressed. This is normally achieved through coordinated bargaining at national (N) or sector level (S). The second axis addresses the changing role of the state in regulation and asks whether a country moves towards a 'weak state' (one that is only oriented towards competitive interests of employers), or towards an 'engaged state' (one that initiates and/or supports attempts to achieve a kind of Post-Fordist compromise).

While there is a general trend towards improving the competitive position of national locations through the transition from a demand-oriented towards a supply-oriented mode of regulation, there are important differences as to whether this shift is carried out in order to increase short-term capital valorization in the first instance or in a kind of compromise that combines supply-oriented changes with reforms in the interest of employees.[14] With regard to wage determination processes and types of socio-economic regulation, reforms in the UK and Germany can be understood as having served the interests of employers in the first instance ('capital-oriented' growth strategy). In the UK, earlier attempts to establish a degree of wage coordination were terminated and capital-oriented reforms were carried out against resistance from the trade unions. German trade unions, in contrast, turned out to be strong enough to prevent the formal abolition of the wage determination and regulation system, which was traditionally much more advanced than in the UK. The increased use of 'opening clauses', however, appears to have resulted in the weakening of collective agreements at sector level and to the stealth relativization of the *Flächentarifvertrag*. Recent labour market reforms one-sidedly aimed at diminishing labour costs for employers and lacked elements that could be interpreted as being in the interest of employees or the unemployed. On the opposite side of the spectrum, we found three cases that can be seen as compromises (or 'negotiated' growth strategies). The trajectories of Sweden, the Netherlands, and Spain have in common that, after a

---

13 This is why neo-liberal authors always claim their ideas were not realised enough, when political and economic development does not proceed as predicted. For the ideological dimension of the neo-liberal perspective, see Bourdieu (2003), Herkommer (2004) and Koch (2006).

14 See Sections 4.1.2, 4.2.2, 4.3.2, 4.4.2 and 4.5.2 (Deregulation and re-regulation in …).

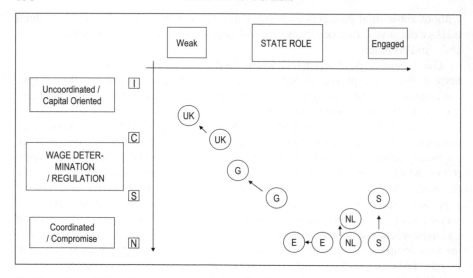

Figure 5.1   Wage determination and state regulation during and after Fordism

UK:	*Continuing lack of coordination in wage determination / capital-oriented reforms of regulatory system / transition from a weak Keynesian state towards a weak Schumpeterian state.*
Sweden (S):	*Transition of wage determination system from bargaining at national level to a new compromise with bargaining at sector level / the state engaged in bringing about and supporting both models.*
The Netherlands (NL):	*Transition in wage determination from automatic indexation to more flexible principles / the state as crucial actor in negotiating new compromise.*
Germany (G):	*Undermining of wage determination system by stealth / transition from a moderating state towards a weak state.*
Spain (E):	*Fall and rise of central level bargaining in relation to wage determination and regulation / transition from a strong state that monopolizes regulation power towards a moderating state.*

Source: Koch, 2005, p.333.

temporary breakdown of wage determination at the national level and a period of decentralized bargaining, wage coordination was resumed in some form. In Sweden, bipartite bargaining at the national level was relinquished and replaced by sector-level bargaining. In the Netherlands and Spain, tripartite bargaining was resumed. While strict and automatic forms of wage indexation were avoided in recent reshapings of wage determination processes, all three countries established or continued with existing tripartite institutions that are designed to facilitate the discussion of wage issues in wider socio-economic contexts. After rather negative experiences with decentralized bargaining, collective actors (including employers) started to revalue setting wage norms that are related to productivity development and economic growth. Specific compromises in socio-economic regulation vary from country to country: Sweden's 'Alliance for Growth' combines a technological upgrading of industry with investments in training for employees, the expansion of the education system and the retention of the welfare state on a high quantitative level. In the Netherlands, supply-oriented policies to facilitate labour market flexibility were complemented with more security for 'flexible workers', while the welfare state was reformed but not downsized. In Spain, dismissal costs for employers were reduced, while the conditions for the use of fixed-term employment were tightened, and the entitlements to unemployment benefits for fixed-term employees were improved.

With regard to the changing role of the state in socio-economic governance, this study has theoretically argued for an open concept that does not reduce national governments to mere executers of real or alleged constraints brought about by globalization and considers state strategies that combine supply-orientation with the consideration of employment rights. Two cases come close to the ideal-type of a 'weak state' (one that intervenes to make itself redundant in the interest of market forces): the UK and Germany. In the 1980s and 1990s, British governments directly intervened in the industrial relations system with the goal of achieving a pure market society: one that develops 'undisturbed' by external influences. The improvement of the profitability of UK companies was thereby largely identified with the structural debilitation of the trade unions, the termination of industrial policies, and the privatization of public property. In Germany, under Helmut Kohl, the government attempted to preserve the traditional growth strategy by maintaining the role of the 'moderating' state, while under the SPD/Green government, the 'urgent need' for far-reaching reforms was emphasized, and capital interests were increasingly supported. In Sweden, the Netherlands, and, to a lesser extent, in Spain, governments played a more inclusive role in combining supply-oriented growth strategies with reforms that were in the interest of employees ('engaged state'). In Sweden and the Netherlands, governments took the initiative of carrying out modifications of the regulatory systems, while employers and trade unions played more passive roles. In both cases, governments were crucial in finding ways out of the crisis, and they remain active in current socio-economic governance. The Spanish state, which had basically monopolized regulation power under Franco, dispensed parts of this competence to the labour market parties. Governments became increasingly 'moderating' in their attempts to reach central agreements.

5.5   Recomposed labour markets and social structures?

According to the fourth and final hypothesis made in relation to the transition from Fordism to Post-Fordism, the decomposition of labour markets and social structures (5.3) is followed by their recomposition. It was claimed that the latter was moulded by the particular growth strategy a country follows: capital-oriented or negotiated. Are there indications of an 'upswing' of social structures in correspondence with the implementation of Post-Fordist growth strategies? In 2003, the last year consulted, the five countries were in different phases of their transition from Fordism. In the Netherlands and the UK, far-reaching reforms in the labour market and welfare state had already been initiated in the early 1980s; in Sweden and Spain, this was done in the 1990s, while Germany's *Agenda 2010* was not adopted until 2003. As a consequence, on the basis of the data available, the postulated recomposition of the social structure can be validated for Sweden, the UK, the Netherlands, and less so for Spain, while this cannot be done for Germany. At the beginning of the new millennium, Germany, more than the other countries, was shaped by the socio-economic crisis that began in the late 1970s and which was accompanied by a decomposition of the occupational and social structure. Whether, in Germany, the postulated restructuring will actually take place or whether the country's crisis will continue in the long-term cannot be decided on the basis of the data available for this book. This issue must therefore be raised in future research.

In this section, the most relevant results are summarized and interpreted against the background of the thesis of a recomposition of the social structure. Theoretically (3.2), we postulated that a capital-oriented growth strategy creates employment through an extensive usage of the labour force. This was claimed to be accompanied by slow growth rates in productivity, high wage inequality, and a low level of state expenditure on labour market affairs. The decrease in unemployment is accompanied by an increase in poverty, at times in the form of the working poor, as well as by rising self-employment. Conversely, in negotiated growth strategies, full employment is a result of a combination of rising growth in productivity and regulated forms of the reduction of working hours. Poverty and social exclusion are kept within certain limits by supporting state policies in the areas of labour market and welfare.

Two countries have been found to follow capital-oriented growth strategies (5.4): the UK and Germany. While in Germany this is a rather recent phenomenon, in the UK, this has been the case since the 1980s. There, the changes in labour market and social structure largely follow the assumed pattern. In relation to the period of 1996 to 2005, the comparatively high average number of hours worked per person (1695) in combination with an increasing economic activity rate (77.4 per cent) indicates an extensive accumulation regime.[15] At the same time, unemployment decreased to 5.8 per cent and productivity growth remained relatively slow. The increase of both the Gini coefficient (from 0.270 to 0.345) and relative poverty (from 17.3 per cent to 21.3 per cent) in the period 1979-99 supports the thesis of growing income inequalities in capital-oriented growth strategies.[16] The number of wealthy people and millionaires in the UK has increased, but so has the number of the working poor. The creation of employment coincides with an increase in poverty, and economic participation with social exclusion. The modest and decreasing level of

---

15 See Table 4.4.16 (Selected empirical results).
16 See Table 4.4.15 (Income inequality and relative poverty).

state expenditure on labour market policies (from 1.98 per cent in 1991 to 0.75 per cent in 2002/3)[17] can well be interpreted as expression of the neo-liberal philosophy of treating unemployment as a result of employee's 'exaggerated' wage demands in the first place. Finally, accelerated de-industrialization and increasingly unattractive perspectives for employees have contributed to the rise of self-employment to 12.8 per cent in 2003 – a percentage almost twice as high as in the early 1970s.[18] Here, our theoretical discussion and empirical results encourage further qualitative research into the socio-psychological motivations for this new trend towards self-employment. Despite the need for more detailed research, the evaluation of the data used in this study points to a recomposed socio-economic space that is characterized by comparatively great inequalities.

As a result of the late introduction of socio-economic reforms, there is little evidence for any Post-Fordist recovery in the German case. On the contrary, by 2003, labour market and social structure continued to be moulded by the decomposition during the crisis of Fordism. This was aggravated by the adjustment problems of German unification. In the period 1996 to 2003, growth in both GDP (1.3 per cent) and productivity (1.0 per cent) continued to be slow, while real wages practically stagnated.[19] The employment crisis of Germany is best expressed in the parallel decrease of both the activity and employment rate in the period of 1994 to 2003, while unemployment continued to move at levels over the 10 per cent mark.[20] On the one hand, less people are economically active, and, on the other, of those remaining economically active increasingly more are unemployed. There is also a tendency towards long-term unemployment: in the period 1996 to 2003, every second unemployed person continued to be so after one year.[21] In addition to the indicators mentioned, the comparatively high proportion of jobs in the industrial sector indicates that the decomposition of the social structure is far from over. The positive aspect of the late implementation of the capital-oriented reforms is that both relative poverty (13.1 per cent in 2002) and Gini coefficient (0.270 in 2002) remained at levels far below the UK. However, recent changes in both labour market and tax system will presumably further increase income inequalities leading to a new concentration of wealth in the top deciles of the income pyramid, and to the emergence of a stratum of working poor hitherto unknown in Germany. The reduction of working hours and the frequent use of early retirement schemes, with which during the 1980s and 1990s, the labour market parties reacted to mass unemployment, are likely to be reversed. The new government resulting from the general elections in September 2005 will presumably further aggravate these trends as it is led by the Christian Democrats

---

17 See Table 4.4.14 (Public expenditure on labour market policies as percentage of GDP).

18 See Table 4.4.16 (Selected empirical results).

19 See Table 4.1.19 (Selected empirical results).

20 See Table 4.1.2 (Population, economic activity, occupational system and unemployment).

21 See Table 4.1.19 (Selected empirical results).

who have supported the changes suggested by the SPD/Green government and have indeed already called for more radical initiatives.

In contrast to the UK and Germany, the reforms in the other three countries were not carried out one-sidedly but rather constitute compromises between the interests of both employers and employees. Among these cases, Sweden comes closest to the ideal-type of a negotiated growth strategy (4.2.2). After negative growth in GDP and productivity, the 'explosion' of unemployment, and the short spell of Christian Democratic governance in the early 1990s, there are clear indications of recovery since the mid-1990s. As in the UK, there was a healthy growth in GDP (2.6 per cent), productivity (2.0 per cent), and real wages (2.4 per cent) in the period of 1995 to 2005. Tertiarization continued, and unemployment decreased to levels below 5 per cent after 2000.[22] Unlike the UK, however, these developments were accompanied only by a very slight increase in income inequalities and relative poverty. The Gini coefficient increased from 0.229 in 1992 to 0.252 in 2000 and was hence well below the UK value, while relative poverty remained almost constant and stood at 12.3 per cent in 2000 – about half that of the UK.[23] Finally, the role of the state in the Swedish Social Democratic growth strategy is different from the UK, where supply-oriented forms of state intervention are accompanied much less often by measures to arrest the advanced processes of social exclusion. The Swedish 'engaged' state is, *inter alia*, expressed in the relatively high level of public expenditure on labour market policies, which stood at 2.45 per cent in 2002 – three and a half times as high as in the UK.[24] In a nutshell, the Swedish case supports our hypothesis that fast economic growth rates can be combined with low levels of poverty and inequality in a Post-Fordist growth strategy based on negotiations and cooperation. Unlike capital-oriented growth strategies, economic inclusion does not necessarily go hand in hand with increasing social exclusion.

The Dutch growth path can also be labelled *negotiated* since all the relevant actors have come to agree on the dual strategy of a reduction in working hours plus wage restraint, and the preservation of the welfare state on a high level (4.5.2). In the 1990s, the volume of work rose as the increase in labour market participation and the reduction of unemployment overcompensated for the decrease in individual working hours to the lowest level within the countries compared (1323 hours in 2003). It marks a qualitative difference to the UK that the Dutch return to full employment has not been accompanied by an increase of relative poverty and of working poor. On the contrary, the Netherlands is the only country, where both Gini coefficient and relative poverty decreased in the course of the 1990s.[25] The fact that part-time workers, in particular, are entitled to receive additional state transfer income on

---

22 See Tables 4.2.17 (Selected empirical results) and 4.2.3 (Population, economic activity, occupational system and unemployment).

23 See Table 4.2.16 (Income inequality and relative poverty).

24 See Table 4.2.15 (Public expenditure on labour market policies as percentage of GDP).

25 See Table 4.5.15 (Income inequality and relative poverty).

top of their wages crucially contributed to this positive development. Furthermore, reductions in working hours do normally not lead to poverty in old age since the basic pension scheme has not been affected by recent reforms. The broad societal consensus not only on qualitative restructuring but also on the admittedly expensive preservation of the welfare state apparatus is reflected in the comparatively highest public expenditures on labour market policies as percentage of the GDP. In 2002, this was 3.56 per cent, roughly five times as much as in the UK and over 1 per cent more than in Sweden.[26] The Dutch experience, like the Swedish, confirms our hypothesis that the balancing act between social policies oriented towards social inclusion and participation, on the one hand, and the optimization of a national location in intensified international competition can be achieved.

There is one, not unimportant, point in which the Dutch road deviates from the ideal type of a negotiated growth strategy. While the period of 1996 to 2005 was characterized, as assumed, by relatively fast growth rates (2.2 per cent) and a drastic reduction in unemployment (4.1 per cent), the continuing weakness in productivity growth (0.9 per cent) could hinder future development.[27] The employment 'miracle' appears, to a large extent, to have been established thanks to a first extensive phase in which jobs were created on the basis of relative low wages (1.1 per cent growth between 1996 and 2005). The sustainability of the Dutch model will depend on whether the country succeeds with the transition from this first phase towards a second intensive one. The circumstances for this to happen do not seem to be unfavourable: compared to the 1980s, when unemployment was at its peak, the trade unions are in a much better bargaining position. If there is full employment, then organized labour will hardly hold on to the wage restraint concessions, and this should in turn motivate employers sufficiently to invest in qualitative optimization of the technical basis of the production process. Rationalization and, eventually, an increase in productivity growth should follow as a result.

The Spanish population did not experience the 'golden' decades associated with the heyday of Fordism. In the 1980s, when most European countries had already entered the phase of deregulation, de-industrialization and the decomposition of the social structure, institutions of labour market and welfare regulation were still to be established and the dominance of the agricultural sector was still to be overcome. Unlike in other countries, the decrease in agricultural employment was not compensated by an expansion of the industrial sector, since the latter was itself under pressure of rationalization and modernization in the light of the integration into the European economic space. The service sectors, which initially grew very slowly, neither absorbed the redundant population of agriculture and industry, nor the mainly female social groups that became economically active for the first time. The decline of the labour market and social structure of the Franco era is made obvious by the fact that in the first two decades after its termination the number of

---

26 See Table 4.5.14 (Public expenditure on labour market policies as percentage of GDP).

27 See Table 4.5.16 (Selected empirical results).

the economically active population increased, while the number of the employed population decreased. Mass unemployment was the inevitable result.[28]

The most recent period in Spain brought not only a resurgence of collective bargaining and central agreements (4.3.2), but also an economic recovery and a recomposition of the social structure. The position of the trade unions in negotiations at the central level, however, was not strong, due to the fact that they were concentrated in declining industries, the divided labour force (along the lines of permanent/ fixed term contracts), and the high levels of unemployment. Under these conditions a trajectory was agreed upon, which, like in the UK, attempted to create GDP growth and employment based on an extensive use of the labour force. Rising wage inequalities were the price to be paid. In the period of 1996 to 2005, the GDP growth rate was the fastest within the five countries compared (3.2 per cent), while unemployment decreased from 19.0 per cent to 11.3 per cent in 2003.[29] The extensive character of the growth strategy is best expressed in the slowest productivity growth (0.6 per cent) and the highest workload per person. The average number of hours worked per person and year continued at a level over 1800. On average, Spaniards work nearly 500 hours more than the Dutch. Indicators for rising inequality and poverty are the Gini coefficient, which rose from 0.303 in 1990 to 0.325 in 2001, and relative poverty increasing from 17.3 per cent in 1990 to 20.0 per cent in 1997.[30]

---

28 See Table 4.3.2 (Population, economic activity, occupational system and unemployment).

29 See Tables 4.3.2 (Population, economic activity, occupational system and unemployment) and 4.3.16 (Selected empirical results).

30 See Table 4.3.15 (Income inequality and relative poverty).

Concluding Remarks

In this book, I have developed a theoretical notion of the restructuring process of labour markets and social structures in advanced capitalist countries. Against the background of Marx's and Weber's classical sociological theories, we began by raising the issue of whether or not there are general links between inclusion, exclusion and capitalism. Subsequently, we focused on the transition from Fordism to Post-Fordism, and we applied key concepts from the regulation approach to the changes in labour markets and social structures in Western Europe. On this theoretical basis, we raised hypotheses about the UK, Spain, the Netherlands, Sweden and Germany and then examined these in light of empirical studies of the countries.

The point of departure was Marx's notion of the relationship between the accumulation of capital and the development of employment (1.1). From this perspective, the existence of unemployment, labour market marginality and exclusion is not an accidental phenomenon but belongs to the core features of a capitalist market economy. Though growth of productivity decreases the volume of work necessary to produce a given quantity of commodities, wage-earners benefit from this indirectly at best – via reductions in working hours that normally have to be fought through against the resistance of employers. The direct result of such progress in productivity, however, is that a part of the original workforce becomes 'superfluous'. The original level of employment can only be maintained through the expansion of the overall scale of production in greater proportion than the increase in the 'organic composition' of capital resulting from the substitution of workers. During such 'happy' stages of capitalist development, for which the Fordist growth strategy is a prime example, the employers' interest in a maximum of capital valorization is temporarily harmonized with the employees' interest in employment stability, and the degree of social cohesion is high. Such a harmonious combination is, however, not the normal case. More often, increases in labour productivity are accompanied by labour market marginality of part of the workforce, the main forms of which are precarious working conditions, and temporal or permanent unemployment. This distinction between permanent and sporadic participation in, and total exclusion from, the production process is also linked to different conditions for the representation of interests of these groups. While the employers' dependence on their staff allow the latter a representation of interests within the economic field, the furtherance of interests of the unemployed and of those who are only partly active in the production process is largely limited to the political sphere.

Our notion of inclusion and exclusion in capitalism was expanded by considering the level of the distribution of wealth and resources in the Weberian tradition (1.2). Defined as a dynamic balance of power between 'excluding' and 'usurping' groups, the analysis of very different aspects of stratification such as gender, class, and ethnic groups can be carried out in the one and same theoretical terms of reference. Parkin's and Murphy's theories, in particular, provide us with a non-linear and multi-dimensional notion of the process of extending citizenship rights and inequality. As the balance of power between excluding and usurping groups in a particular social field is always unstable since both parties attempt to champion their interests – if necessary against the will of the opposition – a historically given distribution of wealth and resources and the resulting degree of social cohesion is always a fragile arrangement. The amount of resources groups hold are not set in stone, both their increase and decrease remain a constant possibility. If we think Marx and Weber together, the social structure appears as a dynamic plurality of exclusionary social relationships within which the capital–labour relation has a particular status insofar as the privileged position of employers is directly connected to the labour effort of his or her employees (Wright). This is not the case in non-exploitative exclusionary relationships where the welfare of ruling groups solely relies on the exclusion of other groups from access to certain resources. Our general discussion of inclusion and exclusion under capitalist auspices was completed by considering the state and the international dimension (1.3). At the international level, the process of accumulation of capital proceeds by combining different forms of the organization of labour and different types and levels of socio-economic regulation. Different locations compete with each other so that multi-national corporations tend to be in the advantageous position of being able to choose the most suitable combination of the factors of production from many national economic spaces. This competition of locations is mediated by (mainly) national governments, which represent national economic spaces in the international arena and refocus the international balance of power onto internal debates. While the international division of labour allows for the promotion and demotion of single locations, a kind of dynamic core–periphery structure appears nevertheless to be reproduced: the simultaneous existence of economic prosperity and a high level of social security and inclusion in the centres, and of stagnation, social antagonisms, and disintegration in the peripheries seems a historical constant.

The regulation approach (Chapter Two) takes a mediating position between general theories of capitalist development and empirical research on labour markets, welfare systems and social structures. From the perspective of a sociology of economic and social cohesion, this approach is of interest as, on the one hand, it takes those structural tensions seriously that are inherent in a capitalist organization of the division of labour and that make socio-economic regulation necessary. On the other hand, it has developed intermediate concepts located at a level of abstraction that are sufficiently 'concrete' to address the institutional, political and ideological forms of embedding by which capitalist development proceeds. Hence, issues such as wage relations, forms of enterprise and money, the state, and the international aspect of regulation can be examined, at the same time, theoretically and empirically, and over time and space (2.1).

Stable economic growth is dependent on compatible socio-economic regulation, both in the national and international context. While the correspondence of an accumulation regime and a mode of regulation leads to the temporary stability of a social formation, this institutional stabilization always remains limited because it does not, once and for all, dispose of the underlying dimensions of crisis at the level of the mode of production. This is aggravated since both accumulation regimes and modes of regulation contain specific dynamics of their own. Crises happen as a result of a disarticulation between the two. The – however temporary – 'solution' of such a crisis consists in their reshaping and re-articulation. However, whether or not such a new articulation emerges cannot not be taken for granted but is an historical *objet trouvé* (Lipietz): it is perfectly possible that tendencies within an accumulation regime and a mode of regulation do not converge and, hence, that a stable growth strategy does not arise.

Social cohesion in Western Europe after World War II was tied to the Fordist accumulation and regulation context (2.2). As a growth strategy, Fordism rested predominantly on the productivity growth associated with the general achievement of economies of scale. This growth was the basis for the simultaneous and proportionate development of the two departments of social production. The percentage of wages within the total costs of employers decreased, but the real wages of workers increased. Employment grew to its full potential because the total volume of capital rose by a greater proportion than the increase in the number of workers made redundant due to productivity gains in the work process. The cheapening of industrial products raised the purchasing power of wage labourers, so that both the employers' profits and the employees' consumption increased. The state benefited from this favourable situation and used its growing income from taxation for the expansion of a welfare state system, which, in turn, provided a guaranteed minimum standard of living for those who, for whatever reason, could not participate in the labour market. Since most social groups benefited from this growth model, the level of both system and social integration was correspondingly high.

In the course of the 1970s, the Fordist growth model became crisis-prone. The dimensions of the crisis were multi-layered and ranged from the exhaustion of the productivity potential of economies of scale, through the changing demand structures for industrially manufactured goods and the spatial reorganization of the work process, to the new role of financial capital and investment practices (2.3). All these separate factors combined to undermine the crucial structural basis for the ascendancy of the Fordist mode of societalization: the parallel enhancement of profits and wages. With the decline of growth rates in both GDP and wage levels and the corresponding loss in tax revenue, public funds became increasingly unbalanced, and the particular Fordist formula for system and social integration (2.2) was no longer viable. Those labour markets and social structures that had emerged as an integral part of the Fordist stage of capitalist development fell into a long-term decline resulting in the destabilization of economy and society.

While most authors agree that the Fordist growth model has reached its limits, there is no agreement yet on the issue of whether a Post-Fordist growth model has materialized, or is in the process of doing so, nor is there any consensus on the mechanism by which it could be regulated. In view of the relatively open stage of the debate, I proposed in this book that space must be left for different roads to Post-Fordism and I outlined two ideal-types (3.1). Capital-oriented growth strategies abolish the Fordist class compromise from the top down, favour the employers' short-term competitive interests and are mainly aimed at lowering labour costs. Wage determination takes place at the individual or company level, leading to a de-indexation of wages and a structural weakening of trade unions. Flexibility in working hours is implemented in ways that make it increasingly difficult for employees to combine professional and private life. Employers, who themselves contribute little to public funds, enjoy state economic and social policies that are directed towards the promotion of short-term competitiveness. Negotiated growth strategies, by contrast, are the results of collective bargaining at sector or social levels. They actively embrace the participation of workers in reorganizing the work process at a high level of productivity and do not depend so much on 'cheap labour' and the (over-)exploitation of workers, but more on their active integration and skills. They are not based on conflict but on consensus, since the employers' interest in optimal competitiveness is not divorced from the employees' interest in long-term employment contracts, training, etc. Unlike capital-oriented growth strategies, the welfare state survives and is adjusted to meet new challenges.

In the next stage, four hypotheses were suggested in relation to the long-term changes in the labour market, welfare system and social structure Western European countries have been confronted with during their transition from Fordist to Post-Fordist growth strategies (3.2). The first hypothesis postulated a homology between the rise and fall of the Fordist development stage and social structure. More precisely, the second hypothesis stated that the growth period of Fordism was accompanied by labour market and inequality structures that were shaped along the following lines:

- fast GDP growth
- fast labour productivity growth
- rising economic activity (especially of men)
- full employment of the economically active
- rising real wages
- industrialization
- increasing percentage of dependent employment
- dominance of full-time jobs
- expansion of state labour market and welfare programs.

According to the third hypothesis, the crisis of Fordism corresponded with a decomposition of the social structure. The main features of that decline are:

- slow GDP growth
- slow labour productivity growth
- rising economic activity (now especially of women)
- rising unemployment
- stagnating or slow growth of real wages
- de-industrialization/tertiarization
- reduction of state labour market and welfare programs.

Finally, the fourth hypothesis postulated that the decomposition of the social structure is followed by its recomposition depending on the road to Post-Fordism a country follows. Countries that favour a capital-oriented growth strategy tend to develop social structures along the following lines:

- stabilization of GDP growth rates
- slow productivity growth due to extensive use of workforce (long working hours) and frequent usage of unskilled labour power
- decreasing unemployment
- low level of state labour market and welfare polices
- rising wage inequalities; many working poor
- rising part-time work (unregulated)
- rising self-employment.

Negotiated growth strategies coincide with the following socio-structural features:

- stabilization of GDP growth rates
- fast productivity growth
- decreasing unemployment due to intensive use of workforce (short working hours) and frequent use of skilled labour power
- high level of state labour market and welfare policies
- lower wage inequalities than in capital-oriented growth strategies; fewer working poor
- rising part-time work (regulated and with entitlements to additional welfare payments)
- rising self-employment.

Since the empirical results gathered on the basis of these hypotheses have been already summarized – both in a country-specific (Sections 4.1.4, 4.2.4, 4.3.4, 4.4.4 and 4.5.4) and comparative (Chapter Five) way – at this stage, I would like to provide some concluding remarks. On the basis of the literature, interviews with experts in the five countries, and the statistical material, the scrutiny of the first two hypotheses was relatively easy. In all five countries, institutions of labour market and welfare regulation had been established. These had not developed as an outcome of particular interests of single social classes or groups but rather were the results of compromises between different interest groups (5.1). The notion of a 'Fordist class compromise' expresses well the extraordinary broad social basis on which growth strategies in the different countries developed. Against the historical background of the experiences with authoritarian regimes before and during World War II and the competition with the 'real-existing' socialist world, the attempt to shape the capitalist market economy for the greatest possible benefit of all citizens and to orientate it towards the ideals of participation and social cohesion was welcomed by a huge majority of Western European populations. Despite the fact that Fordism as an ideal-typical growth strategy shaped all of the observed national trajectories to a greater or lesser degree, the comparative perspective also revealed that, in terms of real-types, we should speak of Fordisms rather than of Fordism as a uniform model.

Notwithstanding the many differences in detail (5.2), in the 1960s and 1970s, Sweden, the Netherlands, and Germany came close to the ideal-type of a Fordist social structure. For this group of countries, the concurrence of growth of GDP, productivity and real wages, on the one hand, and the achievement of full employment, on the other hand, could be proven. The same applies to the dominance of the industrial sector and the increasing percentage of dependent work within economic activity. In the British case, the distance to the Fordist ideal-type is greater. While the necessity of socio-economic regulation and for the creation of an encompassing welfare state was part of the post-war consensus, particular lines of segmentation and conflict in the industrial relations system nevertheless survived. The realization of the productivity potential normally associated with the implementation of Taylorist management methods was therefore hampered. Nonetheless, other indicators, assumed to be typical for a Fordist social structure, were found in the UK in similar ways as in the three cases mentioned above. Finally, in Spain, political and economic development deviates most from the theoretically constructed model, since the abolishing of the authoritarian industrial relations regime, for example, took place thirty years later than in Germany. At times when the other countries selected for this book enjoyed the 'golden age' of capitalism, Spain followed a development model that was heavily shaped by the agricultural sector and partially oriented towards socio-economic autarchy. The implementation of labour market and welfare institutions equalling the Western European regulatory standard was not carried out until the 1980s and so the social structure did not show those characteristics of Fordist growth that we have associated with Sweden, the Netherlands, Germany, and, less so, the UK. Labour market and social structure were shaped much more by the decline of the Francoist development stage and the adjustment problems of a previously separate economy having to integrate into the international division of labour. Redundancies, particularly in the agricultural and previously protected industrial sector, followed and resulted in mass unemployment.

The third hypothesis, of a decomposition of the social structure following the crisis of Fordism, was likewise supported by the empirical material (5.3). In all five countries, the growth rates of GDP and productivity declined significantly and, in the 1980s, they stagnated at this low level. Problems in employment arose from two fronts and could not be compensated for by the opposing trend towards continuing tertiarization. On the one hand, the at times rapid de-industrialization made many thousands of workers redundant so that the demand for labour, for manual labour in particular, decreased; and, on the other hand, the supply of labour increased in four of the five countries due to the first labour market entry of women. The exception is Sweden where the activity rate of women was already high in the 1960s and 1970s and where, throughout the 1980s, the labour market parties held on to economic and social polices oriented towards the maintenance of full employment. Finally, the crisis in economic growth and the labour market negatively influenced the bargaining power of those still in employment in the sense that increases in real wages like those of the 1970s could no longer be achieved. Wages stagnated as did profits; and the previously successful growth strategy, originally based on consensus and compromise, began to fracture.

It was feared that social partnership was neglected when the institutional welfare compromises of the post-war era were renegotiated in the 1980s and 1990s. The fourth hypothesis therefore pointed towards new roads in socio-economic development, assuming that these roads proceed along and between the two ends of the Post-Fordist spectrum of 'negotiated' and 'capital-oriented' growth strategies. While it is true that there is generally some tendency to strengthen the supply side within industrial relations and socio-economic regulation, which can be traced to increasing international competition, this should not be generalized to the notion of a irreversible shift towards neo-liberalism. In most of the observed countries, the concrete outcomes of deregulation and re-regulation processes are – in the final analysis – compromises in which trade union positions are more or less reflected; and even where neo-liberalism had been tested in pure form – as in the UK under the Conservatives – it was somewhat moderated afterwards (under New Labour). Rather, the comparative perspective indicates that there is no simple and direct connection between developments at the international level and changes in the regulatory systems of the nation-states under observation in this book: if we assume for a moment that 'globalization' has more or less the same impact for all Western European countries, the great discrepancy between the reforms in labour market and welfare system among the five countries is remarkable. Of these countries, two came close to the capital-oriented road: the UK and Germany. While wage determination processes, in particular, and socio-economic regulation, in general, were decentralized, the role of the state was classified as 'weak' insofar as it remained oriented mainly towards the support of market forces. Three countries took positions closer to the 'negotiated' ideal-type: Sweden, the Netherlands, and, to a lesser extent, Spain. In these cases, forms of wage coordination (at the social or sector level) and of re-regulation of wider socio-economic development were resumed after a previous period of ongoing decentralization and deregulation. In Sweden and the Netherlands, governments took the initiative in finding ways out of the crisis, and they remain active in current socio-economic governance. The Spanish state dispensed parts of this competence to the labour market parties so that it became increasingly 'moderating' in its attempts to reach central agreements.

The fourth hypothesis further postulated a link between the kind of Post-Fordist growth strategy a country follows – negotiated or capital-oriented – and the ways in which labour markets and social structures are recomposed after their previous decomposition. This hypothesis was also supported in the sense that where reforms in labour market and welfare system had been implemented early enough to be measured in this inquiry (by 2003), the expected consequences for the social structure more or less materialized (5.5). While in the Netherlands and the UK, such adaptations in the regulatory apparatus were carried out in the 1980s, in Sweden and Spain this took place in the 1990s. However, Germany's U-turn towards supply orientation without compensation for employees was only made in 2003 so that the social consequences of this decision must be a topic for future research. In 2003, the German occupational and social structure continued to be shaped by decomposition following the crisis of Fordism and socio-economic depression following reunification.

The example of the UK confirms our assumption that full employment on the basis of a capital-oriented growth strategy can be achieved but at the cost of huge wage inequalities and rising income poverty. An extensive accumulation regime, exemplified by the coexistence of long working hours and slow productivity growth rates, does not provide sufficient dependent employment at wages that allow people to leave the ranks of the working poor. In capital-oriented growth strategies the extent of economic inclusion might be high; but this does not alter the fact that more people are marginalized and excluded from a decent standard of living than in the 1970s. It was not least because of increasing wage inequality, rising poverty rates and social exclusion that New Labour re-established the minimum wage and introduced redistribution of primary incomes via taxation. Spain exemplifies the rare case of an extensive growth strategy that was negotiated at the central level. Confronted with high unemployment, the labour market parties agreed on a course that massively reduced unemployment in combination with long working hours and slow growth rates in productivity. Like in the UK, income inequalities and relative poverty grew despite the creation of employment.

At the other end of the spectrum, the experiences in the Netherlands and in Sweden support our assumption that a return to full employment is possible without the emergence of millions of working poor and a general disintegration of society. Sweden comes closest to a negotiated growth strategy. State investments in Research & Development and into the higher education sector with the aim of accelerating productivity growth go hand in hand with labour market and welfare state reforms that include quantitative cuts in the level of welfare without qualitatively altering the comparatively generous system: a high productivity/high tax/high wage road to Post-Fordism. Relatively fast growth rates in GDP and productivity are combined with a return to full employment and poverty rates of half the level of the UK. The fact that egalitarian ambitions do not necessarily hamper the competitive position of a national location is illustrated by the fact that Sweden came fifth in the annual Global Competitive Report at the World Economic Forum in Davos in November 2002 – way ahead of, among other countries, the UK (Benner, 2003).

The Netherlands, too, follows a negotiated road as the dual strategy of reducing working hours plus wage restraint was carried out in combination with a preservation of the welfare state at a high level. This country has also returned to full employment, inter alia, by redistributing work in the form of an expansion of part-time work; but, in contrast to the UK, this did not lead to an increase in the number and percentage of the working poor due to the possibilities of combining dependent employment (part-time) work with state transfers. The extent of economic inclusion is even higher than in Fordist times since more and more women have become economically active and no longer participate in social wealth exclusively via their status as the wives of male breadwinners. However, the future of the Dutch growth strategy could be hampered by the weak productivity growth to date, since continuing wage restraint and relatively cheap labour might well function as obstacles for the qualitative optimization of the technological basis of the production process.

Due to the temporal differences in the implementation of reforms in industrial relations, labour markets and welfare system, the assumption of a close link between the type of Post-Fordist development strategy, on one hand, and socio-structural change, on the other, can, for the time being, be regarded as empirically assured for the Netherlands, Sweden, and the UK. In order to further scrutinize and, if necessary, modify this assumption, the two latecomers (Germany, in particular, and Spain) should remain in the focus of research. Further information could be obtained by considering other counties such as the US, France or Denmark. However heterogeneous future growth strategies of national locations turn out to be; in the present study, two utterly different roads to Post-Fordism have been theoretically constructed and empirically identified; this can serve as an orientation for countries in earlier development stages. Against the background of a globalization discourse that often ends in fatalism, this result cannot be reiterated enough. While it is beyond dispute that the processes of international economic interdependence will continue and probably intensify in the future, it does not follow that the role of national governments in areas such as labour market and social policy is reduced to one of a 'transmission belt' of global 'constraints'. In contrast, both the theoretical discussion and the empirical analysis of this study point to the perspective that even under circumstances of increased international competition and a general under-regulation of the global arena, national governments and policy-makers in Western Europe do not have to compete against each other by undercutting social and ecological standards. While it is true that large corporations invest in those countries and regions that promise the greatest net profit, profit margins depend not only on the costs of the factors of production, but also on their comparative productivity. A country with relatively high taxes can therefore remain attractive to international capital as long as it offers a highly qualified labour force that is able to produce high quality commodities. It is therefore within the political and economic area of influence of national decision-makers to define a growth strategy that proceeds somewhere between capital-oriented and negotiated growth strategies. And, depending on the approximation to one of the two ideal-types, this definition will be linked to different and particular modi of economic and social inclusion.

Further research into long-term capitalist development, labour markets and social structures should not only consider other countries and extend the period of time of observation but should also address the European and international levels in regulation more directly. While this book dealt with a comparison of changes in socio-economic regulation at the level of the nation-state, the sustainability of national growth strategies also depends on whether or not Post-Fordist national trajectories can be complemented by a re-regulation of the international economic space. Though this is a topic for future projects, the regulation theoretical perspective taken in this book suggests that national governments are not just at the receiving end of 'global constraints', but are – via their representation in international agencies such as the International Monetary Funds, the World Bank, the Organization of Economic Cooperation and Development and International Labour Organization – potentially crucial actors in the reconstitution of the international sphere. In contrast to the Fordist prosperity model, which was mainly geared to the internal market and complemented by a relatively stable international system, the present situation appears to be characterized as one in which national locations in Western Europe have begun to be restructured and re-regulated while the international level remains somewhat under-regulated.

For the time being, this leaves European locations with the problem of having to continue to open up and internationalize their own national economies. Bob Jessop has referred to the corresponding transition in national socio-economic regulation as one towards 'Schumpeterian' regimes: national governments increasingly opt for providing the necessary conditions for systemic competitiveness, permanent innovation and flexibility. Elaborating on this, in this book, I have tried to show that – in contrast to the neo-liberal orthodoxy, which is unremittingly brought into the public sphere by a particular kind of 'intellectual' in government and business think-tanks and, like a mantra, is reiterated by influential parts of the media (Bourdieu, et al., 2002; Bourdieu, 2005, Koch, 2006) – the Post-Fordist alternative for European nation-states is not between a market and capital-oriented model that provides the maximum of economic efficiency but ('unfortunately') requires the lowering of standards of system and social integration, and a semi-philanthropic approach that is committed to social cohesion but, at the same time, inefficient and, in times of aggravated international competition, unaffordable. On the contrary, the Swedish and, to a lesser extent, the Dutch experience proves that economic competitiveness and social cohesion can be achieved at the same time. Not only do normative orientations such as welfare and social inclusion take centre stage in their negotiated growth strategies – also with regard to competitiveness, both countries perform at least as well as the UK, which follows a capital-oriented road. With particular respect to the current debate on the future European economic and social model, it will be a matter of political will and not of economic 'constraints' whether this model will follow capital-oriented or negotiated principles.

References

Åberg, R. (1994), 'Wage Control and Cost-Push Inflation in Sweden since 1960', in Ronald, D. *et al.* (eds.), *The Return to Incomes Policy*, London: Pinter.

Aglietta, M. (1987), *A Theory of Capitalist Regulation: The US Experience*, 2nd edition, London: Verso.

Aglietta, M. (2002), 'The International Monetary System', in Boyer, R. and Saillard, Y. (eds.), *Regulation Theory. The State of the Art*, London: Taylor & Francis.

Althusser, E. and Balibar, E. (1998), *Reading Capital*, London: Verso.

Altvater, E. and Mahnkopf, B. (1996), *Grenzen der Globalisierung. Ökonomie, Ökologie und Politik in der Weltgesellschaft*, Münster: Westfälisches Dampfboot.

Bader, V. M., Berger, J., Ganßmann, H. and v.d. Knesebeck, J. (1983), *Einführung in die Gesellschaftstheorie. Gesellschaft, Wirtschaft und Staat bei Marx und Weber*, Frankfurt/Main and New York: Campus.

Balibar, E. and Wallerstein, I. (1998), *Rasse, Klasse, Nation. Ambivalente Identitäten*, Berlin: Argument Verlag.

Beardwell, I. (1996), '"How do We Know How it Really is?" An Analysis of the New Industrial Relations', in Beardwell, I. (ed.), *Contemporary Industrial Relations: A Critical Analysis*, Oxford: Oxford University Press.

Becker, J. (2002), *Akkumulation, Regulation, Territorium. Zur kritischen Rekonstruktion der französischen Regulationstheorie*, Marburg: Metropolis.

Becker, U. (2001), '"Miracle" by Consensus? Consensualism and Dominance in Dutch Employment Development', *Economic and Industrial Democracy*, **22**, 453–83.

Benner, M. (1997), *The Politics of Growth. Economic Regulation in Sweden 1930–1994*, Lund: Arkiv.

Benner, M. (2003), 'The Scandinavian Challenge. The Future of Advanced Welfare States in the Knowledge Economy', *Acta Sociologica*, **46** (2), 132–46.

Bertrand, H. (2002), 'The Wage-Labour Nexus', in Boyer, R. and Saillard, Y. (eds.), *Regulation Theory. The State of the Art*, London: Taylor & Francis.

Bischoff, J. (1999), *Der Kapitalismus des 21. Jahrhunderts. Systemkrise oder Rückkehr zur Prosperität?* Hamburg: VSA.

Björklund, A. (2000), 'Going Different Ways: Labour Market Policy in Denmark and Sweden', in Esping-Andersen, G. and Regini, M. (eds.), *Why Deregulate Labour Markets?* Oxford: Oxford University Press.

Blanchflower, D. and Freeman, R. (1994), 'Did the Thatcher Reforms Change British Labour Market Performance?', in Barrell, R. (ed.), *The UK Labour Market. Comparative Aspects and Institutional Developments*, Cambridge: Cambridge University Press.

Boix, C. (1998), *Political Parties, Growth and Equality. Conservative and Social Democratic Economic Strategies in the World Economy*, Cambridge: Cambridge University Press.

Bourdieu, P. (1977), *Reproduction in Education, Society and Culture*, Beverley Hills: Sage.

Bourdieu, P. (1986), 'The Forms of Capital', in Richardson, J. G. (ed.), *Handbook of Theory and Research in the Sociology of Education*, New York: Greenwood Press.

Bourdieu, P. (2003), *Firing Back. Against the Tyranny of the Market 2*, London & New York: Verso.

Bourdieu, P. (2005), *The Social Structures of the Economy*, Cambridge: Polity.

Bourdieu, P. *et al.* (2002), *The Weight of the World. Social Suffering in Contemporary Society*, Cambridge: Polity.

Boyer, R. (1990), *The Regulation School*, New York: Columbia University Press.

Boyer, R. (1995), 'Capital-Labour Relations in OECD Countries: From the Fordist Golden Age to Contrasted National Trajectories', in Schor, J. and You, J.-L. (eds.), *Capital, the State and Labour. A Global Perspective*, Aldershot: United Nations University Press.

Boyer, R. (2002a), 'Perspectives on the Wage-Labour Nexus', in Boyer, R. and Saillard, Y. (eds.), *Régulation Theory. The State of the Art*, London: Taylor & Francis.

Boyer, R. (2002b), 'From Canonical Fordism to Different Modes of Development', in Boyer, R. and Saillard, Y. (eds.), *Régulation Theory. The State of the Art*, London: Taylor & Francis.

Boyer, R. (2005), 'How and Why Capitalisms Differ', *Economy and Society*, **34** (4), 509–557.

Brewer, M., Goodman, A., Myck, M., Shaw, J. and Shephard, A. (2004), *Poverty and Inequality in Britain: 2004*, The Institute for Fiscal Studies, Commentary 96.

Cardoso, F. H. and Faletto, E. (1978), *Dependency and Development in Latin America*, Berkeley: University of California.

Crouch, C. (2003), 'The State: Economic Management and Incomes Policy', in Edwards, P. (ed.), *Industrial Relations. Theory and Practice*, Oxford: Blackwell.

Dangschat, J. (1998), 'Klassenstrukturen im Nach-Fordismus', in Berger, P. A. and Vester, M. (eds.), *Alte Ungleichheiten. Neue Spaltungen*, Opladen: Leske & Budrich.

Detje, R. (1998), 'Auswege aus der Arbeitslosigkeit', *Sozialismus*, **25** (5), 38–43.

Durkheim, E. (1964), *The Division of Labour in Society*, New York: Free Press.

Ebbinghaus, B. and Visser, J. (1997), 'Der Wandel der Arbeitsbeziehungen im westeuropäischen Vergleich', in Hradil, S. and Immerfall, S. (eds.), *Die westeuropäischen Gesellschaften im Vergleich*, Opladen: Leske & Budrich.

Eicker-Wolf, K. (2004), *(Um-)Steuern für Arbeit und soziale Gerechtigkeit. Alternativen zu leeren Kassen und zur Umverteilung von unten nach oben*, Hamburg: VSA.

Esping-Andersen, G. (1990), *The Three Worlds of Welfare Capitalism*, Cambridge: Polity Press.

Esping-Andersen, G. (ed.) (1996), *Welfare States in Transition,* London: Sage.

European Commission (2001), *The EU Economy: 2001 Review,* Luxembourg: Office for Official Publications of the EC.

European Commission (2004), *European Economy* 73 (and various volumes), Luxembourg: Office for Official Publications of the EC.

EUROSTAT (2002), *European Social Statistics: Income, Poverty and Social Exclusion,* Theme 3, Series E, Eurostat, Luxembourg: Office for Official Publications of the EC.

Feldbauer, P., Gächter, A., Hardach, G. and Novy, A. (eds.) (1999), *Industrialisierung. Entwicklungsprozesse in Afrika, Asien und Lateinamerika,* Frankfurt/Main & Wien: Brandes and Apsel/Südwind.

Fina, Ll. (1996), 'Creación de empleo, retos y oportunidades para Europa y para España', *Economista,* No. 69, 309–318.

Friedman, A. L. (2000), 'Microregulation and Post-Fordism: Critique and Development of Regulation Theory', *New Political Economy,* 5 (1), 59–76.

Fröbel, F., Heinrichs, J. and Kreye, O. (1981), *Krisen in der kapitalistischen Weltökonomie,* Reinbek: Rowohlt.

Ganßmann, H. (1999), 'Arbeitmarkt und Ausgrenzung', in Herkommer, S. (ed.), *Soziale Ausgrenzungen. Gesichter des neuen Kapitalismus,* Hamburg: VSA.

Ganßmann, H. and Haas, M. (1999), *Arbeitsmärkte im Vergleich. Deutschland, Japan, USA,* Marburg: Schüren.

Garrett, G. (1998), *Partisan Politics in the Global Economy,* Cambridge: Cambridge University Press.

Geißler, R. (1992), *Die Sozialstruktur Deutschlands. Ein Studienbuch zur Entwicklung im geteilten und vereinten Deutschland,* Opladen: Westdeutscher Verlag.

Golsch, K. (2003), 'Employment Flexibility in Spain and its Impact on Transitions to Adulthood', *Work, Employment and Society,* 17 (4), 691–718.

Gorter, C. (2000), 'The Dutch Miracle?', in Esping-Andersen, G. and Regini, M. (eds.), *Why Deregulate Labour Markets?* Oxford: Oxford University Press.

Gottschalk, P. and Smeeding, T. (1997), 'Cross-national Comparisons of Earnings and Income Inequality', *Journal of Economic Literature,* 35 (2), 633–87.

Gramsci, A. (1971), *Selections from the Prison Notebooks,* Basingstoke: Macmillan.

Guttmann, R. (2002), 'Money and Credit in Régulation Theory', in Boyer, R. and Saillard, Y. (eds.), *Regulation Theory. The State of the Art,* London: Taylor & Francis.

Hagelstange, T. (1988), *Die Entwicklung von Klassenstrukturen in der EG und in Nordamerika,* Frankfurt/Main and New York: Campus.

Hall, A. and Midgley, J. (2004), *Social Policy for Development,* London: Sage.

Hall, P. A. and Soskice, D. (ed.) (2001), *Varieties of Capitalism. The Institutional Foundations of Comparative Advantage,* Oxford: Oxford University Press.

Haller, M. (1997), 'Klassenstruktur und Arbeitslosigkeit. Die Entwicklung zwischen

1960 und 1990', in Hradil, S. and Immerfall, S. (eds.), *Die westeuropäischen Gesellschaften im Vergleich*, Opladen: Leske & Budrich.

Harrysson, L. and Petersson, J. (2004), 'Revealing the Traits of Workfare: The Swedish Example', in Glorieux, I. Jönsson, I. and Littlewood, P. (eds.), *The Future of Work in Europe* , Aldershot: Ashgate.

Hassel, A. (1999), 'The Erosion of the German System of Industrial Relations', *British Journal of Industrial Relations*, **37** (3), 484–505.

Heidenreich, M. (1997), 'Arbeit und Management in den westeuropäischen Kommunikationsgesellschaften', in Hradil, S. and Immerfall, S. (eds.), *Die westeuropäischen Gesellschaften im Vergleich*, Opladen: Leske & Budrich.

Heinrich, M. (1999), *Die Wissenschaft vom Wert. Die Marxsche Kritik der politischen Ökonomie zwischen wissenschaftlicher Revolution und klassischer Tradition*, Münster: Westfälisches Dampfboot.

Hemerijck, A. (1995), 'Corporatist Immobility in the Netherlands', in Crouch, C. and Traxler, F. (eds.), *Organized Industrial Relations in Europe: What Future?* Aldershot: Avebury.

Herkommer, S. (1985), *Einführung Ideologie*, Hamburg: VSA.

Herkommer, S. (2004), *Metamorphosen der Ideologie. Zur Analyse des Neoliberalismus durch Pierre Bourdieu und aus marxistischer Perspektive*, Hamburg: VSA.

Herkommer, S. and Koch, M. (1999), 'The "Underclass": A Misleading Concept and a Scientific Myth? Poverty and Social Exclusion as Challenges to Theories of Class and Social Structure', in Glorieux, I., Herkommer, S., Jönsson, I. and Littlewood, P. (eds.), *Social Exclusion in Europe. Problems and Paradigms*, Aldershot: Ashgate.

Hinrichs, K. (2002), 'What can be Learned from Whom? Germany's Employment Problem in Comparative Perspective', *Innovation*, **15** (2), 77–97.

Hirsch, J. (1995), *Der nationale Wettbewerbsstaat. Staat, Demokratie und Politik im globalen Kapitalismus*, Berlin & Amsterdam: Edition ID-Archiv.

Hirsch, J. (2000), 'The Concept of Materialist State Theory and Regulation Theory', in Schmidt, J. D. and Hersh, J. (eds.), *Globalization and Social Change*, London: Routledge.

Hirsch, J. and Roth, R. (1986), *Das neue Gesicht des Kapitalismus: vom Fordismus zum Postfordismus*, Hamburg: VSA.

Hirst, P. and Thompson, G. (1996), *Globalization in Question. The International Economy and the Possibilities of Governance*, Cambridge: Polity.

Hurtienne, T. (1988), 'Entwicklungen und Verwicklungen – methodische und entwicklungstheoretische Probleme des Regulationsansatzes', in Mahnkopf, B. (ed.), *Der gewendete Kapitalismus. Kritische Beiträge zur Theorie der Regulation*, Münster: Westfälisches Dampfboot.

Hyman, R. (2003), 'The Historical Evolution of British Industrial Relations', in Edwards, P. (ed.), *Industrial Relations. Theory and Practice*, Oxford: Blackwell.

ILO (International Labour Organization) (1973-2003), *Yearbook of Labour Statistics* (various volumes), Geneva: International Labour Office.

Initiativgruppe Regulationstheorie (1997), 'Globalisierung und Krise des Fordismus. Zur Einführung', in Becker, S., Sablowski, T. and Schumm, W. (eds.), *Jenseits der Nationalökonomie? Weltwirtschaft und Nationalstaat zwischen Globalisierung und Regionalisierung*, Berlin: Argument Verlag.

Jessop, B. (1990), 'Regulation Theories in Retrospect and Prospect', *Economy and Society*, **19** (2), 153–216.

Jessop, B. (1999), 'The Changing Governance of Welfare: Recent Trends in its Primary Functions, Scale, and Modes of Coordination', *Social Policy and Administration*, **33** (4), 348–359.

Jessop, B. (2001), 'Kritischer Realismus, Marxismus und Regulation', in Candeias, M. and Deppe, F. (eds.), *Ein neuer Kapitalismus?* Hamburg: VSA.

Jessop, B. (2002), *The Future of the Capitalist State*, Cambridge: Polity.

Jones, G. and Wallace, C. (1992), *Youth, Family and Citizenship*, Buckingham: Open University Press.

Katzenstein, P. J. (1985), *Small States in World Markets, Industrial Policy in Europe*, Ithaka: Cornell University Press.

Keller, B. and Seifert, H. (eds.) (1998), *Deregulierung am Arbeitsmarkt. Eine empirische Zwischenbilanz*, Hamburg: VSA.

Klickauer, T. (2002), 'Stability in Germany's Industrial Relations: A Critique on Hassel's Erosion Thesis', *British Journal of Industrial Relations*, **40** (2), 296–303.

Klodt, H. (1998), 'Großbritannien: Die marktwirtschaftliche Strategie', *Mitteilungen aus der Arbeitsmarkt- und Berufsforschung*, No. 2, 277–93.

Koch, M. (1998a), *Unternehmen Transformation. Sozialstruktur und gesellschaftlicher Wandel in Chile*, Frankfurt am Main: Vervuert.

Koch, M. (1998b), *Vom Strukturwandel einer Klassengesellschaft. Theoretische Diskussion und empirische Analyse*, 2nd edition, Münster: Westfälisches Dampfboot.

Koch, M. (2000), 'The Theory of Sociological Thought and the Research Process', in Kinloch, G. C. and Mohan, R. P. (eds.), *Ideology and the Social Sciences*, New York: Greenwood Press.

Koch, M. (2001), 'In Search of a Class Theory of Marginality and Exclusion', *International Journal of Contemporary Sociology*, **38** (2), 193–212.

Koch, M. (2003), *Arbeitsmärkte und Sozialstrukturen in Europa. Wege zum Postfordismus in den Niederlanden, Schweden, Spanien, Großbritannien und Deutschland*, Wiesbaden: Westdeutscher Verlag.

Koch, M. (2004a), 'European Reactions to Global Challenges: The Cases of the Netherlands, UK, Sweden, Spain, and Germany', *New Global Development. Journal of International and Comparative Social Welfare (from 2006: Journal of Comparative Social Welfare)*, **20** (1), 15–22.

Koch, M. (2004b), 'Labour Market Regulation after Fordism: Five Countries Compared', in Glorieux, I. Jönsson, I., and Littlewood, P. (eds.), *The Future of Work in Europe*, Aldershot: Ashgate.

Koch, M. (2005), 'Wage Determination, Socio-Economic Regulation and the State', *European Journal of Industrial Relations*, **11** (3), 327–346.

Koch, M. (2006), 'Pierre Bourdieu as a Sociologist of the Economy and Critic of "Globalisation"', *International Journal of Contemporary Sociology*, **43** (1), forthcoming.

Kondratieff, N. M. (1946), 'Die langen Wellen der Konjunktur', *Archiv für Sozialwissenschaft und Sozialpolitik*, **56**, 573–609.

Lane, C. (1994), 'Industrial Order and the Transformation of Industrial Relations: Britain, Germany, and France Compared', in Hyman, R. and Ferrer, A. (eds.), *New Frontiers in European Industrial Relations*, Oxford: Blackwell.

Lapp, S. and Lehment, H. (1997), 'Lohnzurückhaltung in Deutschland und den Vereinigten Staaten', *Die Weltwirtschaft*, No. 1, 67–83.

Lindbeck, A. and Snower, D. (1986), 'Wage Setting, Unemployment, and Insider-Outsider Relations', *American Economic Review*, **76** (2), 235–39.

Lipietz, A. (1985), 'Akkumulation, Krisen und Auswege aus der Krise. Einige methodologische Anmerkungen zum Begriff der "Regulation"', *PROKLA*, No. **58**, 109–37.

Lipietz, A. (1987), *Mirages and Miracles: The Crisis of Global Fordism*, London: Verso.

Lipietz, A. (1998), *Nach dem Ende des "Goldenen Zeitalters". Regulation und Transformation kapitalistischer Gesellschaften*, Berlin: Argument Verlag.

Lister, R. (1997), *Citizenship. Feminist Perspectives*, Houndsmills: Macmillan.

Lockwood, D. (1992), *Solidarity and Schism. "The Problem of Disorder" in Durkheimian and Marxist Sociology*, Oxford: Oxford University Press.

Lutz, B. (1989), *Der kurze Traum immerwährender Prosperität*, Frankfurt/Main and New York: Campus.

Luxemburg, R. (2004), *The Accumulation of Capital*, Oxford: Routledge.

Mackert, J. (1998), 'Jenseits von Inklusion/Exklusion', *Berliner Journal für Soziologie*, **8** (4), 561–76.

Marimón, R. (Ed.) 1996, *La Economía Española, una visión diferente*, Barcelona: Antoni Bosch.

Marsden, D. (1992), 'Incomes Policy for Europe? Or will Pay Bargaining Destroy the Single European Market?', *British Journal of Industrial Relations*, **30** (4), 587–604.

Marshall, T. H. (1977), *Class, Citizenship and Social Development*, Chicago and London: Chicago University Press.

Marshall, T. H. (1981), *The Right to Welfare and Other Essays*, London: Heinemann Educational.

Marx, K. (1973), *Grundrisse. Foundations of the Critique of Political Economy (Rough Draft)*, Harmondsworth, Middlesex: Penguin.

Marx, K. (1977), *Capital. A Critique of Political Economy. Volume One: The Process of Production of Capital*, London: Lawrence & Wishart.

Meidner, R. (1999), 'Zurück zur Vollbeschäftigung: Ein alternativer makroökonomischer Politikentwurf', *Sozialismus*, **26** (12), 15–22.

Murphy, R. (1988), *Social Closure. The Theory of Monopolization and Exclusion*, Oxford: Clarendon.

Novy, A., Parnreiter, C. and Fischer, K. (1999), *Globalisierung und Peripherie. Umstrukturierung in Lateinamerika, Afrika und Asien*, Frankfurt/Main: Brandes und Apsel; Vienna: Südwind.

OECD (Organization for Economic Cooperation and Development) (1991–2004), *Employment Outlook* (various volumes), Paris.

OECD (1998–2004), *Economic Outlook* (various volumes), Paris.

Parkin, F. (1972), *Class Inequality and Political Order*, Frogmore: Paladin.

Parkin, F. (1979), *Marxism and Class Theory: A Bourgeois Critique*, Cambridge: Tavistock.

Paschukanis, E. (1929), *Allgemeine Rechtslehre und Marxismus. Versuch einer Kritik der juristischen Grundbegriffe*, Vienna: Verlag für Literatur und Politik.

Pestoff, V. A. (1995), 'Towards a New Swedish Model of Collective Bargaining and Politics', in Crouch, C. and Traxler, F. (eds.) *Organized Industrial Relations in Europe: What Future?* Aldershot: Avebury.

Piachaud, D. (1998), 'Changing Dimensions of Poverty', in Ellison, N. and Pierson, C. (eds.), *Developments in British Social Policy*, London: Macmillan.

Polanyi, K. (1944), *The Great Transformation: The Political and Economic Origins of Our Time*, Boston: Beacon Press.

Pontusson, J. (1997), 'Between Neo-Liberalism and the German Model: Swedish Capitalism in Transition', in Crouch, C. and Streeck, W. (eds.), *Political Economy of Modern Capitalism. Mapping Convergence & Diversity*, London: Sage.

Pontusson, J. and Swenson, P. (1996), 'Labour Markets, Production Strategies, and Wage-Bargaining Institutions', *Comparative Political Studies*, **29** (2), 223–50.

Poulantzas, N. (1978), *State, Power and Socialism*, London: NLB.

Purcell, J. (1995), 'Ideology and the End of Institutional Industrial Relations: Evidence from the UK', in Crouch, C. and Traxler, F. (eds.), *Organized Industrial Relations in Europe: What Future?* Aldershot: Avebury.

Reich, R. B. (1997), *Die neue Weltwirtschaft*, Munich: Fischer.

Remery, C., van Doorne-Huiskes, A., Schippers, J. (2002), 'Labour Market Flexibility in the Netherlands: Looking for Winners and Losers', *Work, Employment and Society*, **16** (3), 477–95.

Revelli, M. (1997), Vom 'Fordismus' zum 'Toyotismus'. *Das kapitalistische Wirtschafts- und Sozialmodell im Übergang*, Hamburg: VSA.

Reynauld, B. (2002), 'Diversity and Rules in Wage Determination', in Boyer, R. and Saillard, Y. (eds.), *Regulation Theory. The State of the Art*, London: Taylor & Francis.

Rhodes, M. (2000), 'Restructuring the British Welfare State: Between Domestic Constraints and Global Imperatives', in Scharpf, F. W. and Schmidt, V. A. (eds.), *Welfare and Work in the Open Economy*, Vol. 2, Oxford: Oxford University Press.

Ritsert, J. (1998), *Soziale Klassen*, Münster: Westfälisches Dampfboot.

Royo, S. (2002), 'A New Century of Corporatism? Corporatism in Spain and Portugal', *West European Politics*, **25** (3), 77–104.

Sabour, M. (1999), 'The Socio-Cultural Exclusion and Self-Exclusion of Foreigners in Finland', in Glorieux, I., Herkommer, S., Jönsson, I. and Littlewood, P. (eds.), *Social Exclusion in Europe. Problems and Paradigms*, Aldershot: Ashgate.

Sagardoy, J. A., del Valle, J. M., Gill, J. L. and Gete, P. (1995), *Prontuario de Derecho del Trabajo*, Madrid: Editorial Civitas.

Sakowsky, D. (1992), 'Die Wirtschaftspolitik der Regierung Thatcher', *Wirtschaftswissenschaftliche Monographien 10*, University of Göttingen.

Samek, L. (2000), 'The Dynamics of Labour Market Reform in European Countries', in Esping-Andersen, G. and Regini, M. (eds.), *Why Deregulate Labour Markets?* Oxford: Oxford University Press.

Scharpf, F. W. (2000), 'The Viability of Advanced Welfare States in the International Economy: Vulnerabilities and Options', *Journal of European Public Policy*, **7** (2), 190–228.

Schmid, G. (1996), 'Beschäftigungswunder Niederlande? Ein Vergleich der Beschäftigungssysteme in den Niederlanden und in Deutschland', *Working Paper FS I 96–206*, Wissenschaftszentrum Berlin für Sozialforschung.

Scholz, F. (2000), Perspektiven des 'Südens' im Zeitalter der Globalisierung, *Geographische Zeitschrift*, **88** (1), 1–20.

Schulte, T. (1999), 'Lohnzurückhaltung: Grundlage für eine solidarische Lohn- und Beschäftigungspolitik in Europa? Erfahrungen aus Deutschland und den Niederlanden im Vergleich', *Sozialismus*, **26** (10), 38–41.

Soskice, D. (1990), 'Reinterpreting Corporatism and Explaining Unemployment: Coordinated and Non-coordinated Market Economies', in Brunetta, R. and Dell'Aringa, C. (eds.), *Labour Relations and Economic Performance*, London: Macmillan.

Soskice, D. (1994), 'Reconciling Markets and Institutions: The German Apprenticeship System', in Lynch, L. M. (ed.), *Training and the Private Sector*, Chicago: Chicago University Press.

Spithoven, A. H. G. M. (2002), 'The Third Way: The Dutch Experience', *Economy and Society*, **31** (3), 333–68.

Statistisches Bundesamt (2004), *Datenreport 2004. Zahlen und Fakten über die Bundesrepublik Deutschland*, Berlin: Bundeszentrale für politische Bildung.

Stille, F. (1998), 'Der niederländische Weg: Durch Konsens zum Erfolg', *Mitteilungen aus der Arbeitsmarkt- und Berufsforschung*, No. 2, 294–311.

Streeck, W. (1997), 'German Capitalism: Does it Exist? Can it Survive?', in Crouch, C. and Streeck, W. (eds.), *Political Economy of Modern Capitalism*, London: Sage.

Swensson, L. (2003), 'Explaining Equalization. Political Institutions, Market Forces, and Reduction of the Gender Wage Gap in Sweden, 1920-1995', *Social Science History*, **27** (3), 371–95.

Taylor, F. W. (1947), *Scientific Management*, New York: Harper & Row.

Ter Weel, B. (2003), 'The Structure of Wages in the Netherlands, 1986–98', *Labour*, **17** (3), 361–82.

Théret, B. (2002), 'The State, Public Finance and Régulation', in Boyer, R. and Saillard, Y. (eds.), *Regulation Theory. The State of the Art*, London: Taylor & Francis.

Tickel, A. and Peck, J. (1995), 'Social Regulation after Fordism: Regulation Theory, Neo-Liberalism and the Global-Local Nexus', *Economy and Society*, **24** (3), 357–86.

Toharia, L. (1997), *Labour Market Studies: Spain*, Report to the European Commission, Brussels.

Toharia, L. and Malo, M. A. (2000), 'The Spanish Experiment: Pros and Cons of Flexibility at the Margin', in Esping-Andersen, G. and Regini, M. (eds.), *Why Deregulate Labour Markets?* Oxford: Oxford University Press.

Torfing, J. (1997), 'Die Zukunft des skandinavischen Wohlfahrtskapitalismus: Der Fall Dänemark', in Becker, S., Sablowski, T. and Schumm, W. (eds.), *Jenseits der Nationalökonomie? Weltwirtschaft und Nationalstaat zwischen Globalisierung und Regionalisierung*, Berlin: Argument Verlag.

Turner, B. (1993), 'Contemporary Problems in the Theory of Citizenship', in Turner, B. (ed.), *Citizenship and Social Theory*, London: Sage.

Van der Meer, M. (1996), 'Aspiring Corporatism? Industrial Relations in Spain', in Van Ruysseveldt, J. and Visser, J. (eds.), *Industrial Relations in Europe*, London: Sage.

Van Oorschot, W. (2002), 'Miracle or Nightmare? A Critical Review of Dutch Activation Policies and their Outcomes', *Journal of Social Policy*, **31** (3), 399–420.

Van Riel, B. (1995), *Unemployment Divergence and Coordinated Systems of Industrial Relations*, Frankfurt/Main: Peter Lang.

Visser, J. (2002), 'The First Part-Time Economy in the World: A Model to be Followed?', *Journal of European Social Policy*, **12** (1), 23–42.

Visser, J. and Hemerijck, A. (1997), 'A Dutch Miracle'. *Job Growth, Welfare Reform and Corporatism in the Netherlands*, Amsterdam: Amsterdam University Press.

Vring, v. d., T. (1999), *Arbeitsangebot und Arbeitsnachfrage. Statistische Analyse der Erwerbstätigkeit in Westdeutschland 1970-1996*, Hamburg: VSA.

Walker, A. and Walker, C. (eds.) (1997), *Britain Divided: The Growth of Social Exclusion in the 1980s and 1990s*, London: CPAG.

Wallerstein, I. (1979), 'Aufstieg und künftiger Niedergang des kapitalistischen Weltsystems', in Senghaas, D. (ed.), *Kapitalistische Weltökonomie*, Frankfurt/Main: Suhrkamp.

Weber, M. (1978), *Economy and Society. An Outline of Interpretive Sociology*, Berkeley: University of California Press.

Weber, M. (1986), 'Die protestantische Ethik und der Geist des Kapitalismus', in Weber, M. (ed.), *Gesammelte Aufsätze zur Religionssoziologie*, Vol. 1, Tübingen: Mohr.

Weber, M. (1991), in Gerth, H. and Wright Mills, C. (eds.), *From Max Weber*, London: Routledge.

Wright, E. O. (1994), *Interrogating Inequality: Essays on Class Analysis, Socialism and Marxism*, London and New York: Verso.

Wright, E. O. (1997), *Class Counts. Comparative Studies in Class Analysis*, Cambridge: Cambridge University Press.

Zukunftskommission der Friedrich-Ebert-Stiftung (1998), *Wirtschaftliche Leistungsfähigkeit, sozialer Zusammenhalt, ökologische Nachhaltigkeit. Drei Ziele – ein Weg*, Bonn: Dietz.

Index

Date Due

MAR 14 2011

MAY 09 2011